NAGC Pre-K–Grade 12

Gifted Education
Programming Standards

A Guide to Planning and
Implementing High-Quality Services

NAGC Pre-K–Grade 12

Gifted Education
Programming Standards

A Guide to Planning and
Implementing High-Quality Services

Edited by
Susan K. Johnsen, Ph.D.

a service publication of the
NATIONAL ASSOCIATION FOR
Gifted Children

PRUFROCK PRESS INC.
WACO, TEXAS

Library of Congress Cataloging-in-Publication Data

NAGC pre-K-grade 12 gifted education programming standards : a guide to planning and implementing high-quality services / edited by Susan K. Johnsen.
  p. cm.
 ISBN 978-1-59363-845-0 (pbk.)
 1. Gifted children--Education--Standards--United States. 2. Curriculum planning--United States. I. Johnsen, Susan K. II. National Association for Gifted Children (U.S.)
 LC3993.9.N34 2012
 371.950973--dc23
                        2011034795

Edited by Jennifer Robins

Production design by Raquel Trevino

ISBN-13: 978-1-59363-845-0

Prufrock Press Inc.
P.O. Box 8813
Waco, TX 76714-8813
Phone: (800) 998-2208
Fax: (800) 240-0333
http://www.prufrock.com

Contents

Foreword
Ann Robinson
Past President
National Association
for Gifted Children

The appearance of *NAGC Pre-K–Grade 12 Gifted Education Programming Standards: A Guide to Planning and Implementing High-Quality Services* is a testament to what a productive group of people can do in a short period of time when they have deep knowledge of the field and a powerful commitment to improving the infrastructure of school services for gifted learners.

Education has become enmeshed with the standards movement: in some cases, with enthusiasm; in others, with measured acceptance; and in still others, with truculence. In this instance, the new programming standards represent a productive collaboration between two advocacy organizations—the National Association for Gifted Children (NAGC) and The Association for the Gifted, Council for Exceptional Children (CEC-TAG). These are standards the field can embrace with enthusiasm, and this insightful and practical publication on ways to implement them is a resource we soundly applaud.

The team of leaders who took on the challenge of writing this useful book represents a wealth of diversity. Among the authors, the reader will find individuals who have devoted decades to the field and young up-and-comers. Among the authors, the reader will find individuals from higher education, state departments of education, central office administration, program coordination, and association advocacy. Their broad range of experiences and perspectives ensure that readers from any of these roles will find themselves and their issues addressed in this book.

Currently, the greatest challenge facing the field of gifted education is one of underresourced and disappearing infrastructure at all levels—local, state, and national. The programming standards and the solid guidance given for implementing them are a bright spot for advocates for gifted children and adolescents. The standards point the way to what we *should* be doing for gifted learners, provide examples from states and schools where such work is being done, and offer scenarios to engage us in possibilities for using the standards on behalf of our most advanced learners.

In addition to guiding pre-K–grade 12 practices, the programming standards are articulated with the teacher standards for university preparation programs used by the National Council for the Accreditation of Teacher Education (NCATE) and the Teacher Education Accreditation Council (TEAC), now joining to form the Council for the Accreditation of Educator Preparation (CAEP), and with the recently developed expectations for preparing preservice teachers embedded in the language of the recently reauthorized Higher Education Opportunity Act. What all of this means for the field is that the standards have consistency across students and educators and thus provide a coherent approach for the field of gifted education.

One of the key issues on which the programming standards focus our attention is the vital question of the "dosage" problem of school interventions for gifted students. What level of intensity, duration, and scope of programs and services is required to make a difference in a gifted child's cognitive, social, emotional, and motivational outcomes? Gifted education has been criticized for weak, ineffective, or undifferentiated services, but often these criticisms ignore the reality of severe budgetary constraints. In most cases, the dosage problem can be attributed to a lack of enabling policy and solid fiscal support. If decision makers allocate no or limited resources, then the programmatic dosage will be too little (and probably too late) to demonstrate effects—either immediate or long-term. In other cases, the dosage problem may be the result of substandard program quality or the lack of implementation fidelity. Programs will have few effects if teachers, counselors, and administrators are not trained and are disinterested, if curriculum is shoddy, or if student outcomes for advanced learners are misguided, obscured, or poorly understood.

NAGC Pre-K–Grade 12 Gifted Education Programming Standards: A Guide to Planning and Implementing High-Quality Services provides practical strategies, long-range planning tools, and a great deal of wisdom with respect to the provision of high-quality programs. During my term as President of NAGC, it was my great pleasure to work with Dr. Susan Johnsen and Dr. Joyce VanTassel-Baska as Co-Chairs of the NAGC Professional Standards Committee. Their leadership, the leadership of the individuals on the programming standards workgroup, and the able authors of the chapters in this volume have made a wonderful and necessary contribution to the field of gifted education. To the authors and editor Susan Johnsen: Thank you. To the readers: Enjoy!

Preface
Overview of the NAGC Pre-K–Grade 12 Gifted Programming Standards

by Susan K. Johnsen

Growing out of the need for more rigorous and measurable standards and higher expectations for academic performance, standards have been developed for teacher preparation, programming, and specific content or discipline areas. These standards have been used for the design of assessment-based accountability systems and the accreditation of both teacher preparation and K–12 programs.

Gifted education has been and continues to be an integral part of this standards movement. The National Association for Gifted Children/Council for Exceptional Children, The Association for the Gifted (NAGC/CEC-TAG) have developed teacher preparation standards that provide guidelines for professional development and for developing education programs at the undergraduate and graduate levels (see http://www.nagc.org and http://www.cectag.org). Using the teacher preparation standards and the 1998 Pre-K-Grade 12 Gifted Program Standards, a workgroup comprised of members from CEC-TAG and NAGC developed the NAGC Pre-K–Grade 12 Gifted Programming Standards, which were related to the previous sets of standards (see Appendix A for the complete set of standards). The six standards focus on student outcomes in learning and development, assessment, curriculum planning and instruction, learning environments, programming, and professional development. All of the standards are aligned with evidence-based practices, which are known to be effective in working with gifted and talented students, and are sensitive to the dual goals of equity and excellence. These programming standards are the focus of this book, *NAGC Pre-K–Grade 12 Gifted Education Programming Standards: A Guide to Planning and Implementing High-Quality Services*. The authors of these chapters were guided by the following questions:

» What standards relate to the focus area (e.g., social-emotional development, curriculum, identification)?
» How are these standards supported by research and effective practices?
» How might teachers, schools, and school districts use these standards?

> » How might teachers, schools, and school districts assess student outcomes?

Along with addressing these questions, each author has provided specific examples of ways that the standards might be implemented.

In Chapter 1, "Introduction to the NAGC Pre-K–Grade 12 Gifted Programming Standards," Susan K. Johnsen examines where these standards fit within the national context, identifies the needs for Gifted Programming Standards, explains the process used for developing the standards, identifies the general principles underlying the Gifted Programming Standards, contrasts the 1998 Program Standards with the 2010 Gifted Programming Standards, describes each of the standards and its related research, and makes recommendations for their use. Uses include self-assessment, professional development, program evaluation, and advocacy.

In Chapter 2, "Creating Environments for Social and Emotional Development," Thomas P. Hébert identifies four themes emerging in the Gifted Programming Standards related to social and emotional development: self-understanding; awareness of learning and affective needs in gifted students; personal, social, and cultural competence; and appreciation of talents within gifted young people and their recognition of ways to support the development of their gifts and talents. For each of these themes, Hébert provides research that supports specific practices. He concludes his chapter by describing ways that a teacher might create a classroom environment that is designed to support the social and emotional development of students.

In Chapter 3, "Using the NAGC Gifted Programming Standards to Create Programs and Services for Culturally and Linguistically Different Gifted Students," Donna Y. Ford and Tarek C. Grantham examine the six standards using a multicultural lens and a gifted lens. They provide a cultural framework for interpreting, conceptualizing, and building upon the newly revised standards. The authors discuss culture in terms of position statements by the National Association for Multicultural Education (NAME) and expand upon each standard with examples using a culturally responsive frame of reference. They conclude their chapter by providing recommendations and specific strategies to increase the representation of culturally different students in gifted education.

In Chapter 4, "The Assessment Standard in Gifted Education: Identifying Gifted Students," Susan K. Johnsen identifies the foundational principles that inform the standards on identification and then describes ways of establishing equal access (Student Outcome 2.1), using and interpreting a variety of assessment evidence (Student Outcome 2.2), and representing gifted students from diverse backgrounds (Student Outcome 2.3). She includes criteria and an example form to use in organizing data for placement and guidelines from the Office for Civil Rights for examining bias in the overall identification procedure.

In Chapter 5, "The Curriculum Planning and Instruction Standard in Gifted Education: From Idea to Reality," Joyce VanTassel-Baska provides an overview of curriculum planning, a definition of differentiation, necessary curriculum planning documents (curriculum framework, scope and sequence), and curricular emphases within the standard. She then reviews research that supports the curriculum planning and instruction standard and provides two curriculum models that respond to the demands of the Gifted Programming Standards. Next, she adds methods for assessing student outcomes and ways that the curriculum planning and instruction standard might be used. She concludes the chapter by providing recommendations for getting started.

In Chapter 6, "Instructional Strategies for Differentiation Within the Classroom," Julia Link Roberts focuses on instructional strategies for differentiation in classrooms. These instructional strategies include planning for differentiation, preassessing to ensure that each student is learning, and implementing learning experiences that match each student's interest, learning preferences, and readiness. She emphasizes the importance of educators working together to implement the standards and the instructional goal of continuous progress. She concludes the chapter by providing specific differentiation strategies, programming options, and needed policies and procedures for implementing the standards.

In Chapter 7, "Programming Models and Program Design," Cheryll M. Adams, Chrystyna V. Mursky, and Bill Keilty provide information that allows school personnel to make appropriate choices for programming for gifted students. They initially describe effective programming and services that have clearly articulated elements (i.e., philosophy, goals, definition, identification plan, curriculum, professional development, and evaluation). They then provide programming options for acceleration, enrichment, and grouping. They conclude by describing state-level initiatives and two programming examples.

In Chapter 8, "Professional Development Standard in Gifted Education: Creating Priorities," Sandra N. Kaplan begins by describing the purposes and historical background of professional development and its use as a catalyst for change. She acknowledges problems of practice and how they can become an initial step in reforming professional development. Next, she provides ways for developing teachers' expertise in gifted education, assessing the needs for planning and implementing professional development, methods for establishing relationships with potential participants, and example program models. She concludes the chapter by providing methods for prioritizing the Gifted Programming Standards for professional development.

In Chapter 9, "Using the NAGC Gifted Programming Standards to Evaluate Progress and Success: Why and How," Reva Friedman-Nimz focuses on the two evaluation outcomes within Standard 2. She describes a process for translating these standards, evidence-based practices, and learner outcomes into a coherent program development, implementation, and evaluation plan. To demonstrate how to develop an overall plan, she integrates a series of campus-level scenarios within a discussion of evidence-based programming, conducting a gap analysis, and developing an action plan. She concludes her chapter by describing the positive effects of program evaluation.

In Chapter 10, "State Models for Implementing the Standards," Chrystyna V. Mursky describes how state departments of education use national standards for evaluating and improving state standards, approving gifted plans and programs, and monitoring compliance with state regulations. She then describes how three states (Alabama, Maryland, and Texas) are implementing the standards and suggests more ideas of ways the standards might be used.

In Chapter 11, "Action Plans: Bringing the Gifted Programming Standards to Life," Alicia Cotabish and Sally Krisel focus on ways that educators might use the standards and where they might begin. They provide a Snapshot Survey of Gifted Programming Effectiveness Factors, which allows educators to assess the extent to which their programs use best practices, rate the extent to which they need to change to improve student outcomes, and determine needed resources. Following the survey description, they provide model examples of ways to use a gap analysis and action plan charts in implementing the standards. They conclude the chapter by describing two scenarios of ways that a program coordinator and a classroom teacher used the standards.

In Chapter 12, "Off the Page and Into Practice: Advocating for Implementation of the Gifted Programming Standards," E. Wayne Lord and Jane Clarenbach discuss how collaboration with education colleagues helps to ensure a receptive environment. Next, they describe how leaders in gifted education can advocate for the standards' use. They suggest three advocacy strategies when presenting the standards and provide a sample scenario for each.

The appendices also offer rich resources for practitioners. The programming standards appear in Appendix A. Each standard is preceded by a description and followed by student outcomes and evidence-based practices. Appendix B provides assessments for measuring student outcomes and evaluating programs in these areas: creativity, critical thinking, curriculum, interests, learning and motivation, multicultural, products and performances, social/emotional, and program planning.

As chair of the workgroup, I would like to thank the following members for their development of the programming standards: Alicia Cotabish, University of Arkansas at Little Rock; Todd Kettler, Coppell (TX) ISD; Margie Kitano, San Diego State University; Sally Krisel, Hall County (GA) Public Schools; E. Wayne Lord, Augusta State University; Michael S. Matthews, University of North Carolina at Charlotte; Chrystyna Mursky, Wisconsin Department of Public Instruction; Christine Nobbe, Center for Creative Learning (MO); Elizabeth Shaunessy, University of South Florida; and Joyce VanTassel-Baska, The College of William and Mary. They continue to work on developing resources and making presentations related to these standards. I would also like to acknowledge Jane Clarenbach at the National Association for Gifted Children; Margie Kitano, San Diego State University; and Jennifer Robins, Prufrock Press, for their editorial assistance. I hope that you find this book helpful in implementing the NAGC Pre-K–Grade 12 Gifted Programming Standards.

Chapter 1
Introduction to the NAGC Pre-K–Grade 12 Gifted Programming Standards

by Susan K. Johnsen

The standards movement has grown exponentially since 1983, when the National Commission on Excellence in Education published *A Nation at Risk*. The Commission recommended that schools, colleges, and universities adopt more rigorous and measurable standards and set higher expectations for academic performance. Since that time, all states have adopted some form of a standards-based education system, professional associations have approved content standards in most subject areas, and the No Child Left Behind Act of 2001 has required that states report results on standards-related accountability measures (U.S. Department of Education, 2008). More recently, the U.S. Education Department's competitive grant program, Race to the Top, which has billions of dollars in federal monies, requires that states that are competing for these funds have standards in place to improve teaching and learning. Clearly, the standards movement is not going away. Because gifted and talented students deserve to be included, gifted educators must have standards to become actively involved in the national conversation.

Currently, gifted educators have two sets of standards—those that address teacher preparation and those that address pre-K–12 programs. This chapter will (a) examine where these gifted education standards fit within the national context, (b) recognize the need for gifted programming standards, (c) explain the process used for developing the 2010 Pre-K–Grade 12 Gifted Programming Standards, (d) identify the general principles underlying the Gifted Programming Standards, (e) contrast the 1998 Gifted Program Standards with the 2010 Gifted Programming Standards, (f) describe each of the Gifted Programming Standards, and (g) make recommendations for their use.

Gifted Education Standards Within the National Context

The standards in gifted education are part of a wider network of professional preparation and programming standards that influence the education of all teachers and students (see Figure 1.1). At the top of Figure 1.1 are the Interstate Teacher Assessment and Support Consortium (InTASC) Standards (Council of Chief State School Officers [CCSSO], 1992, 2010, 2011). InTASC is a consortium of state education agencies and national educational organizations interested in the reform of the preparation, licensing, and ongoing professional development of teachers and is a part of the CCSSO (see http://www.ccsso.org). InTASC has developed common standards in the core subject areas of English-language arts and mathematics (e.g., CSSO, 2010) and in teacher preparation (CSSO, 1992, 2011). The influence of InTASC standards is noteworthy: 41 states have adopted the 2010 common core standards and 38 states have adopted the 1992 InTASC teacher preparation standards (see http://www.corestandards.org/in-the-states).

The InTASC standards were used as guidelines for the development of the initial teacher preparation certificate in gifted education (National Association for Gifted Children [NAGC] & Council for Exceptional Children, The Association for the Gifted [CEC-TAG], 2006). Initial certificates may be offered at both the undergraduate and graduate levels and focus on educators who may have other certificates but are seeking their first one in gifted education. The National Council for Accreditation of Teacher Education (NCATE) uses the NAGC/CEC-TAG initial standards to accredit teacher education programs (see http://www.ncate.org). Teacher preparation programs that meet these standards are nationally recognized by NCATE. Recently, the InTASC model core teaching standards and the NCATE recommendations for standards have been changed and will influence the next revision of the NAGC/CEC-TAG teacher preparation standards in 2013 (CCSSO, 2011; NCATE, 2009).

Gifted educators are also developing an advanced set of standards for teachers who already have an initial certificate, which should be available in 2012 (see http://www.cectag.org and http://www.nagc.org). These standards are based on the National Board for Professional Teaching Standards (NBPTS, 2011) and the Council for Exceptional Children's (CEC, 2009) Advanced Common Core Standards. When approved, they will provide guidelines for teacher preparation programs and schools that are interested in developing teacher leaders in gifted education. Moreover, the NBPTS (2011) has a certificate for teachers in gifted education, which is a pathway within the Exceptional Needs Certificate.

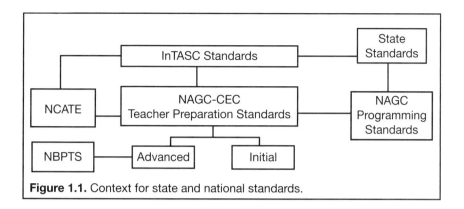

Figure 1.1. Context for state and national standards.

Although only 20 states require credentialing or licensure for professionals working in gifted education programs, the majority of states have requirements for programs and services in gifted education (NAGC, 2008–2009). State rules, regulations, and/or guidelines include characteristics of definitions, procedures for identification, programs and services, personnel preparation, and other practices such as acceleration, early entrance, dual enrollment, and high school graduation alternative.

All of these teacher preparation and state standards have influenced the development of the 2010 NAGC Pre-K–Grade 12 Gifted Programming Standards. The national Gifted Programming Standards provide the next layer of support to schools so that they are aware of not only quality teachers in gifted education, but also the characteristics of quality programs. The remainder of this chapter will describe these new standards and their value to the field of gifted education.

Need for Gifted Programming Standards

The 2010 NAGC Pre-K–Grade 12 Gifted Programming Standards are important to professional fields and provide benefits to all educators. They provide coherence, structures, guidelines for professional development, attention to underserved populations, ways to improve programming, and a foundation for advocacy.

Given the lack of a federal mandate and variations in services across states, the Gifted Programming Standards can identify the characteristics of effective programming in gifted education and ensure a degree of consistency across schools and school districts so that all students receive a quality education (Johnsen, VanTassel-Baska, & Robinson, 2008). Educators in gifted education can point to evidence-based practices that are important to implement. Without standards, services to gifted and talented students are left to the discretion of decision makers who may or may not have a background or even an interest in gifted education.

The Gifted Programming Standards can also provide a structure for defining critical benchmarks; developing policies, rules, and procedures; and identifying practices that are the most effective for students with gifts and talents (Johnsen, 2011a). In this way, policymakers can focus on what is important in gifted education, and schools are able to evaluate all aspects of their programs and set benchmarks for improvement.

With the Gifted Programming Standards, professionals in gifted education are more aware of evidence-based classroom practices essential to improving outcomes for gifted and talented students. They can be used as a guide for professional development of individual teachers and for entire school districts. Educator preparation institutions and agencies can also use the standards for identifying relevant theory, research, and pedagogy for designing courses and coherent programs.

The Gifted Programming Standards also reveal the importance that the field of gifted education places on serving underrepresented populations in the areas of assessment, curriculum planning, establishing learning environments, and programming. They reinforce the idea that diversity exists in our society and in each individual's expression of gifts and talents (Johnsen, 2006).

Finally, Gifted Programming Standards can be used for advocacy and effect new initiatives at the local, state, and national levels. They may then direct educators' efforts toward adequately recognizing students with gifts and talents, developing and implementing programming, and ultimately raising the quality of services provided to gifted students and their families.

Process Used to Develop the Gifted Programming Standards

The 2010 NAGC Pre-K–Grade 12 Gifted Programming Standards are the result of many years' effort on the part of NAGC members in collaboration with CEC-TAG members and others who have sought to improve the education of gifted and talented students. The effort began more than 10 years ago with the development of the 1998 Pre-K–Grade 12 Gifted Program Standards (Landrum, Callahan, & Shaklee, 2001; NAGC, 2000).

When the NAGC/CEC-TAG (2006) teacher preparation standards were developed, the NAGC Board wanted to revise the 1998 Gifted Program Standards so that they were aligned with the new teacher preparation standards and recent research. The NAGC Board created the Professional Standards Committee in 2007 to provide leadership in not only creating awareness of the new teacher preparation standards but also in developing an appropriate alignment of the NAGC/CEC-TAG teacher preparation standards to other standards within and outside of the gifted education field, including the 1998 Pre-K–12 Gifted Program Standards (NAGC, 2007).

On September 15, 2007, NAGC approved a Governance Policy that created the NAGC Professional Standards Committee (PSC) and charged this new committee with "develop[ing] appropriate alignment of the NCATE standards to other standards in and out of the gifted education field, including the *NAGC Pre-K–12 Gifted Program Standards.*" The PSC met for the first time at the 2007 NAGC annual convention in Minneapolis, MN. Susan Johnsen and Claire Hughes assumed the leadership roles for aligning the teacher preparation standards with the 1998 NAGC Pre–K–Grade 12 Gifted Program Standards and identifying its research base. The alignment and research support for each of the 1998 program standards was completed by August 2008. The research support included theory/literature-based, research-based, and practice-based research (CEC, 2010, pp. 9–10):

» *Theory/literature-based.* Knowledge or skills are based on theories or philosophical reasoning. They include knowledge and skills derived from sources such as position papers, policy analyses, and descriptive reviews of the literature.

» *Research-based.* Knowledge or skills are based on peer-reviewed studies that use appropriate research methodologies to address questions of cause and effect, and that researchers have independently replicated and found to be effective.

» *Practice-based.* Knowledge and skills are derived from a number of sources. Practices based on a small number of studies or nomination procedures, such as promising practices, are usually practice-based. Practice-based knowledge or skills also include those derived primarily from model and lighthouse programs. Practice-based knowledge and skills include professional wisdom. These practices have been used so widely with practical evidence of effectiveness that there is an implicit professional assumption that the practice is effective. Practice-based knowledge and skills also include "emerging practice," practices that arise from teachers' classroom experiences and are validated through some degree of action research.

Areas that were not aligned between the two sets of standards (e.g., teacher preparation and the 1998 Gifted Program Standards) included differences in themes (e.g., diversity, special education, technology, differentiation), in lack of specificity, and in the tone of the program guidelines (e.g., more advocacy than standards). The PSC made recommendations for aligning the two sets of standards and for updating the program standards to the NAGC Board. The NAGC Board accepted the PSC's recommendations and approved a Pre-K–Grade 12 Gifted Program Standards Revision Workgroup (Workgroup).

At the annual NAGC meeting in Tampa, FL, on October 31, 2008, the Workgroup, which was chaired by Susan Johnsen, met for the first time. Its charge was to (a) revise and update the 1998 Gifted Program Standards to reflect the current research in the field; (b) align the program standards with the teacher preparation standards so that they shared common themes (diversity, twice-exceptional learners, technology, differentiation); (c) integrate special education and recent special education regulations into the standards; (d) provide more specificity within all of the program standards; (e) consider the variations among state policy, rules, and regulations that influences the standards' language; and (f) establish criteria for the categories of "minimal" and "exemplary" standards. The PSC developed a set of questions to identify the current use of the program standards and future areas for improvement. Margie Kitano and Wayne Lord field tested these survey questions with gifted education coordinators and directors.

In February 2009, NAGC sent the piloted survey to its members and had 32 states respond, which included 68 administrators, district coordinators, full-time gifted teachers, school-level gifted coordinators, state directors, and university faculty. These results were reported: only 15 (22%) of the respondents mentioned a strong alignment between state standards and the NAGC program standards, 39 (57%) said the standards didn't interface with their states' accountability systems, 68 (100%) thought that curriculum and instruction and student identification were essential standards, 49 (72%) didn't differentiate their standards (e.g., acceptable to exemplary), and the majority felt it was important to include diversity ($n = 52, 76\%$) and collaboration ($n = 44, 65\%$).

During five subsequent conference calls in 2009, the Workgroup agreed to organize the revised standards around student outcomes so that schools might be more accountable in showing evidence that their programs were effective for students with gifts and talents. Because of NCATE's recommendations to reduce the number of standards and indicators for reviewing teacher preparation programs, the Gifted Programming Standards were collapsed into six areas and assigned to different Workgroup members for development. Using the 1998 Gifted Program Standards, state program standards, and the NAGC/CEC-TAG teacher preparation standards, the Workgroup developed a draft set of student outcomes and evidence-based practices. They then identified the research base for each of the evidence-based practices.

At the 2009 NAGC annual convention in St. Louis, MO, a draft of the revised Gifted Programming Standards was presented to the University Network and at a special session. Again, a wide variety of stakeholders were present, including university faculty, administrators, teachers, and parents. Comments regarding the standards were collected and summarized and shared at the Workgroup's meeting. The participants (a) liked the change to student outcomes; (b) felt that a minimum of three studies from a variety of sources and disciplines should be used for retaining an evidence-based practice; (c) suggested that empirical, literature-based, and practice-based research could be used; (d) identified areas that might be missing and areas of overlap; and (f) recommended the development of specific resources for student assessments and implementing specific strategies. Feedback was mixed on having "developing, acceptable, exemplary" ratings. Some wanted these ratings, others suggested that an overall rating might be provided, and still others thought that the focus should be on student outcomes, not on the completion of a certain number of standards.

The Workgroup members met in San Diego in January 2010 to examine all of the programming standards as a whole, modify the standards based on the feedback from the NAGC annual meeting in St. Louis, and create a final draft copy for the NAGC Board to review at its next meeting. The NAGC Board unanimously approved the new Gifted Programming Standards at its March 2010 meeting. Subsequently, the CEC-TAG Board unanimously approved the new standards at its April 2010 meeting. The programming standards were then disseminated at the 2010 NAGC annual meeting in Atlanta, GA.

General Principles Underlying the Gifted Programming Standards

During the process of developing the Gifted Programming Standards, the Workgroup reviewed the research base and developed the following principles to guide the revision of the 1998 Gifted Program Standards (NAGC, 2010, p. 4):

1. *Giftedness is dynamic and is constantly developing; therefore, students are defined as those having gifts and talents rather than those with stable traits.* Instead of endorsing a static definition of giftedness (e.g., a student is either gifted or not), more researchers have acknowledged the developmental nature of giftedness, which includes a set of interacting components such as general intelligence, domain-related skills, creativity, and nonintellective factors (Cattell, 1971; Gagné, 1999; Renzulli, 1978; Tannenbaum, 1991). A developmental perspective strongly influences identification and programming practices.

2. *Giftedness is found among students from a variety of backgrounds; there-fore, a deliberate effort was made to ensure that diversity was included across all standards.* Diversity was defined as differences among groups of people and individuals based on ethnicity, race, socioeconomic status, gender, exceptionalities, language, religion, sexual orientation, and geographical area. Because the underrepresentation of diverse students in gifted education programs is well documented (Daniels, 1998; Ford & Harris, 1999; Morris, 2002), specific evidence-based practices needed to be incorporated to ensure that identification procedures were equitable (Ford & Harmon, 2001; Frasier, Garcia, & Passow, 1995; Harris, Plucker, Rapp, & Martinez, 2009), curriculum was culturally responsive (Ford, Tyson, Howard, & Harris, 2000; Kitano & Pedersen, 2002a, 2002b), and learning environments fostered cultural understanding for success in a diverse society (Harper & Antonio, 2008; Zirkel, 2008).

3. *Standards should focus on student outcomes rather than practices.* The number of practices used or how the schools used the practices were not as important as whether or not the practice was effective with students. Consequently, the Workgroup decided not to identify acceptable versus exemplary standards because the distinction would be difficult to support with research.

4. *All educators are responsible for the education of students with gifts and talents.* Educators were defined as administrators, teachers, counselors, and other instructional support staff from a variety of professional backgrounds (i.e., general education, special education, gifted education). Research suggests that collaboration enhances talent development (Gentry & Ferriss, 1999; Landrum, 2002; Purcell & Leppien, 1998) and improves the likelihood that gifted students with disabilities receive services in gifted education programs (Coleman & Johnsen, 2011).

5. *Students with gifts and talents should receive services throughout the day and in all environments that are based on their abilities, needs, and interests.* Therefore, the Workgroup decided to use the word "programming" rather than the word "program," which might connote a unidimensional approach (e.g., a once-a-week type of program option). This emphasis is critical given the patchwork of programs and services that are currently provided to gifted and talented students, which vary from state to state and from school to school (NAGC, 2008–2009).

Along with the stakeholders' input, these principles informed the Workgroup's revisions of the 1998 Gifted Program Standards and assisted in maintaining consistency throughout the revision process.

Differences Between the 1998 Gifted Program Standards and the 2010 Gifted Programming Standards

NAGC released the first set of pre-K–grade 12 standards to the field in 1998. These standards were organized within seven areas (i.e., program design, program administration and management, socio-emotional guidance and counseling, student identification, curriculum and instruction, professional development, program evaluation) and included minimum and exemplary performance levels. The major differences between the 1998 Gifted Program Standards and the 2010 Gifted Programming Standards center on the following areas (Johnsen, 2011a; NAGC, 2010):

1. *The 2010 Gifted Programming Standards are aligned to the 1998 Gifted Program Standards and the NAGC/CEC-TAG teacher preparation standards.* The 2010 Gifted Programming Standards adhere very closely to the language in the NAGC/CEC-TAG teacher preparation standards and the 1998 Gifted Program Standards and integrate the two sets of standards within evidence-based practices. This alignment is helpful to schools that want to build on previously implemented standards and that want to ensure that gifted educators are using best practices. On the other hand, the 2010 Gifted Programming Standards include teacher preparation standards that were not addressed in the 1998 Gifted Program Standards such as language and communication, learning environments, social interaction, diversity, collaboration between gifted education and special education, and ongoing assessment (see Table 1.1). Moreover, the number of standards were reduced and combined into cohesive categories that reflect the research literature and other sets of professional standards (e.g., NCATE, InTASC; see Table 1.2).

2. *The 2010 Gifted Programming Standards' focus is on student outcomes.* The revised standards reflect the national landscape and movement toward accountability based on student performance. Student outcomes require schools to examine the effectiveness of their practices and the value of gifted education programming. When educators are able to show programming's effects on gifted and talented students'

Table 1.1

2010 NAGC Pre-K–Grade 12 Student Outcome Alignments With NAGC/CEC-TAG Teacher Preparation Standards and the 1998 NAGC Pre-K–Grade 12 Gifted Program Standards

2010 NAGC Pre-K–Grade 12 Outcomes	NAGC/CEC-TAG Teacher Preparation Standards										1998 NAGC Pre-K–Grade 12 Gifted Program Standards						
	1	2	3	4	5	6	7	8	9	10	1	2	3	4	5	6	7
1.1		*	*														
1.2		*	*														
1.3			*		*												
1.4		*															
1.5		*	*														
1.6	*	*	*										*				
1.7			*														
1.8													*				
2.1								*			*						
2.2	*							*		*	*	*		*	*		
2.3								*				*			*		
2.4				*				*		*		*					
2.5											*	*	*	*			
2.6											*	*	*	*			
3.1	*			*			*				*	*	*	*	*		*
3.2				*			*					*					
3.3				*			*					*	*		*		
3.4				*			*										
3.5				*			*										
3.6				*			*										
4.1	*				*	*											
4.2					*												
4.3					*												
4.4	*				*												
4.5						*											
5.1				*		*	*								*	*	*
5.2										*					*	*	
5.3										*						*	
5.4															*	*	

Table 1.1, continued

5.5							*								*		
5.6	*								*						*		
5.7							*							*	*		
6.1	*			*					*	*	*	*	*	*			
6.2									*		*	*	*	*			
6.3									*								
6.4	*								*		*						

Table 1.2

Relationships Among the NAGC/CEC-TAG Teacher Preparation Standards, the 1998 NAGC Pre-K–Grade12 Gifted Program Standards, and the 2010 NAGC Pre-K–Grade 12 Programming Standards

NAGC/CEC-TAG Teacher Preparation Standards	1998 NAGC Pre-K–Grade 12 Gifted Program Standards	2010 NAGC Pre-K–Grade 12 Programming Standards (Relationships to Standards)
1. Foundations 2. Development and Characteristics of Learners 3. Individual Learning Differences 4. Instructional Strategies 5. Learning Environments and Social Interactions 6. Language and Communication 7. Instructional Planning 8. Assessment 9. Professional and Ethical Practice 10. Collaboration	1. Student Identification 2. Professional Development 3. Socio-Emotional Guidance and Counseling 4. Program Evaluation 5. Program Design 6. Program Administration and Management 7. Curriculum and Instruction	1. Learning and Development (combined NAGC/CEC-TAG #2, #3; 1998 Gifted Program Standards #3) 2. Assessment (combined NAGC/CEC-TAG #8, 1998 Gifted Program Standards #1, #4) 3. Curriculum Planning and Instruction (combined NAGC/CEC-TAG #4, #7; 1998 Gifted Program Standards #7) 4. Learning Environments (combined NAGC/CEC-TAG #5, #6) 5. Programming (combined NAGC/CEC-TAG #10; 1998 Gifted Program Standards #5, #6) 6. Professional Development (combined NAGC/CEC-TAG #9, #10; 1998 Gifted Program Standards #2)

Note. The Foundations Standard from the NAGC-CEC/TAG Teacher Preparation Standards was integrated throughout all of the Pre-K-Grade 12 Gifted Programming Standards.

performance, they are more likely to have data that provide the basis for improving laws and policies related to gifted education and to access greater resources.

3. *The 2010 Gifted Programming Standards emphasize evidence-based practices that are based on research.* Although the 1998 Gifted Program Standards were developed to reflect the best practices at the time, the field has evolved since their creation more than 10 years ago. The revised standards have support from research, literature, and practice-based studies for each of the evidence-based practices. Only evidence-based practices that had research support from at least three studies were included. The research base also provides gifted educators with the necessary evidence needed for advocacy.

4. *The 2010 Gifted Programming Standards reflect a much stronger emphasis on diversity.* The new standards use a broader definition of diversity that includes cultural, linguistic, intellectual, sexual orientation, and disabilities, and overtly stress the importance of student outcomes and evidence-based practices in this area. For example, within the Learning and Development standard, students "recognize the influences of their beliefs, traditions, and values on their learning and behavior" (see 1.2); within the Learning Environments standard, students "possess skills in communicating, teaming, and collaborating with diverse individuals and across diverse groups" (see 4.4); and within the Curriculum Planning and Development criterion, teachers use "challenging, culturally responsive curriculum" (see 3.5.1). Because students from diverse backgrounds continue to be underrepresented in gifted education programs, this emphasis is critical for their inclusion and their ability to access quality programming.

5. *The 2010 Gifted Programming Standards emphasize stronger relationships between gifted education, general education, and special education.* The revised standards stress the importance of partnerships among all educators in addressing the needs of all students. With the inclusion of twice-exceptional students within a Response-to-Intervention model (Coleman & Johnsen, 2011), gifted educators have opportunities to collaborate with special and general educators in implementing rigorous differentiated curriculum, recognizing strengths early, scaffolding learning, and using data to make decisions about more intensive services (see 5.2). The Gifted Programming Standards stress the importance of partnerships among all educators (administrators, teachers, counselors, and other instructional support staff) in addressing the needs of all students (see Standard 6: Professional Development).

6. *The 2010 Gifted Programming Standards are more specific and integrate cognitive science research.* Based on recent research on learning, the Gifted Programming Standards emphasize metacognition, higher level thinking, and problem solving within the evidence-based practices. The evidence-based practices are also more specific and provide guidance to educators on the types of practices to implement. For example, educators are encouraged to use critical and creative thinking strategies and problem-solving and inquiry models (see 3.4.1–3.4.4).

An Overview of the 2010 Pre-K–Grade 12 Gifted Programming Standards

The 36 student outcomes are organized within six programming standards: learning and development, assessment, curriculum planning and instruction, learning environments, programming, and professional development (see Appendix A). Each of the six standards represents an important emphasis in developing and implementing effective programming for students with gifts and talents. Practices that are based on research evidence are also included and aligned with each student outcome. These evidence-based practices provide guidance to educators in specific strategies that might be implemented to achieve the student outcomes. Following is a brief overview of each standard and its related student outcomes and evidence-based practices.

Standard 1: Learning and Development

The first standard is foundational to the remaining standards because educators must understand the population's characteristics and needs before they plan and implement assessments, curriculum, instructional strategies, learning environments, programming, and professional development. The student outcomes within this standard recognize the learning and developmental differences of students with gifts and talents, and encourage the students' ongoing self-understanding, awareness of their needs, and cognitive and affective growth in the school, home, and community. To achieve these outcomes, educators (a) help students identify their interests, strengths, and gifts (Lee & Olszewski-Kubilius, 2006; Simonton, 2000; VanTassel-Baska, 2009); (b) develop activities, culturally responsive classrooms, and special interventions that match each student's characteristics (Ford, 2006; Hébert, 1991; Shade, Kelly, & Oberg, 1997); (c) use research-based grouping practices (Gentry & Owen, 1999; Kulik & Kulik, 1992; Rogers, 1991); (d) provide role models and mentors within and outside the school (Bloom & Sosniak, 1981; VanTassel-Baska, 2006); (e) collaborate with families (Moon, Jurich, & Feldhusen, 1998; Williams & Baber, 2007); and (f) provide students with college and career guidance (Greene, 2003; Maxwell, 2007).

Standard 2: Assessment

This standard incorporates knowledge of all forms of assessments including identification, the assessment of learning progress and outcomes, and evaluation of programming because they are inextricably linked to one another. The student outcomes within this standard relate to equal access, representation of students from diverse backgrounds, and the expression of individual differences in gifts and talents during the identification process. Students with gifts and talents also demonstrate advanced and complex learning and progress as a result of ongoing assessments and evaluation. To achieve these outcomes, evidence-based practices include (a) developing environments where students can show diverse gifts and talents (Borland & Wright, 1994; Grantham, 2003; Hertzog, 2005); (b) using comprehensive, cohesive, ongoing, and technically adequate procedures during the identification process that do not discriminate against any student with potential (Ford & Trotman, 2000; Johnsen, 2011b; Ryser, 2011); (c) using various types of assessments such as performances, products, off-level tests, and other types of pre/post measures (Baker & Schacter, 1996; Baum, Owen, & Oreck, 1996; Reis, Burns, & Renzulli, 1992; VanTassel-Baska, 2007); and (d) implementing an evaluation that is purposeful, reliable, and valid for examining the effectiveness of practices on student outcomes (Avery, VanTassel-Baska, & O'Neill, 1997; Callahan & Reis, 2004; Moon, 1996).

Standard 3: Curriculum Planning and Instruction

The third standard not only addresses curricular planning but also talent development, instructional strategies, culturally relevant curriculum, and accessing appropriate resources to engage a variety of learners. Desired outcomes include students demonstrating growth commensurate with their aptitude, becoming competent in talent areas and as independent investigators, and developing knowledge and skills for being productive in a multicultural, diverse, and global society. To achieve these outcomes, educators (a) develop comprehensive, cohesive programming for students with a variety of gifts and talents that is based on standards, incorporate differentiated curricula in all domains, and use a balanced assessment system (Kitano, Montgomery, VanTassel-Baska, & Johnsen, 2008; Tomlinson, 2004; Stiggins, 2008; VanTassel-Baska, 2004); (b) use specific strategies such as critical and creative thinking, metacognitive, problem-solving, and inquiry models (Anderson & Krathwohl, 2001;

Elder & Paul, 2004; Hartman, 2001); (c) develop and use culturally responsive curriculum (Ford, 2006; Ford et al., 2000); and (d) use high-quality resources that integrate technology (Pyryt, 2003; Siegle, 2004).

Standard 4: Learning Environments

The fourth standard focuses on the creation of safe learning environments where students are able to develop personal, social, cultural, communication, and leadership competencies. Specific student outcomes include the development of self-awareness, self-advocacy, self-efficacy, confidence, motivation, resilience, independence, and curiosity. Students also learn how to develop positive peer relationships, social interactions, and interpersonal and technical communication skills with diverse individuals and across diverse groups. In their development of leadership skills, they also demonstrate personal and social responsibility. To achieve these outcomes, educators create environments that (a) not only have high expectations, but also honor effort (Cross, Stewart, & Coleman, 2003; Dweck & Kamins, 1999; McKown & Weinstein, 2008); (b) are safe and welcoming for exploring issues and for risk taking (Brody, 1999; Neihart, 2002); (c) provide opportunities for self-exploration and leadership (Frey, 1998; Hensel, 1991; Ross & Smyth, 1995); (d) promote positive interactions with artistic/creative and chronological-age peers (Enersen, 1993; Olszewski-Kubilius, Grant, & Seibert, 1994); (e) support diverse learners (Cline & Schwartz, 2000; den Brok, Levy, Rodriguez, & Wubbels, 2002); and (f) teach positive coping, social, and communication skills (Berger, 2003; Kitano & Lewis, 2005; Kolesinski & Leroux, 1992).

Standard 5: Programming

The fifth standard includes a variety of programming options that are coordinated and implemented by teams of educators who have adequate resources and policies and procedures to implement comprehensive services, which include talent development and career planning. Outcomes include students demonstrating growth and enhanced performance in cognitive and affective areas and identifying future career pathways and talent development pathways to reach their goals. To achieve these outcomes, educators (a) create policies and procedures (Ford & Trotman, 2000; Zeidner & Schleyer, 1999); (b) provide sufficient funding (Baker & Friedman-Nimz, 2003; NAGC, 2008–2009); (c) coordinate services and collaborate with families and other professionals (Campbell & Verna, 2007; Coleman & Johnsen, 2011); and (d) develop and implement a comprehensive set of services such as acceleration, enrichment, grouping, individualized learning, mentorships, internships, and technology that develop relevant student talent areas (Berger, 2003; Colangelo, Assouline, & Gross, 2004; Johnsen & Johnson, 2007; Kulik & Kulik, 1992; Renzulli & Reis, 2003; Siegle & McCoach, 2005).

Standard 6: Professional Development

This standard examines the preparation of educators and the knowledge and skills needed to develop their students' talent and socioemotional development. It also emphasizes high-quality educator development that creates lifelong learners who are ethical in their practices. Student outcomes include the development of their talents and focus on the social and emotional areas. To achieve these outcomes, educators (a) participate in ongoing, research-supported, and multiple forms of professional development that model how to develop environments and instructional activities for students with gifts and talents (Garet, Porter, Desimone, Birman, & Yoon, 2001; Kitano et al., 2008); (b) provide sufficient human and material resources for professional development (Guskey, 2000; Johnsen, Haensly, Ryser, & Ford, 2002); (c) become involved in professional organizations (Callahan, Cooper, & Glascock, 2003; Landrum et al., 2001); (d) assess their practices and identify areas for personal growth (Bain, Bourgeois, & Pappas, 2003; Gubbins et al., 2002); (e) respond to cultural and personal frames of reference (Ford & Trotman, 2001; Frasier et al., 1995); and (f) comply with rules, policies, and standards of ethical practice (Copenhaver, 2002; Klein & Lugg, 2002).

Use of the Gifted Programming Standards

How might educators use the 2010 Pre-K–Grade 12 Gifted Programming Standards? The Gifted Programming Standards may be used for self-assessment, professional development, selecting teachers, program evaluation, and advocacy.

> » *Self-assessment.* First, they can be used for self-assessment at the classroom, school, school district, and/or state levels. At the classroom and school levels, teachers might consider which evidence-based practices are being implemented, how these are affecting student progress, and other practices they might want to implement (see Table 1.3). In Table 1.3, the educators have identified a practice (i.e., use of inquiry models within interdisciplinary units) that is being implemented but not assessed. The next step might be for them to identify some possible assessments, review these, and identify which ones might be used across grade levels to determine students' progress in becoming independent investigators.

Table 1.3

Gap Analysis Chart

Standard	Evidence-Based Practices	What We Do to Support This Practice	Desired Student Outcomes	What Evidence Do We Have That Current Practices Are Leading to Desired Student Outcomes?	What Additional Evidence Do We Need? (Gaps)
3. Curriculum Planning and Instruction	3.4.3 Use inquiry models	Interdisciplinary units of study are built around inquiry model.	3.4 Students with gifts and talents become independent investigators.	No formal assessments are used to determine if students are becoming more competent as independent investigators.	Need to develop a way of assessing increasing competence in this area (e.g., product and performance rubrics).

Note. Adapted from *NAGC Pre-K–Grade 12 Gifted Programming Standards: A Blueprint for Quality Gifted Education Programs* (p. 5), by National Association for Gifted Children, 2010, Washington, DC: Author. Copyright 2010 by National Association for Gifted Children. Adapted with permission.

At the school, school district, and state levels, educators may self-assess by aligning the standards with local and state programming standards, similar to Table 1.1, and examine these questions: What standards are addressed? Which ones may need to be addressed? What assessments are being used to examine the student outcomes and the effectiveness of practices? Assessments that might be considered include off-level standardized achievement measures; end-of-course or Advanced Placement (AP) exams; rubrics for assessing complex products and performance; critical or creative thinking measures to assess process skills; pre/post assessments, portfolio assessments, or student self-assessments such as journals, written products, or surveys to examine students' performances over time (see Appendix B for a listing of assessments). It's important that educators remember to match "the desired outcome to the student's knowledge and skills and level of interest" (NAGC, 2010, p. 7).

» *Professional development.* Following self-assessment, educators can target specific evidence-based practices for professional development. For example, using the information in Table 1.3, educators across grade levels might select and/or design comprehensive and cohesive assessment tools that might be used to examine how well students are progressing in becoming independent investigators in a variety of domains. These assessments then might be used to drive more professional development in specific practices related to research such as formulating questions, gathering information, analyzing data and summarizing information, developing products, and so on.

» *Selection of gifted educators.* Along with the NAGC/CEC-TAG teacher preparation standards, these standards might also be used for selecting teachers and other educators who would be effective in planning programming and serving students with gifts and talents. For example: Do educators engage students in identifying their interests, strengths, and gifts (see 1.1.1)? Do they use differentiated pre- and post-performance-based assessments that measure the progress of students (see 2.4.1)? Do they use critical thinking strategies (see 3.4.1)? Do they establish a safe and welcoming climate for addressing social issues (see 4.3.1)? Do they collaborate with other educators in planning programs for students with gifts and talents (see 5.2.1)? Are they aware of the foundations of gifted education and research-supported practices (6.1.1)?

» *Program evaluation.* The standards can help educators establish school- or district-wide benchmarks to monitor the progress of implementing specific evidence-based practices over time. Because the Gifted Programming Standards are also written in terms of student outcomes, educators involved in evaluation can assess the effect of implemented practices on students with gifts and talents. For example, to what degree are students demonstrating self-knowledge (Standard 1); accessing resources to support their needs (Standards 1 and 2); demonstrating competence in talent areas (Standards 3 and 6); demonstrating skills in communicating, teaming, and collaborating across diverse groups (Standard 4); and demonstrating learning progress commensurate with their abilities (Standards 3 and 5)? Collecting these assessment data will not only improve programming, but also will show the value added by having specialized programming for students with gifts and talents, which can be used for requesting adequate human and material resources.

» *Advocacy.* The standards can be used to inform educators, policymakers, and the community about the characteristics of effective programming for students with gifts and talents. Presentations can be made to teachers, instructional support staff, administrators, school boards, parent groups, and other community organizations in describing the important practices and related outcomes for gifted education programming.

Building both grass-roots and administrative-level supports can assist in policy development at the district and state levels, which ultimately builds a foundation for gifted education programming that will not disappear during lean economic times.

Summary

Since the 1980s, education has been influenced by the standards movement and the need for accountability. The field of gifted education needs standards, not only to be a part of national conversations, but also to provide leadership to educators who are wanting to develop programming that is effective for gifted and talented students. The 2010 NAGC Pre-K–Grade 12 Gifted Programming Standards provide a foundation for developing consistency across schools and school districts, a structure for defining critical benchmarks, guidelines for professional development, and a basis for advocacy efforts. Moreover, the standards' attention to underserved populations demonstrates the field's commitment to each individual's expression of gifts and talents.

Informed by national standards, research, and more than 2 years of collaborative work among associations, administrators, district coordinators, full-time gifted teachers, school-level gifted coordinators, state directors, and university faculty, the Gifted Programming Standards focus on student outcomes that are organized within six areas: learning and development, assessment, curriculum planning and instruction, learning environments, programming, and professional development. Their use in self-assessment, professional development, selection of gifted educators, program evaluation, and advocacy will help in the development and implementation of quality programming so that all students with gifts and talents have opportunities for enhancing their performance.

References

Anderson, L. W., & Krathwohl, D. R. (Eds.). (2001). *A taxonomy for learning, teaching, and assessing: A revision of Bloom's taxonomy of educational objectives.* New York, NY: Longman.

Avery, L. D., VanTassel-Baska, J., & O'Neill, B. (1997). Making evaluation work: One school district's experience. *Gifted Child Quarterly, 41,* 124–132.

Bain, S., Bourgeois, S., & Pappas, D. (2003). Linking theoretical models to actual practices: A survey of teachers in gifted education. *Roeper Review, 25,* 166–172.

Baker, B. D., & Friedman-Nimz, R. (2003). Gifted children, vertical equity, and state school finance policies and practices. *Journal of Education Finance, 28,* 523–555.

Baker, E. L., & Schacter, J. (1996). Expert benchmarks for student academic performance: The case for gifted children. *Gifted Child Quarterly, 40,* 61–65.

Baum, S. M., Owen, S. V., & Oreck, B. A. (1996). Talent beyond words: Identification of potential talent in dance and music in elementary students. *Gifted Child Quarterly, 40,* 93–101.

Berger, S. (2003). Technology and gifted learners. In W. A. Owings & L. S. Kaplan (Eds.), *Best practices, best thinking, and emerging issues in school leadership* (pp. 177–190). Thousand Oaks, CA: Corwin Press.

Bloom, B. S., & Sosniak, L. A. (1981). Talent development vs. schooling. *Educational Leadership, 39,* 86–94.

Borland, J. H., & Wright, L. (1994). Identifying young, potentially gifted, economically disadvantaged students. *Gifted Child Quarterly, 38,* 164–171.

Brody, L. (1999). The talent searches: Counseling and mentoring activities. In N. Colangelo & S. Assouline (Eds.), *Talent development III: Proceedings from the 1995 Henry B. and Jocelyn Wallace National Research Symposium on Talent Development* (pp. 153–157). Scottsdale, AZ: Great Potential Press.

Callahan, C., Cooper, C., & Glascock, R. (2003). *Preparing teachers to develop and enhance talent: The position of national education organizations.* (ERIC Document Services No. ED477882)

Callahan, C., & Reis, S. (2004). *Program evaluation in gifted education: Essential readings in gifted education series.* Thousand Oaks, CA: Corwin Press.

Campbell, J. R., & Verna, M. A. (2007). Effective parental influence: Academic home climate linked to children's achievement. *Educational Research and Evaluation, 13,* 501–519.

Cattell, R. B. (1971). *Abilities: Their structure, growth, and action.* Boston, MA: Houghton Mifflin.

Cline, S., & Schwartz, D. (2000). *Diverse populations of gifted children: Meeting their needs in the regular classroom and beyond.* Columbus, OH: Prentice-Hall.

Colangelo, N., Assouline, S. G., & Gross, M. U. M. (2004). *A nation deceived: How schools hold back America's brightest students* (Vol. 1). Iowa City: The University of Iowa, The Connie Belin & Jacqueline N. Blank International Center for Gifted Education and Talent Development.

Coleman, M. R., & Johnsen, S. K. (Eds.). (2011). *RtI for gifted students.* Waco, TX: Prufrock Press.

Copenhaver, J. (2002). *Primer for maintaining accurate special education records and meeting confidentiality requirements when serving children with disabilities—Family Educational Rights and Privacy Act (FERPA).* Logan: Utah State University, Mountain Plains Regional Resource Center.

Council for Exceptional Children. (2009). *What every special educator must know: Ethics, standards, and guidelines* (6th ed.). Retrieved from http://www.cec.sped.org/Content/NavigationMenu/ProfessionalDevelopment/ProfessionalStandards/default.htm

Council for Exceptional Children. (2010). *Validation study resource manual.* Arlington, VA: Author.

Council of Chief State School Officers. (1992). *InTASC model core teaching standards.* Washington, DC: Author.

Council of Chief State School Officers, & National Governors Association. (2010). *Common core state standards initiative.* Retrieved from http://www.corestandards.org

Council of Chief State School Officers. (2011). *InTASC model core teaching standards: A resource for state dialogue.* Retrieved from http://www.ccsso.org/Documents/2011/InTASC_Model_Core_Teaching_Standards_2011.pdf

Cross, T., Stewart, R. A., & Coleman, L. (2003). Phenomenology and its implications for gifted studies research: Investigating the *lebenswelt* of academically gifted students attending an elementary magnet school. *Journal for the Education of the Gifted, 26,* 201–220.

Daniels, V. I. (1998). Minority students in gifted and special education programs: The case for educational equity. *Journal of Special Education, 32,* 41–44.

den Brok, P., Levy, J., Rodriguez, R., & Wubbels, T. (2002). Perceptions of Asian-American and Hispanic-American teachers and their students on teacher interpersonal communication style. *Teaching and Teacher Education, 18,* 447–467.

Dweck, C. S., & Kamins, M. L. (1999). Person versus process praise and criticism: Implications for contingent self-worth and coping. *Developmental Psychology, 35,* 835–847.

Elder, L., & Paul, R. (2004). *The art of asking essential questions.* Dillon Beach, CA: The Foundation for Critical Thinking.

Enersen, D. L. (1993). Summer residential programs: Academics and beyond. *Gifted Child Quarterly, 37,* 169–176.

Ford, D. Y. (2006). Creating culturally responsive classrooms for gifted students. *Understanding Our Gifted, 19*(1), 10–14.

Ford, D. Y., & Harmon, D. A. (2001). Equity and excellence: Providing access to gifted education for culturally diverse students. *Journal of Secondary Gifted Education, 12,* 141–148.

Ford, D. Y., & Harris, J. J., III. (1999). *Multicultural gifted education.* New York, NY: Teachers College Press.

Ford, D. Y., & Trotman, M. F. (2000). The Office for Civil Rights and non-discriminatory testing, policies, and procedures: Implications for gifted education. *Roeper Review, 23,* 109–112.

Ford, D. Y., & Trotman, M. F. (2001). Teachers of gifted students: Suggested multicultural characteristics and competencies. *Roeper Review, 23,* 235–239.

Ford, D., Tyson, C., Howard, T., & Harris, J. J. (2000). Multicultural literature and gifted Black students: Promoting self-understanding, awareness, and pride. *Roeper Review, 22,* 235–240.

Frasier, M. M., Garcia, J. H., & Passow, A. H. (1995). *A review of assessment issues in gifted education and their implications for identifying gifted minority students.*

Storrs: University of Connecticut, The National Research Center on the Gifted and Talented.

Frasier, M. M., Hunsaker, S. L., Lee, J., Finley, V. S., Frank, E., Garcia, J. H., & Martin, D. (1995). *Educators' perceptions of barriers to the identification of gifted children from economically disadvantaged and limited English proficient backgrounds* (Report RM-95216). Storrs: University of Connecticut, The National Research Center on the Gifted and Talented.

Frey, C. P. (1998). Struggling with identity: Working with seventh- and eighth-grade gifted girls to air issues of concern. *Journal for the Education of the Gifted, 21,* 437–451.

Gagné, F. (1999). My convictions about the nature of abilities, gifts, and talents. *Journal for the Education of the Gifted, 22,* 109–136.

Garet, M. S., Porter, A. C., Desimone, L., Birman, B. F., & Yoon, K. S. (2001). What makes professional development effective? Results from a national sample of teachers. *American Educational Research Journal, 38,* 915–945.

Gentry, M., & Ferriss, S. (1999). StATS: A model of collaboration to develop science talent among rural students. *Roeper Review, 21,* 316–320.

Gentry, M., & Owen, S. V. (1999). An investigation of the effects of total school flexible cluster grouping on identification, achievement, and classroom practices. *Gifted Child Quarterly, 43,* 224–243.

Grantham, T. C. (2003). Increasing Black student enrollment in gifted programs: An exploration of the Pulaski County Special School District's advocacy efforts. *Gifted Child Quarterly, 47,* 46–65.

Greene, M. J. (2003). Career adrift? Career counseling for the gifted and talented. *Roeper Review, 25,* 66–72.

Gubbins, E. J., Westberg, K. L., Reis, S. M., Dinnocenti, S. T., Tieso, C. L., Muller, L. M., . . . Burns, D. E. (2002). *Implementing a professional development model using gifted education strategies with all students* (Report RM02172). Storrs: University of Connecticut, The National Research Center on the Gifted and Talented.

Guskey, T. R. (2000). *Evaluating professional development.* Thousand Oaks, CA: Corwin Press.

Harper, S. R., & Antonio, A. (2008). Not by accident: Intentionality in diversity, learning and engagement. In S. R. Harper (Ed.), *Creating inclusive campus environments for cross-cultural learning and student engagement* (pp. 1–18). Washington, DC: National Association of Student Personnel Administrators.

Harris, B., Plucker, J. A., Rapp, K. E., & Martinez, R. S. (2009). Identifying gifted and talented English language learners: A case study. *Journal for the Education of the Gifted, 32,* 368–393.

Hartman, H. J. (2001). *Metacognition in learning and instruction: Theory, research and practice.* Dordrecht, The Netherlands: Kluwer Academic Publishers.

Hébert, T. P. (1991). Meeting the affective needs of bright boys through bibliotherapy. *Roeper Review, 13,* 207–212.

Hensel, N. H. (1991). Social leadership skills in young children. *Roeper Review, 14,* 4–6.

Hertzog, N. B. (2005). Equity and access: Creating general education classrooms responsive to potential giftedness. *Journal for the Education of the Gifted, 29,* 213–257.

Johnsen, S. K. (2006). New national standards for teachers of gifted and talented students. *Tempo, 26*(3), 26–31.

Johnsen, S. K. (2011a). A comparison of the Texas State Plan for the Education of Gifted/Talented Students and the 2010 NAGC Pre-K–Grade 12 Gifted Programming Standards. *Tempo, 31*(1), 10–28.

Johnsen, S. K. (Ed.). (2011b). *Identifying gifted students: A practical guide.* Waco, TX: Prufrock Press.

Johnsen, S. K., Haensly, P. A., Ryser, G. R., & Ford, R. F. (2002). Changing general education classroom practices to adapt for gifted students. *Gifted Child Quarterly, 46,* 45–63.

Johnsen, S. K., & Johnson, K. (2007). *Independent study program* (2nd ed.). Waco, TX: Prufrock Press.

Johnsen, S. K., VanTassel-Baska, J., & Robinson, A. (2008). *Using the national gifted education standards for university teacher preparation programs.* Thousand Oaks, CA: Corwin Press.

Kitano, M. K., & Lewis, R. B. (2005). Resilience and coping: Implications for gifted children and youth at risk. *Roeper Review, 27,* 200–205.

Kitano, M. K., Montgomery, D., VanTassel-Baska, J., & Johnsen, S. K. (2008). *Using the national gifted education standards for pre-K–12 professional development.* Thousand Oaks, CA: Corwin Press.

Kitano, M. K., & Pedersen, K. S. (2002a). Action research and practical inquiry: Multicultural-content integration in gifted education: Lessons from the field. *Journal for the Education of the Gifted, 26,* 269–289.

Kitano, M. K., & Pedersen, K. S. (2002b). Action research and practical inquiry: Teaching gifted English learners. *Journal for the Education of the Gifted, 26,* 132–147.

Klein, J. P., & Lugg, E. T. (2002). Nurturing young adolescents legally and ethically. *Middle School Journal, 34*(1), 13–20.

Kolesinski, M. T., & Leroux, J. A. (1992). The bilingual education experience, French-English, Spanish-English: From a perspective of gifted students. *Roeper Review, 14,* 221–224.

Kulik, J. A., & Kulik, C. C. (1992). Meta-analytic findings on grouping programs. *Gifted Child Quarterly, 36,* 73–77.

Landrum, M. S. (2002). *Resource consultation and collaboration in gifted education.* Mansfield Center, CT: Creative Learning Press.

Landrum, M. S., Callahan, C. M., & Shaklee, B. D. (2001). *Aiming for excellence: Gifted program standards: Annotations to the NAGC Pre-K–Grade 12 Gifted Program Standards.* Waco, TX: Prufrock Press.

Lee, S.-Y., & Olszewski-Kubilius, P. (2006). The emotional intelligence, moral judgment, and leadership of academically gifted adolescents. *Journal for the Education of the Gifted, 30,* 29–67.

Maxwell, M. (2007). Career counseling is personal counseling: A constructivist approach to nurturing the development of gifted female adolescents. *The Career Development Quarterly, 55,* 206–224.

McKown, C., & Weinstein, R. S. (2008). Teacher expectations, classroom context, and the achievement gap. *Journal of School Psychology, 46,* 235–261.

Moon, S. M. (1996). Using the Purdue three-stage model to facilitate local program evaluation. *Gifted Child Quarterly, 40,* 121–128.

Moon, S. M., Jurich, J. A., & Feldhusen, J. F. (1998). Families of gifted children: Cradles of development. In R. C. Friedman & K. Rogers (Eds.), *Talent in context: Historical and social perspectives on giftedness* (pp. 81–99). Washington, DC: American Psychological Association.

Morris, J. E. (2002). African American students and gifted education. *Roeper Review, 24,* 59–62.

National Association for Gifted Children. (2000). *Pre-K–Grade 12 Gifted Program Standards.* Washington, DC: Author.

National Association for Gifted Children. (2007). *NCATE teacher education standards committee: NAGC governance policy, Policy manual-8.2.2.* Washington, DC: Author.

National Association for Gifted Children. (2008–2009). *State of the nation in gifted education.* Washington, DC: Author.

National Association for Gifted Children. (2010). *NAGC pre-K–grade 12 gifted programming standards: A blueprint for quality gifted education programs.* Washington, DC: Author.

National Association for Gifted Children, & Council for Exceptional Children, The Association for the Gifted. (2006). *NAGC–CEC teacher knowledge and skill standards for gifted and talented education.* Retrieved from http://www.ncate.org/Standards/ProgramStandardsandReportForms/tabid/676/Default.aspx

National Board for Professional Teaching Standards. (2011). *Exceptional needs standards* (2nd ed.). Retrieved from http://www.nbpts.org/for_candidates/certificate_areas1?ID=18&x=42&y=9

National Commission on Excellence in Education. (1983). *A nation at risk: The imperative for educational reform.* Washington, DC: U.S. Government Printing Office.

National Council for Accreditation of Teacher Education. (2009). *Summary of board actions NCATE fall all-boards meeting, October 19–23, 2009.* Retrieved from http://www.ncate.org/LinkClick.aspx?fileticket=6MLImbd3roc%3d&tabid=522

Neihart, M. (2002). Risk and resilience in gifted children: A conceptual framework. In M. Neihart, S. M. Reis, N. M. Robinson, & S. M. Moon (Eds.), *The social and emotional development of gifted children: What do we know?* (pp. 113–122). Waco, TX: Prufrock Press.

No Child Left Behind Act, 20 U.S.C. §6301 (2001).

Olszewski-Kubilius, P., Grant, B., & Seibert, C. (1994). Social support systems and the disadvantaged gifted: A framework for developing programs and services. *Roeper Review, 17,* 20–25.

Purcell, J. H., & Leppien, J. H. (1998). Building bridges between general practitioners and educators of the gifted: A study of collaboration. *Gifted Child Quarterly, 42,* 172–181.

Pyryt, M. C. (2003). Technology and the gifted. In N. Colangelo & G. A. Davis (Eds.), *Handbook of gifted education* (3rd ed., pp. 582–589). Boston, MA: Allyn & Bacon.

Reis, S. M., Burns, D. E., & Renzulli, J. S. (1992). *Curriculum compacting: The complete guide to modifying the regular curriculum for high ability students.* Mansfield Center, CT: Creative Learning Press.

Renzulli, J. (1978). What makes giftedness? Reexamining a definition. *Phi Delta Kappan, 60,* 180–184.

Renzulli, J. S., & Reis, S. M. (2003). The Schoolwide Enrichment Model: Developing creative and productive giftedness. In N. Colangelo & G. A. Davis (Eds.), *Handbook of gifted education* (3rd ed., pp. 184–203). Boston, MA: Allyn & Bacon.

Rogers, K. B. (1991). *The relationship of grouping practices to the education of the gifted and talented learner: Research-based decision making series.* Storrs: University of Connecticut, The National Research Center on the Gifted and Talented.

Ross, J., & Smyth, E. (1995). Differentiating cooperative learning to meet the needs of gifted learners: A case for transformational leadership. *Journal for the Education of the Gifted, 19,* 63–82.

Ryser, G. R. (2011). Fairness in testing and nonbiased assessment. In S. K. Johnsen (Ed.), *Identifying gifted students: A practical guide* (pp. 63–74). Waco, TX: Prufrock Press.

Shade, B. J., Kelly, C., & Oberg, M. (1997). *Creating culturally responsive classrooms.* Washington, DC: American Psychological Association.

Siegle, D. (2004). *Using media and technology with gifted learners.* Waco, TX: Prufrock Press.

Siegle, D., & McCoach, D. G. (2005). Extending learning through mentorships. In F. A. Karnes & S. M. Bean (Eds.), *Methods and materials for teaching the gifted* (2nd ed., pp. 473–518). Waco, TX: Prufrock Press.

Simonton, D. K. (2000). Cognitive, personal, developmental, and social aspects. *American Psychologist, 55,* 151–158.

Stiggins, R. (2008). *Assessment manifesto: A call for the development of balanced assessment systems.* Portland, OR: ETS Assessment Training Institute.

Tannenbaum, A. (1991). The social psychology of giftedness. In N. Colangelo & G. A. Davis (Eds.), *Handbook of gifted education* (pp. 27–44). Boston, MA: Allyn & Bacon.

Tomlinson, C. A. (Ed.). (2004). *Differentiation for gifted and talented students.* Thousand Oaks, CA: Corwin Press.

U.S. Department of Education (2008). *A nation accountable: Twenty-five years after a nation at risk.* Washington, DC: Author. Retrieved from http://www2.ed.gov/rschstat/research/pubs/accountable/accountable.pdf/

VanTassel-Baska, J. (2004). *Curriculum for gifted and talented students.* Thousand Oaks, CA: Corwin Press.

VanTassel-Baska, J. (Ed.). (2006). *Serving gifted learners beyond the traditional classroom: A guide to alternative programs and services.* Waco, TX: Prufrock Press.

VanTassel-Baska, J. (Ed.). (2007). *Alternative assessments with gifted and talented students.* Waco, TX: Prufrock Press.

VanTassel-Baska, J. (Ed.). (2009). *Patterns and profiles of promising learners from poverty.* Waco, TX: Prufrock Press.

Williams, E. R., & Baber, C. R. (2007). Building trust through culturally reciprocal home-school-community collaboration from the perspective of African-American parents. *Multicultural Perspectives, 9*(2), 3–9.

Zeidner, M., & Schleyer, E. J. (1999). Evaluating the effects of full-time vs. part-time educational programs for the gifted: Affective outcomes and policy considerations. *Evaluation and Program Planning, 22,* 413–427.

Zirkel, S. (2008). The influence of multicultural educational practices on student outcomes and intergroup relations. *Teachers College Record, 110,* 1147–1181.

Chapter 2

Creating Environments for Social and Emotional Development

by Thomas P. Hébert

To begin to examine the challenges of creating appropriate school environments for social and emotional development of highly intelligent young people, it is critical to define our terms. The definition of social and emotional development that informs this discussion is that proposed by Moon (2003, as cited in National Association for Gifted Children [NAGC], 2010), who defined it as "those factors from a psychological perspective that assert an affective influence on an individual's self-image, behavior, and motivation; issues such as but not limited to peer relationships, emotional adjustment, stress management, perfectionism, and sensitivity" (p. 15).

The 2010 NAGC Pre-K–Grade 12 Gifted Programming Standards driving the field of gifted education incorporate a number of student outcomes and practices that are related to the social and emotional development of students with gifts and talents. These NAGC student outcomes and evidence-based practices cut across several of the categories including learning and development, curriculum planning and instruction, learning environments, and programming and professional development. They are organized thematically and presented below, followed by a succinct discussion of research support and effective practices to inform gifted education teachers and administrators. This discussion is in no way exhaustive but represents an effort to highlight the major strands of the research literature. This chapter then provides a micro-level description of one classroom to show how teachers might implement strategies to reach these outcomes and concludes with a broader description of the philosophical underpinnings that would guide such an approach in one school.

Student Outcomes and Practices

As one examines the Gifted Programming Standards, it becomes evident that student outcomes in social and emotional development and the practices to support them emerge thematically and include self-understanding; awareness of learning and affective needs; personal, social, and cultural competence; and the appreciation of talents and the recognition of ways to support their development.

Self-Understanding

The first significant theme emerging in the standards related to social and emotional development is self-understanding evident in the lives of gifted young people (e.g., see 1.1–1.3). Within this population there exists self-knowledge regarding their identities, interests, and strengths. Gifted students acquire a developmentally appropriate understanding of how they learn and grow and a respect of similarities and differences between themselves and their peers.

The research within the field of gifted education that best informs the knowledge base on self-understanding is within the areas of identity formation in gifted individuals and their striving for self-actualization. Several studies have examined self-actualization in gifted students. Lewis, Karnes, and Knight (1995) found that gifted elementary and middle school students scored higher on measures of self-actualization than the general population. In addition, Karnes and McGinnis (1996) reported a significant correlation between measures of self-actualization and inner locus of control in gifted teenagers. In a more recent study, Pufal-Struzik (1999) found that gifted students reached higher levels of self-actualization than the control group did. She noted that the gifted students who had a sense of self-actualization had a higher level of self-acceptance. Moreover, a strong need for intellectual stimulation was associated with their self-acceptance. These findings were consistent with a qualitative research study by Hébert and McBee (2007) examining gifted college students in a university honors program. Within this population they found a strong drive to achieve self-actualization. This desire for self-actualization included valuing knowledge and education, a desire to overcome weaknesses, and a need to align one's personal behavior with ethical principles that guided their lives.

Research on identity development in gifted students supports our understanding of this need to strive for self-actualization. In a study of six gifted high-achieving males in an urban high school, Hébert (2000a) identified a strong belief in self as the most significant factor influencing the success of the young men. These males had developed a solid identity that provided them with the drive, energy, and skills they needed to deal with life's challenges in an urban environment. Similar results were found in subsequent studies conducted by Hébert on special populations of gifted males in different contexts. A strong belief in self was found to be significant in shaping the experiences of a group of gifted collegiate males pursuing careers in elementary education (Hébert,

2000b). In addition, Hébert (2002) examined gifted African American first-generation college males in a predominantly White university and discovered that their firm belief in self, combined with strong internal motivation, helped to shape their identity as high achievers. Dole (2001) examined how dual exceptionalities influenced the identity formation of gifted college students with learning disabilities. Within these young adults, she found that "Knowledge of self was ongoing and led to self-acceptance and self-advocacy, not necessarily in that order" (Dole, 2001, p. 122). Their self-understanding and self-acceptance supported them in establishing realistic career goals, and they tapped into their strengths and persisted in accomplishing their goals.

Research studies have shed light on our understanding of the critical need to support gifted and talented students in the process of coming to know and understand themselves and where they want to go in life. Educators can be trained to support them in this journey.

Awareness of Learning and Affective Needs

The second important theme emerging in the Gifted Programming Standards on social and emotional development is an awareness of learning and affective needs in gifted students (e.g., see 1.4–1.8). Advanced learners recognize their preferred approaches to learning, and they require meaningful and challenging school experiences that address their unique characteristics and needs. Gifted students are able to easily interact with others having similar interests, abilities, or experiences and access resources from the community to support their cognitive and affective needs. In doing so, they often identify talent development opportunities to reach their future career goals.

Research literature on the important role of involvement in extracurricular activities sheds light on several of these characteristics. Gifted education scholars have found that gifted students participate actively in academic and athletic extracurricular activities (Bucknavage & Worrell, 2005; Olszewski-Kubilius & Lee, 2004). Such activities serve as outlets for gifts and talents and enable young people to experiment with developing them. Additionally, involvement in clubs, teams, or campaigns provides opportunities for gifted students to build a sense of self-efficacy and experience the joy of success (Calvert & Cleveland, 2006; Hébert & Reis, 1999). Being a member of a group known for accomplishment nurtures a strong belief in self, and successful and productive group experiences also support young people in raising personal aspirations for the future. Moreover, gifted students often discover significant mentors in the adults who facilitate the extracurricular activities.

Researchers have also found that twice-exceptional students who struggle with the challenges of being gifted with a learning disability will discover their strengths in extracurricular activities. Rather than see themselves as struggling learners in mathematics, they prefer to think of themselves as superstars on the theatrical stage or in the athletic arena (Mooney & Cole, 2000; Rodis, Garrod, & Boscardin, 2001).

Offering appropriate outlets for developing talents in gifted young people serves an important role in social and emotional development. As young people engage in talent development, they experience challenges as well as joys of success, and they continue to grow in their self-understanding and self-actualization. Moreover, educators can play important roles in supporting their talent development.

Personal, Social, and Cultural Competence

The third theme emerging in the Gifted Programming Standards on social and emotional development is the personal, social, and cultural competence evident in gifted young people (e.g., see 3.5, 4.1–4.4). Gifted students demonstrate growth in personal and social competence and dispositions for exceptional academic and creative productivity. This competence includes self-advocacy and self-efficacy, confidence, motivation, reliance, curiosity, risk taking, and leadership, which may be manifested in positive relationships with peers and in social interactions with adults. Moreover, gifted students possess skills in cultural sensitivity and are able to communicate and collaborate with diverse individuals and across diverse groups.

In order to appreciate the personal, social, and cultural competence of gifted students, educators must examine research from the 1920s, when Leta Hollingworth contributed significantly to our understanding of the social and emotional development of gifted children. She was the first psychologist to systematically examine peer relationships of gifted students at differing ranges of intellectual giftedness. Hollingworth was fascinated by the differences she uncovered in the cognitive and affective development of moderately and highly gifted children. She defined the IQ range of 125–155 as "socially optimal intelligence" (Hollingworth, 1926). She pointed out that children within this range were well adjusted, self-confident, and outgoing young people who discovered and maintained meaningful friendships with their age peers. She noted, however, that children above the 160 IQ level struggled with problems of social isolation. She discovered the more intelligent the child, the less often he or she was able to find a true companion, and many highly gifted children with IQs of 180 or above developed personal habits of solitary play. Since the work of Hollingworth, research has consistently confirmed her findings (DeHaan & Havighurst, 1961; Gallagher, 1958; Janos, Marwood, & Robinson, 1985).

The work of Miraca Gross (1992, 1993, 2004) on friendships and gifted children has also added a great deal to our understanding of personal and social competence within this population. Gross conducted studies examining the longitudinal effects of acceleration and found important social and emotional benefits. She also found that gifted children's views of friendship undergo a developmental hierarchy of stages that are age-related. She noted that as children mature, their expectations of friendship and beliefs about friendship become more sophisticated and complex. Through her findings, she delineated five linear stages: play partner, people to chat to, help and encouragement, intimacy/empathy, and the sure shelter. Throughout her studies, Gross found that what gifted children seek in friendships is not driven by chronological age as much as mental age. It should be noted that research by Gross is consistent with studies that examined the experiences of gifted students who were accelerated and found no significant negative consequences related to personal or social competence (Colangelo, Assouline, & Gross, 2004; Olszewski-Kubilius, 2002; Rinn, 2008). It remains evident that personal and social competence and the ability to search for and discover meaningful relationships with other young people will often depend on just how superior intellectually one child is over another. Moreover, with development and maturity, gifted students learn personal and social competence and become capable of enjoying important friendships.

Along with their ability to grow in developing meaningful relationships and friendships, evidence of gifted students developing other personal traits and competencies has been reported through research. Internal motivation or an inner locus of control has been highlighted. Individuals who assume control or responsibility for the events in their lives are said to display an inner locus of control. Researchers have found evidence of this trait in gifted young people (Goldberg & Cornell, 1998; Hébert, 2000a; McLaughlin & Saccuzzo, 1997). Such a trait helps to explain the degree to which a student recognizes a relationship between his own behavior and the outcome of that behavior. Understanding this trait and how to develop it within young people would help educators to support gifted underachievers.

Resilience, defined by Neihart (2002) as "the ability to achieve emotional health and social competence in spite of a history of adversity or stress" (p. 114), has also been reported to be a characteristic of gifted young people. Reis, Hébert, Diaz, Maxfield, and Ratley (1995), a team of researchers from The National Research Center on the Gifted and Talented, conducted a 3-year study of high-ability high school students who achieved or underachieved in an urban setting. These researchers found that many of the high-achieving students demonstrated resilience by overcoming problems related to their families, their high school, and their urban community. They reported that the resilience and the courage displayed by these teenagers was remarkable, as these students quietly accepted their difficult circumstances and appreciated opportunities their school and community had to offer them. They made the best of their situations and went on to become valedictorians, school leaders, scholars, and star athletes; graduated with major scholarships; and moved on to Ivy League schools or the most selective colleges in the country.

The study by Reis and her colleagues (1995) is also noteworthy in that the research team found evidence of multicultural awareness and sensitivity within the sample of urban high school students. These young people acknowledged that appreciation for cultural diversity was an important part of their identity. They highlighted the pride they had in the culturally diverse population of their high school and how their appreciation for diversity helped them become better adults.

The development of affective skills associated with personal, social, and cultural competence helps to prepare young people for meaningful lives. Educators may play significant roles in supporting such competencies and can do so through enriched curriculum and classroom environments designed to support social and emotional development.

Appreciation of Talents and the Recognition of Ways to Support Student Development

The final theme in the Gifted Programming Standards on social and emotional development is an appreciation of talents within gifted young people and their recognition of ways to support the development of their gifts and talents (e.g., see 5.1–5.7). Gifted students appreciate being able to develop their strengths in their domain of talent or area of interest that may be aligned with future career goals. For this reason, researchers in gifted education have long recognized the value of providing mentorship opportunities for this population.

Mentoring involves a personal relationship between a young person and an older individual who may be an expert in a field or is knowledgeable about a particular topic. In a mentoring relationship, shared interests, common passions, or career interests may bring the student and the adult together. Mentors work with their protégés in a partnership as they explore their common interest or passion. Gifted education teachers and researchers have often noted that the benefits of mentoring programs on the social and emotional development of gifted students surpass any academic or career objectives. Researchers and practitioners have reported increased self-understanding and self-confidence (Nash, 2001; Siegle, McCoach, & Wilson, 2009); commitment, empathy, and self-trust (Tomlinson, 2001); increased responsibility (Subotnik, 2003); and positive self-image (Goff & Torrance, 1999). Tomlinson (2001) celebrated the benefits of this approach as she maintained that "powerful mentorships help prepare young people to live with greater purpose, focus, and appreciation at a younger age by drawing not only on the knowledge of the past, but on its wisdom as well" (p. 27).

The appreciation of diverse talents and recognition of ways to develop the strengths of gifted and talented students involves a school's effort to design appropriate mentoring opportunities. Such efforts are worthwhile and will benefit our communities in the future.

Designing a Gifted-Friendly Classroom Environment: One Teacher's Approach

The following discussion presents how Kate, a fictionalized eighth-grade teacher of gifted students, incorporated multiple strategies field tested by the author to create a classroom environment designed to support the social and emotional development of her students.[1] Kate's challenge was the critical task of creating an emotional climate in her classroom that enabled her students to feel they were valued for their intelligence and creativity and respected as individuals by both their teacher and their classmates.

Kate was a language arts teacher working with students formally identified as gifted by her school district who selected to enroll in her advanced class. She welcomed her students on the first day of school with a small brown paper sack decorated with ribbons. During the summer, Kate had spent a little time at the local dollar store purchasing inexpensive items that she included in the small paper sack. She attached a simple note to the students welcoming them to her classroom and explaining the following items included in the sack:

- » A blank CD—In this classroom, you will burn your own path to success.
- » Laffy Taffy—Remember to always keep your sense of humor.
- » A jigsaw puzzle piece—Everyone in this classroom is unique, but together we can make something great.
- » A jumbo paper clip—In this classroom, we will all help each other keep it together.
- » Miniature Post-it® Notes—You'll need these to capture your important "Aha!s."

» A free homework pass—For that one day when you will really need to cash it in. (Hébert, 2011, p. 353)

With a little bit of preparation and creativity, Kate designed these treats for her students to help them realize they were about to embark upon a great academic year in advanced language arts. Following the unpacking of the little brown sacks, Kate enjoyed facilitating an activity she referred to as "Little Known Facts." She asked her new students to jot down on an index card five interesting facts or items of information about themselves. She explained that within that list of five, one of the items had to be a lie. Students were then directed to exchange the cards with another classmate, enjoy conversation with each other, and determine which of the items was a lie. Kate included herself in this activity. Her list of interesting bits of information were as follows:

» I enjoy dancing Zumba.
» I am a triplet.
» In my senior year, I was president of my high school's Future Home-makers of America club.
» As a young girl, I enjoyed organizing my friends and putting on puppet shows in my backyard for all of the neighbors on my street.
» I once lived in Zurich, Switzerland.

Kate's students enjoyed sharing their interesting lives with each other and their teacher. They were delighted to learn that their teacher was capable of telling a lie. Although she had never lived in Switzerland, she shared with her students her dream of spending one summer backpacking across Europe. Following their conversation in dyads, Kate had each student introduce his or her new friend to the class. Plenty of good-natured laughter evolved, the students quickly learned a great deal about each other, and this nonthreatening activity provided Kate with plenty of conversation starters at the beginning of the year.

Later that week, Kate implemented another activity she referred to as "Business Cards." She explained to her students how professionals design business cards that present an image to the world of just what they are all about. Kate then shared a collection of business cards that she had collected from her travels and helped her students to see how many of them delivered very clear messages. Kate's students enjoyed seeing how the graphic on a card from Andrew's Lawn Care spoke to them, saying that Andrew was meticulous in his approach to mowing and landscaping. Kate's card from the Boone Bagelry Restaurant in Boone, NC, offered a clear message that folks in Boone had a great place to enjoy a scrumptious breakfast. A card from Lotus Sun Therapeutics in Athens, GA, indicated to Kate's students that their teacher probably enjoyed a well-deserved massage during stressful times of the year from the therapist featured. From the colorful lotus blossom shown on the business card, Kate's students might have assumed that their teacher was in good hands.

Following the discussion of the business cards, Kate had her students reflect on the question "What does a business card say about you?" She distributed large sheets of art paper and crayons and provided them the time to design their personal business cards. Kate's objective behind this activity was to help each gifted student find a friend in that language arts classroom. She wanted the science fiction buffs to discover each other. She wanted the young women who designed step dance routines to find other dancers. She wanted the sports fanatics to locate others like them. She believed that through their common interests, new friendships would emerge. Kate proudly displayed their cards on the classroom walls and enjoyed watching her students as they made new friendship connections.

To reinforce the importance of those friendship connections, Kate incorporated a simple language arts activity that focused on friendships. One morning she paired her students and provided them time to get to know each other in quiet conversation. Once they'd had enough time to learn about each other's lives beyond their middle school, they were directed to write a two-word poem describing their new friend. She explained that each line of the poem was limited to two words. After the poets had completed their work and introduced their new friends to the class, Kate encouraged her students to accompany the poem with original artwork. The poems and illustrations were proudly displayed on a classroom bulletin board. One example of a poem that resulted from this activity is offered below:

Michael Vernon
Twin brother
Skateboard expert
Curly hair
Donut lover
Basketball player
Huskies fan
Awesome guy!

—Clark Oliver

Along with providing strategies designed to have her students come to know each other and their teacher, Kate knew that she needed to learn more important information about her students' interests. In order to design appropriate instructional activities that would engage these bright young people,

Kate conducted interest inventories with her students. Her facilitation of interest surveys enabled her to make connections with the interests of her students and the language arts curriculum she was required to deliver. By learning her students' interests, Kate was able to adjust the curriculum to address their individual needs.

Kate followed Nugent's (2005) recommendation that teachers develop their own interest inventories by asking questions about what they enjoy doing after school, their involvement in sports, important people in their lives, family travels, reading interests, and how they feel about particular literary genres. By applying her personal creativity to a menu of questions for her students, Kate uncovered much helpful information that would inform her language arts instruction while also creating a supportive classroom environment. Kate believed that along with planning her curriculum, having students complete the inventories sent an important message to them that said, "I care about you beyond this classroom and want to know what you're interested in." Kate infused clever questions such as, "What picture is on your screen-saver on your computer? Why?" (Hébert, 2011, p. 361) and "If you could change anything about your middle school, what would it be?" Through these inventory questions, Kate learned a great deal of helpful information about her students' interests, learning styles, personality traits, and lives beyond their middle school.

As a teacher of language arts, Kate was fortunate because her content area allowed for her to address the social and emotional needs of her students through literature. Kate was a proponent of using literature to facilitate discussions with her students about their issues or concerns. Acknowledging that she was not a therapist, Kate recognized that as a classroom teacher she could facilitate quality discussions with middle school students about good books. By doing so, she could help her students draw parallels between their experiences and those of the main characters in the novels, biographies, or short stories they were reading in class. Her objective was to guide gifted students to self-understanding. When she facilitated such discussions, she was always pleased to note that the students were really listening to each other as they shared their feelings about personal experiences related to the central characters in the books. Kate saw this approach as her work in helping her students understand themselves and cope with developmental adolescent problems by offering literature relevant to their personal situations as gifted teenagers.

Kate agreed with Halsted (2009), who maintained that literature engages gifted students emotionally. Kate understood that the therapeutic experience began when young people enjoyed a book and discovered that the main characters were very much like themselves. This interaction is referred to as identification, and the more Kate's gifted students had in common with the characters they met in the books, the more meaningful the identification process became. When that identification process occurred, it was accompanied by a catharsis, an emotional feeling that lets gifted students know that they are not alone in tackling a problem. Kate saw that as her students enjoyed the literature, they learned vicariously through the books' characters and were often able to gain new ways of examining their troublesome issues. As a result of the sensitive manner in which she facilitated the classroom discussions, her students gained insights, and they were often able to apply new problem-solving strategies discussed with their classmates the next time a problematic situation occurred.

In facilitating such discussions, Kate realized that she needed to incorporate meaningful follow-up activities after a class discussion of a book. She included a variety of enjoyable options such as creative writing, journaling, cartooning, blogging, writing song lyrics, writing raps, designing television commercials, or self-selected options that her students generated. Kate discovered that as her students were engaged in these activities, they continued discussion among themselves about the issues they had discussed earlier with the whole class, and they continued to provide each other supportive feedback. Kate smiled to herself after a class discussion when she overheard two eighth-grade boys quietly chatting and one commented, "Jamal, I never knew that Sam Sherlock used to harass you in first grade. Man! It made me feel better to know that I wasn't the only kid he picked on back then."

In her work with this approach, Kate also learned that follow-up activities in her classroom could be either collaborative or private. She discovered that when discussions involved students engaging in rather serious self-disclosure, private journaling as a follow-up activity provided her students the needed time to process their feelings. Kate believed that the follow-up activities were just as important to her students as the discussion of the books, and she found that the more hands-on the follow-up activities, the more her eighth-grade boys would talk. She found it fascinating that engaging in hands-on activities was so critical for the young men in her classroom to be more comfortable in discussing anything personal. Kate noticed that the girls had no problems with this issue.

Kate also discovered that she enjoyed facilitating discussions about social and emotional issues using movies. Kate found that this strategy—referred to in the field of gifted education as guided viewing of film (Hébert & Hammond, 2006; Hébert & Sergent, 2005)—offered several benefits to her students. Kate realized that movies were an important component of adolescent culture. Her students pointed out that being cool meant being knowledgeable about the most current popular films. With movies playing such an influential role in their teenage lives, Kate believed that her gifted students would be receptive to discussing sensitive topics through enjoyable films. Using movies that were aligned with her language arts curriculum, she would occasionally reinforce the study of a novel with a parallel film and address affective issues such as friendship, identity development, peer pressure, and parental and family expectations. As she and her students enjoyed discussions on the films, Kate was able to deliver her language arts content as well as provide healthy classroom guidance.

In her work using movies, Kate found that were times when she wanted to offer guided viewing sessions with small groups of teenagers struggling with a particular issue such as underachievement, perfectionism, or giftedness combined with a learning disability. Other times she chose to organize single-sex groups for films that addressed gender-specific issues in a sensitive manner. Kate offered her students these opportunities during lunch or after school. These smaller groups of students found more comfort in a setting where only their classmates present shared similar challenges. Just as she incorporated follow-up activities in using literature, Kate found it helpful to assist students in processing feelings evoked by the movie through enjoyable, hands-on activities.

Along with the infusion of strategies to address affective development in her students, Kate's design of a gifted-friendly classroom environment incorporated a classroom mailbox that enabled her students to communicate with her privately. Kate's mentor teacher during her year of student teaching had provided her evidence that middle school students often needed outlets for privately sharing what was going on in their lives beyond school. She saw evidence of success with this approach, and she included the mailbox in her classroom every year. She covered a shoe box in brightly colored paper, and explained to her students that if they were to leave a letter in the box, she guaranteed that they would find a letter from her in a sealed envelope the following day.

Throughout the years she implemented "Ms. Kate's Mailbox," she found that students typically communicated their thoughts on aspects of the language arts class that they were enjoying, reviews of her style of fashion, or venting about boy-girl relationships. Occasionally Kate received letters from students that were calls for help with more serious issues that she knew she was not equipped to address. Kate responded to those letters the following day with a private conversation with the student, made a point to introduce the child to the school counselor, and assisted in scheduling some time with the counselor during these difficult periods in eighth grade. Kate's mailbox was an effective approach to student-teacher communication and served as a critical outlet for teenagers when they needed support, encouragement, or adult guidance.

Another important component of Kate's language arts classroom was significant time dedicated throughout the year to involvement in social outreach projects. As Kate observed characteristics within her students such as moral maturity, sensitivity, and empathy, she believed that a natural approach to supporting those qualities was to encourage her students to engage in work that involved reaching out and helping others in the community. Kate believed that for gifted young people, involvement in social action projects addressed their need for consistency between their adolescent values and their actions, and such involvement enabled them to address authentic community problems and become effective voices for change (Hart, Atkins, & Donnelly, 2006).

To provide her students with such opportunities, Kate applied her personal creativity and discovered connections between the language arts curriculum and social action projects. When reading a young adult novel about the challenges faced by a teenager from a family of migrant workers, Kate's students were compelled by the difficult issues facing the family and became involved in several outreach projects to support families living in a nearby migrant community. Another novel centered on a poignant relationship between a young adolescent male and an elderly woman led Kate's students to reach out to the nearby nursing home with visits and projects that connected individual teenagers to their special friends in the senior community. With every outreach project that Kate facilitated, she found that her students discovered volunteering for others less fortunate really made them feel good and helped them to realize how their talents enabled them to make a meaningful difference in their communities.

Support for Creating a Gifted-Friendly Classroom Environment: Philosophical Underpinnings of Kate's School

For school districts interested in applying the Gifted Programming Standards in gifted education to their schools, it may be time for educators and administrators to reflect on the philosophical beliefs that guide the design of classroom environments. Are the classrooms in these schools similar to Kate's? If not, what needs to be changed? Does the school district need to reflect on its philosophical beliefs related to educating gifted learners? What might that philosophy look like?

Kate was fortunate to work in a middle school where her administrators and colleagues appreciated her approach to a supportive classroom environment for social and emotional development. She realized that her school's philosophical approach to middle-grades education was consistent with what she valued in gifted education. Kate believed that teaching gifted middle school students required maintaining academic rigor and providing curriculum that offered intellectual challenge. She also believed that gifted young people would engage in hard intellectual work more effectively if their concomitant social and emotional needs were addressed.

Fortunately, Kate's professional colleagues took that same approach to education. As a faculty, they maintained that gifted students needed appropriate levels of academic challenge and time every day to work with other students of similar abilities, interests, and motivation. They believed in a continuum of services including counseling, acceleration, enrichment, extracurricular activities, and mentorships; however, they worked hard to provide a responsive educational environment matched to the level and pace of students' learning, recognition for excellent work and persistent effort, and opportunities for choice of topics aligned with individual interests (Robinson, Reis, Neihart, & Moon, 2002).

In examining their continuum of services for gifted students, Kate's administrators and colleagues also recognized a need to develop a broad yet comprehensive approach to supporting social and emotional development by designing a scope and sequence of affective skills in educating young adolescents. To pursue such an approach, educators might consider examining the Gifted Programming Standards and developing a menu of affective training skills to integrate into the school's curriculum. The following list of skills serves as a beginning to developing curriculum that addresses social and emotional development:

- » understanding self,
- » understanding others,
- » developing empathy,
- » working collaboratively with others,
- » peer relationships,
- » parental relationships,
- » moral reasoning,
- » interpersonal communication,
- » assertiveness training and self-advocacy,
- » conflict management,
- » identity development,
- » celebrating your strengths,
- » coping with stress,
- » developing a sense of humor,
- » appreciating gender differences,
- » celebrating diversity, and
- » planning for your future.

Kate's school was a model of Parker Palmer's (1993) approach to education. Palmer, a well-known educational theorist, saw teaching as creating a learning space. His poetic metaphor for a learning environment included three important characteristics that are significant in supporting the social and emotional development of young people: openness, boundaries, and a spirit of hospitality. According to Palmer, openness referred to eliminating any barriers to learning. He indicated that educators who designed learning spaces had to define and protect the boundaries of that space. They recognized that learning spaces needed structure, for without it, confusion and chaos would occur. Moreover, learning spaces incorporated a spirit of hospitality that Palmer described as individuals being open to receiving each other and each other's new ideas. He maintained that learning spaces were to be hospitable to make learning enjoyable and flexible enough to provide room for young people to experience difficult challenges involved in learning such as testing one's hypotheses, questioning false information, and dealing with mutual criticism within a community of learners.

Classrooms throughout Kate's school could be viewed as what Kennedy (1995) described were gifted-friendly classroom environments in which bright students "feel valued and comfortable, free to develop socially and emotionally, as well as intellectually" (p. 292). Kennedy described what we have seen in Kate's classroom: "an environment in which a child is encouraged both to ask and answer complex questions . . . an environment in which individual differences are honored, and no one is ostracized . . . an environment in which the child can expect to learn new things every day—and to enjoy learning" (p. 232). Fogarty (1998) was consistent in this view in that she saw such classroom environments as places "that celebrate the joy of the learner's emotional and intellectual world . . . through richness and relationships" (p. 655). More recently, Stephanie Pace Marshall, Founding President and President Emerita of the Illinois Mathematics and Science Academy, captured the essence of this approach with a simple yet thoughtful message to students in today's schools. This message is one that Kate and many more teachers of gifted students will want to post high at the front of their classrooms: "Take care of yourself. Take care of each other. Take care of this place."

References

Bucknavage, L. B., & Worrell, F. C. (2005). A study of academically talented students' participation in extracurricular activities. *Journal of Secondary Gifted Education, 16,* 74–86.

Calvert, E., & Cleveland, E. (2006). Extracurricular activities. In F. A. Dixon & S. M. Moon (Eds.), *The handbook of secondary gifted education* (pp. 527–546). Waco, TX: Prufrock Press.

Colangelo, N., Assouline, S. G., & Gross, M. U. M. (2004). *A nation deceived: How schools hold back America's brightest students* (Vol. 1). Iowa City: The University of Iowa, The Connie Belin & Jacqueline N. Blank International Center for Gifted Education and Talent Development.

DeHaan, R. F., & Havighurst, R. J. (1961). *Educating gifted children* (2nd ed.). Chicago, IL: University of Chicago Press.

Dole, S. (2001). Reconciling contradictions: Identity formation in individuals with giftedness and learning disabilities. *Journal for the Education of the Gifted, 25,* 103–137.

Fogarty, R. (1998, May). The intelligence-friendly classroom: It just makes sense. *Phi Delta Kappan, 79,* 655–657.

Gallagher, J. J. (1958). Peer acceptance of highly gifted children in elementary school. *Elementary School Journal, 58,* 465–470.

Goff, K., & Torrance, E. P. (1999). Discovering and developing giftedness through mentoring. *Gifted Child Today, 22*(3), 14–15, 52–53.

Goldberg, M. D., & Cornell, D. G. (1998). The influence of intrinsic motivation and self-concept on academic achievement in second- and third-grade students. *Journal for the Education of the Gifted, 21,* 179–205.

Gross, M. U. M. (1992). The use of radical acceleration in cases of extreme intellectual precocity. *Gifted Child Quarterly, 36,* 91–99.

Gross, M. U. M. (1993). *Exceptionally gifted children.* London, England: Routledge.

Gross, M. U. M. (2004). *Exceptionally gifted children* (2nd ed.). New York, NY: RoutledgeFalmer.

Halsted, J. W. (2009). *Some of my best friends are books: Guiding gifted readers from preschool to high school* (3rd ed.). Scottsdale, AZ: Great Potential Press.

Hart, D., Atkins, R., & Donnelly, T. M. (2006). Community service and moral development. In M. Killen & J. G. Smetana (Eds.), *Handbook of moral development* (pp. 633–656). Mahwah, NJ: Lawrence Erlbaum.

Hébert, T. P. (2000a). Defining belief in self: Intelligent young men in an urban high school. *Gifted Child Quarterly, 44,* 91–114.

Hébert, T. P. (2000b). Gifted males pursuing careers in elementary education. *Journal for the Education of the Gifted, 24,* 7–45.

Hébert, T. P. (2002). Gifted Black males in a predominantly White university: Portraits of high achievement. *Journal for the Education of the Gifted, 26,* 25–64.

Hébert, T. P. (2011). *Understanding the social and emotional lives of gifted students.* Waco, TX: Prufrock Press.

Hébert, T. P., & Hammond, D. R. (2006). Guided viewing of film with gifted students: Resources for educators and counselors. *Gifted Child Today, 29*(3), 14–17.

Hébert, T. P., & McBee, M. T. (2007). The impact of an undergraduate honors program on gifted university students. *Gifted Child Quarterly, 51,* 136–151.

Hébert, T. P., & Reis, S. M. (1999). Culturally diverse high-achieving students in an urban high school. *Urban Education, 34,* 428–457.

Hébert, T. P., & Sergent, D. (2005). Using movies to guide: Teachers and counselors collaborating to support gifted students. *Gifted Child Today, 28*(4), 14–25.

Hollingworth, L. S. (1926). *Gifted children: Their nature and nurture.* New York, NY: Macmillan.

Janos, P. M., Marwood, K. A., & Robinson, N. M. (1985). Friendship patterns in highly intelligent children. *Roeper Review, 8,* 46–49.

Karnes, F. A., & McGinnis, J. C. (1996). Self-actualization and locus of control with academically talented adolescents. *Journal of Secondary Gifted Education, 7,* 369–372.

Kennedy, D. M. (1995). Plain talk about creating a gifted-friendly classroom. *Roeper Review, 17,* 232–234.

Lewis, J. D., Karnes, F. A., & Knight, H. V. (1995). A study of self-actualization and self-concept in intellectually gifted students. *Psychology in the Schools, 32,* 52–61.

McLaughlin, S. C., & Saccuzzo, D. P. (1997). Ethnic and gender differences in locus of control in children referred for gifted programs: The effect of vulnerability factors. *Journal for the Education of the Gifted, 20,* 268–283.

Mooney, J., & Cole, D. (2000). *Learning outside the lines.* New York, NY: Simon & Schuster.

Nash, D. (2001, December). Enter the mentor. *Parenting for High Potential, 12,* 18–21.

National Association for Gifted Children. (2010). *NAGC pre-K–grade 12 gifted programming standards: A blueprint for quality gifted education programs.* Washington, DC: Author.

Neihart, M. (2002). Risk and resilience in gifted children: A conceptual framework. In M. Neihart, S. M. Reis, N. M. Robinson, & S. M. Moon (Eds.), *The social and emotional development of gifted children: What do we know?* (pp. 113–122). Waco, TX: Prufrock Press.

Nugent, S. (2005). *Social and emotional teaching strategies.* Waco, TX: Prufrock Press.

Olszewski-Kubilius, P. M. (2002). A summary of research regarding early entrance to college. *Roeper Review, 24,* 152–157.

Olszewski-Kubilius, P. M., & Lee, S. (2004). The role of participation in in-school and outside-of-school activities in the talent development of gifted students. *Journal of Secondary Gifted Education, 15,* 107–123.

Palmer, P. J. (1993). *To know as we are known: Education as a spiritual journey.* San Francisco, CA: HarperCollins.

Pufal-Struzik, I. (1999). Self-actualization and other personality dimensions as predictors of mental health of intellectually gifted students. *Roeper Review, 22,* 44–47.

Reis, S. M., Hébert, T. P., Diaz, E. I., Maxfield, L. R., & Ratley, M. E. (1995). *Case studies of talented students who achieve and underachieve in an urban high school* (Research Monograph No. 95120). Storrs: University of Connecticut, The National Research Center on the Gifted and Talented.

Rinn, A. N. (2008). College planning. In J. A. Plucker & C. M. Callahan (Eds.), *Critical issues and practices in gifted education: What the research says* (pp. 97–106). Waco, TX: Prufrock Press.

Robinson, N. M., Reis, S. M., Neihart, M., & Moon, S. M. (2002). Social and emotional issues facing gifted and talented students: What have we learned and what should we do now? In M. Neihart, S. M. Reis, N. M. Robinson, & S. M. Moon (Eds.), *The social and emotional development of gifted students: What do we know?* (pp. 267–288). Waco, TX: Prufrock Press.

Rodis, P., Garrod, A., & Boscardin, M. L. (Eds.). (2001). *Learning disabilities and life stories.* Boston, MA: Allyn & Bacon.

Siegle, D., McCoach, D. B., & Wilson, H. E. (2009). Extending learning through mentorships. In F. A. Karnes & S. M. Bean (Eds.), *Methods and materials for teaching the gifted* (3rd ed., pp. 519–563). Waco, TX: Prufrock Press.

Subotnik, R. (2003). Through another's eyes: The Pinnacle Project. *Gifted Child Today, 26*(2), 14–17.

Tomlinson, C. A. (2001, December). President's column. *Parenting for High Potential, 5,* 27.

End Note

1   The classroom strategies and methods described are featured in Hébert (2011). Readers are encouraged to explore that resource for further discussion and additional examples of affective educational techniques.

Chapter 3

Using the NAGC Gifted Programming Standards to Create Programs and Services for Culturally and Linguistically Different Gifted Students

by Donna Y. Ford and Tarek C. Grantham

The National Association for Gifted Children (NAGC, 2000) issued its original 1998 standards to guide policy and practice with our most able students. Many of these students were and are neglected in the standards movement and in educational policy in general. At that time, the nation and our schools were relatively diverse and different relative to culture (e.g., race, language), but nowhere near as racially and linguistically different as we are today. Then and now, however, students identified and served as gifted remain unjustifiably homogeneous in terms of racial and linguistic background. Despite standards and legislation such as *Brown v. the Board of Education* (1954), the Civil Rights Act of 1964, and the Jacob K. Javits Gifted and Talented Students Education Act of 1988 (Javits), too few students in gifted education are Black, Hispanic, and Native American, with underrepresentation ranging from approximately 50% for Blacks, 40% for Hispanics, and 30% for Native Americans (Ford, 2011c). According to NAGC (2008),

> In particular, the Javits Act was originally passed by Congress in 1988 as part of the Elementary and Secondary Education Act to support the development of talent in U.S. schools. The Javits Act, which is the only federal program dedicated specifically to gifted and talented students, does *not* fund local gifted education programs. The purpose of the act is to orchestrate a coordinated program of scientifically based research, demonstration projects, innovative strategies, and similar activities that build and enhance the ability of elementary and secondary schools

to meet the special educational needs of gifted and talented students. (para. 1)

In 1998, it can be argued that the NAGC standards served their generic and general purpose—to address the needs of gifted students—but they catered primarily to mainstream students rather than others. Change was necessary so that the new standards would be responsive to the needs of all gifted students and cultural groups. As Johnsen (2011) noted,

> giftedness is dynamic and is constantly developing; therefore, students [are] defined as those with gifts and talents rather than those with stable traits . . . and giftedness is found among students from a variety of backgrounds; therefore, a deliberate effort [is] to ensure that diversity [is] included across all standards. (p. 13)

As with standards from any professional organization, they are designed to reflect contemporary society in proactive ways that address students' differences and needs, to address policymakers' interests, and to ultimately improve outcomes for students and our nation at large. Of course, changing times—changing demographics, needs, and issues—beg the question of whether past and current practices have been and are equitable and efficacious for those students who differ from the mainstream and/or who are not experiencing school success. Thus, policies and practices that have worked in the past, at least for mainstream America, may never have worked for others; thus, we must frequently and consistently evaluate policies with an eye toward meeting the needs of all students and groups as much as possible. Specifically, an examination of the 1998 standards will reveal that the focus on diversity was tangential and weak at best; they needed much improvement to be culturally responsive.

Therefore, taking a much-needed proactive and multicultural stance—partly in recognizing that much work is still necessary regarding underrepresentation (Ford, 2011c), that giftedness is dynamic and ever changing (Ford, 2011b), and that our nation has certainly changed in stark ways (Hodgkinson, 2007; U.S. Department of Education, 2010)—NAGC and the Council for Exceptional Children (CEC) acknowledged the need to modify standards in a proactive, visionary, and culturally responsive way (Ford, 2011a). That is, all of the six standards in the Gifted Programming Standards address culture to varying degrees.

Demographers presenting projections on racial and linguistic diversity share the resounding message that our nation and public schools are quite diverse and changes will continue, many times in exponential ways (e.g., Darling-Hammond & Bransford, 2005; Hodgkinson, 2000/2001). A cursory and even substantive look at the 2010 U.S. Census shows that no state or region has been able to escape or avoid the inevitable increase in Hispanic/Latino, Black, Asian, and Native American populations, and our schools are not exempt. Combined, these students represent almost 50% of the student population in our public schools nationally (U.S. Department of Education, 2010).

Accompanying these demographic changes is an increase in culture, poverty, and language and attendant conflicts and dilemmas that our nation and schools are not accustomed to and/or ready to deal with. As they should and must, NAGC and CEC recognized and responded to the current and inevitable diversity—and differences—along racial, cultural, and linguistic lines in the 2010 Gifted Programming Standards. The pervasive and severe underrepresentation of Black, Hispanic, and Native American students in gifted education had to have been central to discussions and changes.

In many respects, the revised 2010 standards are a welcome change from the somewhat color-blind/culture-blind original standards. Each of the revised standards focuses on cultural similarities and differences when it comes to measurable outcomes in particular. The modifications are proactive and specific, and they hold great promise for addressing the development and needs of all students, including racially and linguistically different students (also see Ford, 2011a).

In the pages that follow, using a Venn diagram perspective, we look at the six standards and outcomes through two lenses: (a) a multicultural lens and (b) a gifted lens (Ford, 2011b; Ford & Harris, 1999), resulting in an overlap that speaks and/or responds to the needs and development of students who are gifted *and* culturally different from their White classmates. In other words, students who are Black, Hispanic, Asian, and Native American are similar to and different from their White classmates. These differences cannot and must not be ignored or trivialized in any way, and the revised standards are the ideal mechanism from which to be proactive and responsive to cultural similarities and differences across groups.

Borrowing from the scholarship of proponents of multicultural and/or culturally responsive education such as Mary Frasier, Alexinia Baldwin, James Banks, and A. Wade Boykin, we expound upon the 2010 Gifted Programming Standards to render a cultural framework through which to interpret, conceptualize, and build upon the newly revised standards (Ford, 2011a, 2011b, 2011c). In doing so, we keep in mind the initial and revised standards, supporting research, informative theories, frameworks, and paradigms, as well as the many associated rationales for moving forward in the best interest of all students—without excuses. Next, we discuss culture in terms of a position statement by the

National Association for Multicultural Education (NAME) and expand upon each standard with examples using a culturally responsive (non-culture-blind) frame of reference. After this overview, we apply the standards using a culturally responsive lens, with supporting recommendations and strategies, which appear in tables or figures and the discussion. Our central argument is that students who differ from the mainstream or status quo have been neglected too long in gifted education policies, practices, and programs; this is the time to make amends—to do what is right educationally, legally, and morally for all gifted students, regardless of their race, gender, income, and/or socioeconomic status.

2010 Gifted Programming Standards: General Purpose, Rationale, and Need

We hope that all educators and policymakers interested in equity and excellence recognize that Black and Hispanic students are poorly represented in gifted education for a number of entrenched and indefensible reasons. Attitudes and stereotypes in the form of deficit thinking play a major role (Ford, 2011c; Torrance, 1974; Valencia, 2010) in decisions and call attention to the vital need for teacher and school personnel training (i.e., higher education and professional development) to address and correct many heinous stereotypes and biases that can and do blind educators to recognizing and valuing the gifts and talents of Black and Hispanic students (especially males), those who are not yet English proficient, and those in the process of becoming culturally competent. If implemented equitably, the 2010 Gifted Programming Standards offer much guidance and opportunities for all school personnel to address the development, needs, and wants of their gifted students, with deliberate attention to diversity in the form of culture and language. Throughout the standards, attention is devoted to diversity, with encouragement and direction for educators to always take into account individual and group differences.

Diversity Standards: Culturally Specific Purpose, Rationale, and Need

In this section, we present a brief overview of why standards must be culturally responsive and inclusive. In doing so, we include and go beyond gifted education programming standards to mention perspectives from other organizations dedicated to serving students who are different from the status quo. A number of organizations, often subdivisions of the main organization, have developed standards and position or policy statements that are culturally specific rather than generic. These policies and statements acknowledge and recognize, in one way or another, the fallacies and dangers and the ultimate ineffectiveness of being color-blind in theory and practice. As with gifted education standards, multicultural standards cannot operate in isolation when it comes to meeting the needs of students who are culturally different *and* gifted.

As a case in point, NAME (2001) presented criteria for evaluating state curriculum standards. We concur with their position:

> Curriculum standards designed to guide public education need to include the particular contributions, distinct heritages and values, as well as the multiple ways of knowing that represent our diverse population. Curricula should be designed to facilitate the development of individuals who appreciate the complexity of the human condition and who can effectively negotiate the diverse cultural contexts of U.S. society. Such individuals must acquire critical understanding and appreciation of their own cultural heritage as well as the cultural heritages of the diverse groups that are represented in our collective national identity. (NAME, 2001, para. 1)

Ultimately, curriculum standards must do far more than simply stress the multicultural composition of the United States. Instead, standards must also outline classroom practices that help educators to impart the knowledge, skills, and dispositions necessary for educators to participate fully and meaningfully in a multiethnic and multiracial society. More specifically, as one case in point, Table 3.1 lists how NAME's (2001) curriculum guidelines respond to five key needs and attendant recommendations; readers will see some alignment with NAGC's 2010 Gifted Programming Standards.

As NAME (2001) asserted, the value in articulating curriculum standards is at least twofold:

> First, setting standards represents each state's commitment to hold all students to equally high standards for performance while providing the instructional programs and support functions necessary for all students to meet these standards. All students deserve a quality education [e.g., Barton & Coley, 2009]; curriculum standards define the core knowledge and skills we expect all students to master while providing an impetus for programs that facilitate the processes of learning and instruction. Second, the process of setting state standards itself represents a crucial step in our school systems' attempts to acknowledge the multiple constituencies composing each state's population and by

Table 3.1
NAME's Five Curriculum Guidelines and Recommendations

I.	**Inclusiveness:** Inclusive curriculum guidelines will
	a. Represent the broad range of experiences and peoples that compose the population of the United States;
	b. Acknowledge the ways multicultural experiences have contributed to the knowledge base, value systems, and ways of thinking within disciplines;
	c. Provide an integrated understanding of human experience in its many varieties and complexities by attending to the exceptional as well as the ordinary; and
	d. Promote understanding of the interdependence of groups and the reciprocal ways, both historic and contemporary, in which our collective experiences shape the lives of the diverse peoples in the United States.
II.	**Diverse perspectives:** Curriculum guidelines emphasizing diverse perspectives will
	a. Represent the multiple constituencies and points of view in the United States;
	b. Encourage students to entertain competing constructions and understandings of social, historical, and natural phenomena;
	c. Recognize the ways these constructions are rooted in the cultural and historical experiences of the people who espouse them; and
	d. Facilitate independent, contextual, and critical thinking among students about what they are being taught in schools.
III.	**Accommodating alternative epistemologies/social construction of knowledge:** To provide students with the means to understand the ways knowledge is socially constructed, curriculum guidelines will
	a. Recognize that alternative cultural constructions entail distinct ways of thinking;
	b. Provide a basis for appreciating the differences in traditional ways of knowing, both the content of knowledge and the forms of evidence advanced to support it;
	c. Set out the paradigms and logic that structure knowledge within a community; and
	d. Provide the analytic tools students need to evaluate both the causes and the effects of traditional and alternative belief systems.
IV.	**Self-Knowledge:** In order to foster a sense in students of how their own identities have been constructed by the complex interplay of historical, social, political, economic, and even geographic factors, curriculum guidelines will
	a. Provide a structure that allows students to investigate their own cultural and ethnic identities and to examine the origins and consequences of their attitudes and behaviors toward other groups;
	b. Lead students to a critical understanding and appreciation of their own cultural and ethnic identities, including both their strengths and weaknesses;
	c. Recognize that identity is based on multiple factors, including the diverse and sometimes contradictory realities of membership in multiple groups; and
	d. Foster in students an understanding that identity is dynamic and therefore, that change is possible.
V.	**Social Justice/Equity:** Curriculum guidelines fostering the goals of social justice will
	a. Emphasize the constitutional rights accorded all members of our society and the responsibilities entailed by citizenship in our multicultural society;
	b. Recognize and uphold the statutes set forth by the *Universal Declaration of Human Rights* adopted by the United Nations in 1948, in particular Article 26.2, that "Education shall be directed to the full development of the human personality and the strengthening of respect for human rights and fundamental freedoms. It shall promote understanding, tolerance and friendship among all nations, racial or religious groups, and shall further the activities of the United Nations for the maintenance of peace";

Table 3.1, continued

c.	Prepare students to "think globally and act locally" by fostering a critical understanding of the ways local knowledge and actions are situated within and have an impact on global contexts;
d.	Provide students opportunities to evaluate the results of personal, organizational, corporate, and governmental decisions and to develop a critical understanding of how such decisions may benefit some groups while negatively impacting others; and
e.	Promote social action, creating an engaged, active, and responsible citizenry committed to eradicating bigotry and to developing a fair, just, democratic society responsive to the needs of all our people regardless of race, class, gender, age, sexual orientation, physical appearance, ability or disability, national origin, ethnicity, religious belief or lack thereof.

Note. From NAME (2001).

extension, the United States' multiethnic, multicultural nature. For the process to be meaningful, it must itself be open and inclusive, the standards represent a consensus of opinion reflecting and respecting the broad range of needs, interests, and bodies of expertise that students, parents, educators, representatives of numerous professional organizations, politicians, and our elders bring to the discussion. . . . Examples of specific statements include, but are not limited to, the United Nations' [1948] *Universal Declaration of Human Rights*; . . . the National Council for Social Studies' [1991] "Curriculum Guidelines for Multicultural Education"; *Alaska Standards for Culturally Responsive Schools* adopted by the Assembly of Alaska Native Educators [1998]; the American Speech and Hearing Association's [1983] position paper "Social Dialects and Implications of the Position on Social Dialects." In order to respond to the changing realities of life in our academic disciplines and in our schools, state standards need to be open to regular review and revision. (para. 7)

Having presented an abbreviated discussion of the Gifted Programming Standards and an overview of the NAME (2001) standards as one example, we now focus on the overlap between the two ideal necessities for educators and associated necessities and outcomes for students.

The Ideal: Merging Gifted Education and Multicultural Education Standards

Standard 1: Learning and Development

"Educators, recognizing the learning and developmental differences of students with gifts and talents, promote ongoing self-understanding, awareness of their needs, and cognitive and affective growth of these students in school, home, and community settings to ensure specific student outcomes" (NAGC, 2010, p. 8). This standard focuses on four student outcomes: self-understanding, awareness of needs, cognitive growth, and affective growth aligned with 13 evidence-based practices. To implement this standard effectively and to address these outcomes, educators need training in culture and must acquire the skills to be culturally competent (Darling-Hammond & Bransford, 2005). Professional development will guide educators in understanding and being responsive not only to self-concept, social-emotional needs, and self-understanding, but also to how students are similar to and different from others as individuals and cultural beings.

As written about more extensively elsewhere (e.g., Ford, 2011b, 2011c) and indicated in Evidence-Based Practice 1.2.1, culture significantly affects learning and development, and educators need to develop activities that match each student's developmental and culture-based learning needs. Culture is a way of life for a group of people; culture comprises the behaviors, beliefs, values, attitudes, habits, customs, and traditions that groups accept, often unconsciously, and that are passed along by verbal and nonverbal communication (modeling and imitation) from one generation to the next. With this said, Table 3.2 lists suggestions for ensuring that culture is addressed. Resources to support the above recommendations come from the works of Ford (2011b; multicultural gifted education), Epstein (1995; family involvement model), Boykin (e.g., 1995) and Boykin and Allen (1988, 2003; cultural learning styles), Cross and Vandiver (2001; racial identity theory), and Banks (e.g., 2000, 2009; multicultural education).

An understanding of and appreciation for students' self-concept and self-esteem is incomplete and inadequate when racial identity and pride are excluded. Cross and Vandiver's (2001) Black racial identity theory is but one of several theories that focuses on self-awareness, self-understanding, self-image, and pride through a cultural lens. When educators know about pre-encounter, immersion-emersion, and internalization identities, they will have a greater understanding of their Black students. And when culturally different students

Table 3.2

Learning and Development With Culturally Specific Examples

Evidence-Based Practices	Culturally Specific Examples
1.1.1. Educators engage students with gifts and talents in identifying interests, strengths, and gifts.	• Self-assessments, lesson plans, and activities are created to be engaging and relevant to students from different cultural groups.
1.1.2. Educators assist students with gifts and talents in developing identities supportive of achievement. 1.2.1. Educators develop activities that match each student's developmental level and culture-based learning needs.	• Students are exposed to culturally different individuals who are academically and professionally successful. They read about successful individuals from their cultural background with respect to similarities in age, abilities, and the like. Role models from culturally different backgrounds are invited to speak with students about their experiences and strategies for being academically successful.
1.3.1. Educators provide a variety of research-based grouping practices for students with gifts and talents that allow them to interact with individuals of various gifts, talents, abilities, and strengths.	• Flexible grouping is adopted on a consistent basis with an eye toward cultural, social, and communication styles. Cooperative learning/small-group assignments are used because they build upon the communal/collective style of most culturally different groups.
1.3.2. Educators model respect for individuals with diverse abilities, strengths, and goals.	• A family atmosphere is created so that students are supportive of each other as individuals and as cultural beings.
1.4.1. Educators provide role models (e.g., through mentors, bibliotherapy) for students with gifts and talents that match their abilities and interests.	• To increase identification with the role models, they must come from culturally different backgrounds and be included in all materials. Multicultural literature is used extensively.
1.4.2. Educators identify out-of-school learning opportunities that match students' abilities and interests.	• Out-of-school opportunities take place in the communities of all students in the class. Students attend cultural events representative of their classmates.
1.5.1. Educators collaborate with families in accessing resources to develop their child's talents.	• Special efforts are made to reach out to parents/families who are often uninvolved and intimidated by educators. Joyce Epstein's model of family involvement guides all efforts.
1.6.1. Educators design interventions for students to develop cognitive and affective growth that is based on research of effective practices.	• Being mindful of the achievement gap and factors that contribute to underachievement (e.g., low expectations, discrimination) among culturally different groups, educators design interventions that are culturally relevant rather than generic.

Evidence-Based Practices	Culturally Specific Examples
1.6.2. Educators develop specialized intervention services for students with gifts and talents who are underachieving and are now learning and developing their talents.	• Talent development models and strategies are adopted to prevent and reverse underachievement and close the achievement gap.
1.7.1. Teachers enable students to identify their preferred approaches to learning, accommodate these preferences, and expand them.	• Culturally based learning styles are recognized and addressed with modifications in teaching styles. Teachers adapt their styles to accommodate and capitalize upon differences in how cultural groups learn.
1.8.1. Educators provide students with college and career guidance that is consistent with their strengths.	• Educators are familiar with and share data with students regarding underrepresented groups in college. These data are used to inform and motivate culturally different students. All students learn about minority colleges, such as Historically Black Colleges and Universities. These colleges are included in college tours and field trips, and students write reports or develop projects about them.

have discussions about racial pride and identity, as well as mentors and role models, they are more likely to do well in school (Grantham, 2004).

Likewise, when learning style differences based on culture are ignored, opportunities to be instructionally responsive are compromised and/or forfeited. Boykin's Afro-Centric Cultural Model is useful, informative, and instructively sound for helping educators match or align their teaching styles with culture-based learning orientations. For example, teachers will know how to build upon verve, movement, communalism, and the oral tradition in their lesson plans and interactions with students and their families (Ford, 2011b).

Standard 2: Assessment

"Assessments provide information about identification, learning progress and outcomes, and evaluation of programming for students with gifts and talents in all domains" (NAGC, 2010, p. 9). This standard focuses on two student outcomes targeting identification, equal access, and identification-instructional alignment (Johnsen, 2011).

For assessment, there are six student outcomes and 22 evidence-based practices listed in the revised standards. In Table 3.3, we combine the related evidence-based practices and provide culturally based strategies and recommendations in the six groupings. Ford and Whiting (2006) and Whiting and Ford

Table 3.3

Assessment With Culturally Specific Examples

Evidence-Based Practices	Culturally Specific Examples
2.1.1. Educators develop environments and instructional activities that encourage students to express diverse characteristics and behaviors that are associated with giftedness. 2.1.2. Educators provide parents/guardians with information regarding diverse characteristics and behaviors that are associated with giftedness.	• Educators reach out to families whose children are poorly represented in gifted education. Meetings and trainings are developed based on their interests, concerns, needs, and schedules.
2.2.1. Educators establish comprehensive, cohesive, and ongoing procedures for identifying and serving students with gifts and talents. These provisions include informed consent, committee review, student retention, student reassessment, student exiting, and appeals procedures for both entry and exit from gifted program services. 2.2.2. Educators select and use multiple assessments that measure diverse abilities, talents, and strengths that are based on current theories, models, and research. 2.2.3. Assessments provide qualitative and quantitative information from a variety of sources, including off-level testing, are non-biased and equitable, and are technically adequate for the purpose. 2.2.4. Educators have knowledge of student exceptionalities and collect assessment data while adjusting curriculum and instruction to learn about each student's developmental level and aptitude for learning. 2.2.5. Educators interpret multiple assessments in different domains and understand the uses and limitations of the assessments in identifying the needs of students with gifts and talents. 2.2.6. Educators inform all parents/guardians about the identification process. Teachers obtain parental/guardian permission for assessments, use culturally sensitive checklists, and elicit evidence regarding the child's interests and potential outside of the classroom setting.	• Decisions to reassess, exit, and appeal are comprehensive and proactive. The goal must never be to "un-identify" culturally different students, and this decision would not be an option when identification is defensible—comprehensive and equitable. Thus, reevaluations may not be efficacious and equitable. When culturally different students are (re)assessed, identified, and placed/served, advocacy and retention must be the goal and a priority. If gifted students are underachieving or struggling, we must support rather than disqualify them. This means erring on the side of being inclusive and flexible rather than exclusive and elitist. • All measures (e.g., tests, checklists) are evaluated for their biases and disparate impact. • Test bias, test anxiety, and stereotype threat are considered in interpretations and decisions. • Educators reach out to and advocate for parents/families from different cultural backgrounds so they are informed and feel empowered to advocate for their children.

Evidence-Based Practices	Culturally Specific Examples
2.3.1. Educators select and use non-biased and equitable approaches for identifying students with gifts and talents, which may include using locally-developed norms or assessment tools in the child's native language or in nonverbal formats. 2.3.2. Educators understand and implement district and state policies designed to foster equity in gifted programming and services. 2.3.3. Educators provide parents/guardians with information in their native language regarding diverse behaviors and characteristics that are associated with giftedness and with information that explains the nature and purpose of gifted programming options.	• A bias-free measure is impossible; however, test bias can be reduced. Every effort must be made to ensure that the most valid and reliable qualitative and quantitative measures/instruments are adopted, interpreted, and applied in culturally responsive and equitable ways. • Families are valued and viewed as an important and equal partner in the assessment process. They are informed, and their concerns and suggestions are included in the decision-making process.
2.4.1. Educators use differentiated pre- and post-performance-based assessments to measure the progress of students with gifts and talents. 2.4.2. Educators use differentiated product-based assessments to measure the progress of students with gifts and talents. 2.4.3. Educators use off-level standardized assessments to measure the progress of students with gifts and talents. 2.4.4. Educators use and interpret qualitative and quantitative assessment information to develop a profile of the strengths and weaknesses of each student with gifts and talents to plan appropriate intervention. 2.4.5. Educators communicate and interpret assessment information to students with gifts and talents and their parents/guardians.	• Assessments vary based on students' needs and context. A profile of strengths and weaknesses is developed for students as a way to identify and program rather than to exclude. • Information is gathered from all families (e.g., via checklists and/or interviews). Families are informed about testing issues and outcomes, and assessment is continuously critiqued/revalued with underrepresentation in mind.
2.5.1. Educators ensure that the assessments used in the identification and evaluation processes are reliable and valid for each instrument's purpose, allow for above-grade-level performance, and allow for diverse perspectives. 2.5.2. Educators ensure that the assessment of the progress of students with gifts and talents uses multiple indicators that measure mastery of content, higher level thinking skills, achievement in specific program areas, and affective growth. 2.5.3. Educators assess the quantity, quality, and appropriateness of the programming and services provided for students with gifts and talents by disaggregating assessment data and yearly progress data and making the results public.	• Program evaluation is ongoing and always considers/addresses underrepresentation. • Problems associated with race, gender, and income are addressed in all areas: assessment, programming, professional development, and so forth. • Multiple criteria are used and subjective and objective information are weighed in proactive ways. Multiple criteria are gathered considering equity and access.

Table 3.3, continued

Evidence-Based Practices	Culturally Specific Examples
2.6.1. Administrators provide the necessary time and resources to implement an annual evaluation plan developed by persons with expertise in program evaluation and gifted education. 2.6.2. The evaluation plan is purposeful and evaluates how student-level outcomes are influenced by one or more of the following components of gifted education programming: (a) identification, (b) curriculum, (c) instructional programming and services, (d) ongoing assessment of student learning, (e) counseling and guidance programs, (f) teacher qualifications and professional development, (g) parent/guardian and community involvement, (h) programming resources, and (i) programming design, management, and delivery. 2.6.3. Educators disseminate the results of the evaluation, orally and in written form, and explain how they will use the results.	• When assessment and programming are equitable, students who are performing poorly are supported personally and academically. • Every effort is made to keep underrepresented students in gifted education classrooms and programs/services. The notion of equity (accommodating differences and injustices) outweighs equality (treating everyone as if they are the same and their situations and needs are equal).

(2006) presented and suggested modifications to assessment standards by the American Educational Research Association (AERA), American Psychological Association (APA), and National Council on Measurement in Education (NCME) in 1999, which are under revision (see http://www.apa.org/science/about/psa/2011/01/testing.aspx). The primary differences between the 2010 Gifted Programming Standards and the 1998 edition is the separation of the general text into "foundations," "operations," and "applications" sections; a condensation of several individual chapters dealing with issues of fairness into a single foundations chapter; the inclusion of topics such as educational accountability and technological advances in testing; and the reorganization of chapters concerning workplace testing and credentialing. Resources to address equitably the standards are: APA, AERA, and NCME (1999) and The National Center for Fair and Open Testing (see http://fairtest.org).

Steele's (e.g., 1997) extensive body of work on how stereotype threat—raced-based test anxiety—undermines test performance in extremely informative for understanding the low test scores of many Black students. Knowing this theory and the related research will help to improve educators' interpretations and use of test scores such that decisions are fair and equitable—in the best interest of poorly represented students.

Standard 3: Curriculum Planning and Instruction

Educators apply the theory and research-based models of curriculum and instruction related to students with gifts and talents and respond to their needs by planning, selecting, adapting, and creating culturally relevant curriculum and by using a repertoire of evidence-based instructional strategies to ensure specific student outcomes. (NAGC, 2010, p. 10)

The six student outcomes for curriculum planning and instruction are divided into 20 evidence-based practices. Table 3.4 adds a cultural perspective. Evidence-based practices will be culturally responsive such that activities, lesson plans, curriculum, and materials are multicultural and devoid of stereotypes and biases; it is equally important that instruction be culturally responsive. Frameworks and curriculum grounded in the models of Banks (2000), Boykin (1995), and Ford (2011b) are adopted and used. Banks's (2000, 2009) multicultural education model focuses on four levels of how to infuse multicultural content into the curriculum. The contributions approach is the lowest level. Educators focus on artifacts, holidays, music, art, foods, fashion, and folklore from cultural groups. Students often have fun learning about foods, artifacts, and the like, but they learn little or nothing about the cultural groups. For example, students learn about teepees and Cinco de Mayo, but not about the culture (e.g., values, beliefs, way of life) or the meaning of the holiday, event, and artifact. Oftentimes, stereotypes are learned from or reinforced by the lessons.

The next level, which is still inadequate and insufficient in terms of cultural rigor and depth, is the additive approach. At this level, teachers make minor changes to the curriculum, such as by adding a book or activity about a cultural group. However, like an appendage, the activity or lesson is not an integral part of the curriculum. At this level, topics, issues, concepts, and the individuals or groups studied are often safe and noncontroversial (e.g., Martin Luther King, Jr., is more likely to appear in the curriculum than Malcolm X; sexism is more "appropriate," safer, and comfortable for students to discuss than racism).

The transformation approach is the third level. It is characterized by substantive changes to the curriculum. The structure of the curriculum changes such that in every subject area, multicultural topics, issues, and concepts are taught and discussed. Literature, science, math, history, art, music, physical education, and so forth are infused with multicultural content. A second feature is that students are taught to view all of what is taught from more than one perspective. For example, students are asked to study two viewpoints about or versions of the Civil War: to put themselves in the role of slave and to suggest

Table 3.4

Curriculum Planning Instruction With Culturally Specific Examples

Evidence-Based Practices	Culturally Specific Examples
3.1.1. Educators use local, state, and national standards to align and expand curriculum and instructional plans. 3.1.2. Educators design and use a comprehensive and continuous scope and sequence to develop differentiated plans for PK–12 students with gifts and talents. 3.1.3. Educators adapt, modify, or replace the core or standard curriculum to meet the needs of students with gifts and talents and those with special needs such as twice-exceptional, highly gifted, and English language learners. 3.1.4. Educators design differentiated curricula that incorporate advanced, conceptually challenging, in-depth, distinctive, and complex content for students with gifts and talents. 3.1.5. Educators use a balanced assessment system, including pre-assessment and formative assessment, to identify students' needs, develop differentiated education plans, and adjust plans based on continual progress monitoring. 3.1.6. Educators use pre-assessments and pace instruction based on the learning rates of students with gifts and talents and accelerate and compact learning as appropriate. 3.1.7. Educators use information and technologies, including assistive technologies, to individualize for students with gifts and talents, including those who are twice-exceptional.	• The gifted education and/or general education curricula (lessons, material, topics, issues) are modified/adapted to be rigorous and culturally responsive. • Rigor is defined as being culturally responsive. Therefore, curricula (lessons and materials) are reflective of and responsive to students in the gifted class, building, and district. • Differentiated lessons are culturally grounded and rigorous for all students, especially those who are gifted and culturally different. Ford's (2011b) multicultural gifted education (Bloom-Banks) matrix presents sample lesson plans that merge rigor and culture. • Preassessments are designed to be proactive and inclusive with underrepresented groups. The goal is to cast a wide net, with educators seeking an increase in poorly represented groups.
3.2.1. Educators design curricula in cognitive, affective, aesthetic, social, and leadership domains that are challenging and effective for students with gifts and talents. 3.2.2. Educators use metacognitive models to meet the needs of students with gifts and talents.	• Differentiation attends to culturally based learning styles and materials, as well as students' interests and passion(s). Modifications address the learning styles of those who differ from middle-class White students. • Students' communities are used to secure resources that support cultural differences.

Evidence-Based Practices	Culturally Specific Examples
3.3.1. Educators select, adapt, and use a repertoire of instructional strategies and materials that differentiate for students with gifts and talents and that respond to diversity. 3.3.2. Educators use school and community resources that support differentiation. 3.3.3. Educators provide opportunities for students with gifts and talents to explore, develop, or research their areas of interest and/or talent.	• Critical thinking and problem-solving skills are a focus for students, using problems and examples that focus on culture, conflict, and injustices. • Curriculum matches or aligns with students' culturally based interests as much as possible. • Students are surveyed regarding their interests, and topics, issues, and results are disaggregated by students' race, gender, and income for professional development and training.
3.4.1. Educators use critical-thinking strategies to meet the needs of students with gifts and talents. 3.4.2. Educators use creative-thinking strategies to meet the needs of students with gifts and talents. 3.4.3. Educators use problem-solving model strategies to meet the needs of students with gifts and talents. 3.4.4. Educators use inquiry models to meet the needs of students with gifts and talents.	• Critical thinking and problem-solving activities are related to the experiences of students who are culturally different. Lesson plans and activities have a cultural focus. They are grounded in the daily and real-world experiences of students.
3.5.1. Educators develop and use challenging, culturally responsive curriculum to engage all students with gifts and talents. 3.5.2. Educators integrate career exploration experiences into learning opportunities for students with gifts and talents, e.g. biography study or speakers. 3.5.3. Educators use curriculum for deep explorations of cultures, languages, and social issues related to diversity.	• Students are taught to make connections to what they learn in school and careers and vocational options. Lessons plans are honest and frank about underrepresentation in careers that interest culturally different students and how they can access them.
3.6.1. Teachers and administrators demonstrate familiarity with sources for high quality resources and materials that are appropriate for learners with gifts and talents.	• Culturally different students are provided with comprehensive resources targeting their interests, needs, and experiences.

alternatives to slavery. Teaching with multiple perspectives increases students' critical thinking, problem solving, and empathy and compassion.

The highest level of Banks's model is the social action/justice approach. As its name indicates, students take steps to confront and resolve social injustices. The goal is to help students to feel empowered and capable of being positive agents for change, harmony, peace, and the like. Small acts of kindness, reading others fairly, and resolving conflicts are just a few examples.

Ford and Harris (1999) and Ford (2011b) presented dozens of lesson plans based on Banks's model. Referred to as the Bloom-Banks matrix, lesson plans merge Banks's four levels with the six levels of Bloom's taxonomy. In this 6 x 4 matrix, there are four quadrants: (a) low-level multicultural and low-level critical thinking; (b) low-level multicultural but high-level critical thinking; (c) high-level multicultural but low-level critical thinking; and (d) high-level multicultural and high-level critical thinking. Of course, Quadrant 1 has neither rigor nor depth; Quadrant 4 is ideal as it is rigorous and in-depth in both ways.

Standard 4: Learning Environments

"Learning environments foster personal and social responsibility, multicultural competence, and interpersonal and technical communication skills for leadership in the 21st century to ensure specific student outcomes" (NAGC, 2010, p. 11). The five student outcomes and 17 related evidence-based practices for the learning environments standard target different competencies—personal, social, cultural, communication, and leadership. The learning environment is fundamentally about relationships and expectations. Although the outcomes target student competencies, educators must also be competent; multicultural/cross-cultural self-efficacy is vital. Teachers who are culturally competent believe they can be effective with students who come from cultures that are different from their own. And they work relentlessly to build meaningful relationships with all of their students. As a familiar saying goes, "Students don't care what you know until they know that you care." This philosophy and sense of cultural competence translate into positive, supportive relationships with culturally diverse students, holding them to high standards of achievement, appreciating their differences and nurturing their weaknesses (see Table 3.5).

Standard 5: Programming

Educators are aware of empirical evidence regarding (a) the cognitive, creative, and affective development of learners with gifts and talents, and (b) programming that meets their concomitant needs. Educators use this expertise systematically and collaboratively to develop, imple-

Table 3.5

Learning Environments With Culturally Specific Examples

Evidence-Based Practices	Culturally Specific Examples
4.1.1. Educators maintain high expectations for all students with gifts and talents as evidenced in meaningful and challenging activities. 4.1.2. Educators provide opportunities for self-exploration, development, and pursuit of interests, and development of identities supportive of achievement, e.g., through mentors and role models. 4.1.3. Educators create environments that support trust among diverse learners. 4.1.4. Educators provide feedback that focuses on effort, on evidence of potential to meet high standards, and on mistakes as learning opportunities. 4.1.5. Educators provide examples of positive coping skills and opportunities to apply them.	• Deficit thinking does not exist. Culturally different students are held to high, positive expectations. • Educators expose students to role models and mentors from backgrounds similar to their students'. Students read about and work with mentors and role models who are resilient, confident, and have racial pride. • Educators personalize learning for students; thus, curricula and activities are multicultural and culturally relevant (e.g., books, topics, issues). • Students are provided many academic, social, and cultural opportunities to work with classmates on group projects as a way to learn more about each and cross-cultural borders.
4.2.1. Educators understand the needs of students with gifts and talents for both solitude and social interaction. 4.2.2. Educators provide opportunities for interaction with intellectual and artistic/creative peers as well as with chronological-age peers. 4.2.3. Educators assess and provide instruction on social skills needed for school, community, and the world of work.	• Students from all backgrounds are provided opportunities to work with each other so that that interpersonal skills, social skills, and cross-cultural skills develop. Students learn about other cultures. • Educators recognize, value, nurture, and support individual personalities and cultural characteristics among students.
4.3.1. Educators establish a safe and welcoming climate for addressing social issues and developing personal responsibility. 4.3.2. Educators provide environments for developing many forms of leadership and leadership skills. 4.3.3. Educators promote opportunities for leadership in community settings to effect positive change.	• Educators discuss prejudice and discrimination with students. • Educators do not allow students to discriminate against each other. • Classroom assignments provide opportunities to do service projects (e.g., tutoring, mentoring, fundraising) in low-income and culturally different communities.

Table 3.5, continued

Evidence-Based Practices	Culturally Specific Examples
4.4.1. Educators model appreciation for and sensitivity to students' diverse backgrounds and languages. 4.4.2. Educators censure discriminatory language and behavior and model appropriate strategies. 4.4.3. Educators provide structured opportunities to collaborate with diverse peers on a common goal.	• Students read books (watch movies) about prejudice and discrimination, teasing and treating others unfairly, and avoiding prejudgments based on race, language, income, religion, and culture. • Speakers talk with students about prejudice and discrimination, treating others fairly, and avoiding prejudgments. • Students learn problem-solving and coping skills, including assertiveness and anger management, to address social injustices. • Students work often with classmates and other individuals from another race or culture.
4.5.1. Educators provide opportunities for advanced development and maintenance of first and second language(s). 4.5.2. Educators provide resources to enhance oral, written, and artistic forms of communication, recognizing students' cultural context. 4.5.3. Educators ensure access to advanced communication tools, including assistive technologies, and use of these tools for expressing higher-level thinking and creative productivity.	• Bilingual instruction and programs exist in schools. • Materials, documents, and assessments exist in multiple languages. • Lesson plans and assignments allow opportunities for students to use their preferred learning and cultural styles (e.g., music, speeches, art, drama) to approach and complete tasks. • Students are not allowed to work in racially homogeneous groups. Students work in groups comprised of students from racially and culturally different backgrounds.

ment, and effectively manage comprehensive services for students with a variety of gifts and talents to ensure specific student outcomes. (NAGC, 2010, p. 12)

The seven programming student outcomes target a range of programming options, coordinated services, collaboration, comprehensiveness, adequate resources, policies and procedures, and college and careers. Table 3.6 lists a few examples of ways to be culturally responsive in these programming outcomes and 13 evidence-based practices. Many multicultural suggestions for programming were discussed above in the context of curriculum and instruction.

Table 3.6

Programming With Culturally Specific Examples

Evidence-Based Practices	Culturally Specific Examples
5.1.1. Educators regularly use multiple alternative approaches to accelerate learning. 5.1.2. Educators regularly use enrichment options to extend and deepen learning opportunities within and outside of the school setting. 5.1.3. Educators regularly use multiple forms of grouping, including clusters, resource rooms, special classes, and special schools. 5.1.4. Educators regularly use individualized learning options such as mentorships, internships, online courses, and independent study. 5.1.5. Educators regularly use current technologies, including online learning options and assistive technologies to enhance access to high-level programming. 5.1.6. Administrators demonstrate support for gifted programs through equitable allocation of resources and demonstrated willingness to ensure that learners with gifts and talents receive appropriate educational services.	• Enrichment opportunities take place in culturally different communities and settings. • Programs with students who are culturally different, regardless of the setting, are not underfunded; funds are used equitably in low-income and culturally different classrooms, areas of the community, and schools. • Programs and services are multicultural. • Individualized learning options allow students opportunities to work with individuals from other cultures (e.g., mentors, internships, independent studies).
5.2.1. Educators in gifted, general, and special education programs, as well as those in specialized areas, collaboratively plan, develop, and implement services for learners with gifts and talents.	• These collaborative services include working with culturally different communities and educators for input.
5.3.1. Educators regularly engage families and community members for planning, programming, evaluating, and advocating.	• Educators reach out to culturally different families by holding meetings and events in their communities. • Efforts and steps are made to increase the involvement and input of culturally different families in all aspects of planning, programming, evaluation, and advocacy.

Table 3.6, continued

Evidence-Based Practices	Culturally Specific Examples
5.4.1. Administrators track expenditures at the school level to verify appropriate and sufficient funding for gifted programming and services.	• Administrators ensure that low-income and minority schools are not under-funded; funds are used equitably in low-income and culturally different schools. • Administrators evaluate the absence or existence of gifted education programs in low-income and high-minority schools and communities.
5.5.1. Educators develop thoughtful, multi-year program plans in relevant student talent areas, PK–12.	• Educators ensure that the plans are multicultural.
5.6.1. Educators create policies and procedures to guide and sustain all components for the program, including assessment, identification, acceleration practices, and grouping practices, that is built on an evidence-based foundation in gifted education.	• Policies and procedures are nondiscriminatory. • Underrepresentation is investigated and steps are taken to eliminate barriers. • Instruments are culturally fair, grouping is flexible, and gifted classrooms/programs have representative percentages of culturally different students.
5.7.1. Educators provide professional guidance and counseling for individual student strengths, interests, and values. 5.7.2. Educators facilitate mentorships, internships, and vocational programming experiences that match student interests and aptitudes.	• Counseling focuses on peer relationships, including negative peer pressure. • Counseling focuses on coping with discrimination. • Counseling focuses on racial pride and identity. • Students are exposed to career counseling and counseling about college early on. They are presented with information on underrepresentation.

Standard 6: Professional Development

All educators (administrators, teachers, counselors, and other instructional support staff) build their knowledge and skills using the NAGC-CEC Teacher Standards for Gifted and Talented Education and the National Staff Development Standards. They formally assess professional development needs related to the standards, develop and monitor plans, systematically engage in training to meet the identified needs, and demonstrate mastery of standard. They access resources to provide for release time, funding for continuing education, and substitute support. These practices are judged through the assessment of relevant student outcomes. (NAGC, 2010, p. 13)

This standard's four student outcomes focus on teachers being lifelong learners who continue to get training on ethics, talent development, and social-emotional development. A dozen evidence-based practices appear in this standard. This standard in particular falls under the larger issues of teacher quality and teacher competence (Darling-Hammond & Bransford, 2005). The effectiveness of teachers is compromised when they are not trained in gifted education and multicultural education (Ford, 2011b, 2011c; Grantham et al., 2011). Both in-service and preservice educators require ongoing preparation to engage with and educate (e.g., teach, counsel, advise, assess) culturally different students and to work effectively with their families and communities. At a minimum, professional development (and coursework and degree offerings) should focus on helping educators (a) recognize, confront, and eliminate deficit thinking about culturally different students and families; (b) eliminate unfair and biased instruments; (c) remove discriminatory policies and procedures; (d) eliminate underrepresentation; (e) reverse underachievement and school apathy; and (f) develop and use rigorous multicultural education principles, strategies, and curriculum (see Table 3.7).

A Final Word

As Ford (2011a) noted, with the newest Gifted Programming Standards, the changes are a timely opportunity to be responsive to every gifted student, regardless of race and culture. It is our hope that what is put on paper with the standards and what we have presented herein will provide educators with the philosophy and strategies needed to make progress—to increase the representation of culturally different students (Black, Hispanic, and Native American students) in gifted education, and to ensure that their experiences are positive ones. As we have written and talked about in books, articles, classes, and workshops, educators must do a better job at recruiting and retaining underrepresented groups in gifted education. The Gifted Programming Standards, along with our suggestions, increase the probability that positive change is within our reach.

Table 3.7

Professional Development With Culturally Specific Examples

Evidence-Based Practices	Culturally Specific Examples
6.1.1. Educators systematically participate in ongoing, research-supported professional development that addresses the foundations of gifted education, characteristics of students with gifts and talents, assessment, curriculum planning and instruction, learning environments, and programming. 6.1.2. The school district provides professional development for teachers that models how to develop environments and instructional activities that encourage students to express diverse characteristics and behaviors that are associated with giftedness. 6.1.3. Educators participate in ongoing professional development addressing key issues such as anti-intellectualism and trends in gifted education such as equity and access. 6.1.4. Administrators provide human and material resources needed for professional development in gifted education (e.g. release time, funding for continuing education, substitute support, webinars, or mentors). 6.1.5. Educators use their awareness of organizations and publications relevant to gifted education to promote learning for students with gifts and talents.	• Professional development includes characteristics and needs of gifted students who are culturally different. • Professional development focuses consistently on recruiting and retaining culturally different students in gifted education. • Professional development focuses on ways to eliminate discriminatory assessment and test bias. • Professional development focuses on the negative impact of prejudice and discrimination on expectations for culturally different students, underreferrals to gifted education, relationships, classroom management, and more.
6.2.1. Educators participate in ongoing professional development to support the social and emotional needs for students with gifts and talents.	• Professional development focuses on understanding racial identity and strategies for promoting racial pride in students.
6.3.1. Educators assess their instructional practices and continue their education in school district staff development, professional organization, and higher education settings based on these assessments. 6.3.2. Educators participate in professional development that is sustained over time, that includes regular follow-up, and that seeks evidence of impact on teacher practice and on student learning. 6.3.3. Educators use multiple modes of professional development delivery including online courses, online and electronic communities, face-to-face workshops, professional learning communities, and book talks. 6.3.4. Educators identify and address areas for personal growth for teaching students with gifts and talents in their professional development plans.	• Evaluations or instructional practices focus on matching cultural styles. • Self-evaluations and evaluations from administrators focus on cultural competence and efficacy. • Multicultural literature is used in professional development training. • Culturally different speakers serve as professional development speakers and trainers.

Table 3.7, continued

Evidence-Based Practices	Culturally Specific Examples
6.4.1. Educators respond to cultural and personal frames of reference when teaching students with gifts and talents. 6.4.2. Educators comply with rules, policies, and standards of ethical practice.	• Culturally responsive instruction is valued and practiced. • Discriminatory policies, procedures, rules, and instruments are eliminated. All barriers to access and equity are eliminated.

References

American Psychological Association, American Educational Research Association, and National Council for Measurement in Education. (1999). *The standards of educational and psychological testing.* Retrieved from http://www.apa.org/science/programs/testing/standards.aspx

American Speech and Hearing Association. (1983). *Social dialects and implications of the position on social dialects.* Retrieved from http://www.asha.org/docs/html/PS1983-00115.html#AP1

Assembly of Alaska Native Educators. (1998). *Alaska standards for culturally responsive schools.* Retrieved from http://www.ankn.uaf.edu/publications/standards.html

Banks, J. A. (2000). *Cultural diversity and education: Foundations, curriculum, and teaching.* Boston, MA: Allyn & Bacon.

Banks, J. A. (2009). *Teaching strategies for ethnic studies* (8th ed.). Boston, MA: Allyn & Bacon.

Barton, P., & Coley, R. J. (2009). *Parsing the achievement gap II.* Princeton, NJ: ETS.

Boykin, A. W. (1995, August). *Culture matters in the psychosocial experiences of African Americans: Some conceptual, process, and practical considerations.* Paper presented at the annual meeting of the American Psychological Association, New York, NY.

Boykin, A. W., & Allen, B. A. (1988). Rhythmic movement facilitation of learning in working-class Afro-American children. *Journal of Genetic Psychology, 149,* 335–347.

Boykin, A. W., & Allen, B. A. (2003). Cultural integrity and schooling outcomes of African American schoolchildren from low-income backgrounds. In P. Pufall & R. Undsworth (Eds.), *Childhood revisited* (pp. 104–120). New Brunswick, NJ: Rutgers University Press.

Brown v. Board of Education of Topeka, 347 U.S. 483 (1954).

Civil Rights Act of 1964, Public Law 88-352, 78 stat. 241 (1964).

Cross, W. E., Jr., & Vandiver, B. J. (2001). Nigrescence theory and measurement: Introducing the Cross Racial Identity Scale (CRIS). In J. G. Ponterotto, J. M. Casas, L.

M. Suzuki, & C. M. Alexander (Eds.), *Handbook of multicultural counseling* (2nd ed., pp. 371–393). Thousand Oaks, CA: Sage.

Darling-Hammond, L., & Bransford, J. (2005). *Preparing teachers for a changing world: What teachers should learn and be able to do.* San Francisco, CA: Jossey-Bass.

Epstein, J. L. (1995). School/family/community partnerships: Caring for the children we share. *Phi Delta Kappan, 76,* 701–712.

Ford, D. Y. (2011a). Don't waste trees: Standards must be culturally responsive and their implementation monitored. *Tempo, 31*(1), 35–38.

Ford, D. Y. (2011b). *Multicultural gifted education* (2nd ed.). Waco, TX: Prufrock Press.

Ford, D. Y. (2011c). *Reversing underachievement among gifted Black students* (2nd ed.). Waco, TX: Prufrock Press.

Ford, D. Y., & Harris, J. J., III. (1999). *Multicultural gifted education.* New York, NY: Teachers College Press.

Ford, D. Y., & Whiting, G. W. (2006). Under-representation of diverse students in gifted education: Recommendations for nondiscriminatory assessment (part 1). *Gifted Education Press Quarterly, 20*(2), 2–6.

Grantham, T. C. (2004). Multicultural mentoring to increase Black male representation in gifted programs. *Gifted Child Quarterly, 48,* 232–245.

Grantham, T. C., Ford, D. Y., Henfield, M. S., Trotman Scott, M., Harmon, D., Porchér, S., & Price, C. (2011). *Gifted and advanced Black students in school: An anthology of critical works.* Waco, TX: Prufrock Press.

Hodgkinson, H. (2000/2001). Educational demographics: What teachers should know. *The Changing Context of Education, 58*(4), 6–11.

Hodgkinson, H. (2007). Educational demographics: What teachers should know. In A. C. Ornstein, E. F. Pajak, & S. B. Ornstein (Eds.), *Contemporary issues in curriculum* (pp. 262–272). Boston, MA: Allyn & Bacon.

Johnsen, S. (2011). A comparison of the Texas state plan for the education of gifted/talented students and the 2010 NAGC Pre-K–Grade Gifted Programming Standards. *Tempo, 31*(1), 10–28.

National Association for Gifted Children. (2000). *Pre-K–grade 12 gifted program standards.* Washington, DC: Author.

National Association for Gifted Children. (2008). *Jacob Javits Gifted and Talented Students Education Act.* Retrieved from http://www.nagc.org/index.aspx?id=572

National Association for Gifted Children. (2010). *NAGC pre-K–grade 12 gifted programming standards: A blueprint for quality gifted education programs.* Washington, DC: Author.

National Association for Multicultural Education. (2001). *Criteria for evaluating state curriculum standards.* Retrieved from http://nameorg.org/resolutions/statecurr.html

National Council for Social Studies. (1991). *Curriculum guidelines for multicultural education.* Retrieved from http://www.socialstudies.org/positions/multicultural

Steele, C. M. (1997). A threat in the air: How stereotypes shape the intellectual identities and performance of women and African-Americans. *American Psychologist, 52,* 613–629.

Title V, Part D. [Jacob K. Javits Gifted and Talented Students Education Act of 1988], Elementary and Secondary Education Act of 1988 (2002), 20 U.S.C. sec. 7253 et seq.

Torrance, E. P. (1974). Differences are not deficits. *Teachers College Record, 75,* 471–487.

United Nations. (1948). *Universal declaration of human rights.* Retrieved from http://www.un.org/en/documents/udhr/index.shtml

U.S. Department of Education. (2010). *Condition of education 2010.* Washington, DC: Author.

Valencia, R. R. (2010). *Dismantling contemporary deficit thinking: Educational thought and practice.* New York, NY: Routledge.

Whiting, G. W., & Ford, D. Y. (2006). Under-representation of diverse students in gifted education: Recommendations for nondiscriminatory assessment (part 2). *Gifted Education Press Quarterly, 20*(3), 6–10.

Chapter 4
The Assessment Standard in Gifted Education: Identifying Gifted Students

by Susan K. Johnsen

Overview of the Assessment Standard

Assessment is a process that is used to gather information using effective tests, instruments, and techniques for a particular purpose such as screening, classification or selection, curriculum planning, learning progress evaluation, and program evaluation. In Standard 2: Assessment, three forms of assessment are included—identification, learning progress and outcomes, and evaluation of programming (National Association for Gifted Children [NAGC], 2010). These forms are inextricably linked to one another. Initially, educators set the stage for identifying students; students are identified using nonbiased and equitable approaches. Identified students then receive individual programming that is based on ongoing assessments. Identification procedures and programming effects are then evaluated, and this information is then used to improve both the identification of students with diverse characteristics and backgrounds and the learning progress of students. Because two forms of assessment are addressed in other chapters, this chapter will focus on the identification of students with gifts and talents.

Foundational Principles That Inform the Standards on Identification

One of the principles that informs not only the identification standards but also all of the 2010 NAGC Pre-K–Grade 12 Gifted Programming Standards is that *gifts and talents are dynamic and are developed over time*. Researchers suggest that general intelligence, domain-related skills, creativity, and nonintellective factors interact with one another to develop gifts and talents (Cattell, 1971; Gagné, 1999; Renzulli, 1978; Tannenbaum, 2003). This view is in contrast to those who believe that intelligence is primarily innate and does not change over time (e.g., Spearman's *g*—general intelligence; Jensen, 1980; Spearman, 1904). Educators who believe the latter are less likely to place weight on assessments other than intelligence tests. Because the assessment programming standards incorporate a more inclusive, developmental viewpoint, a broader range and more dynamic set of assessments are used in the identification process (Budoff, 1987; Lidz, 1991; McCoach, Kehle, Bray, & Siegle, 2001).

A principle related to the developmental nature of giftedness is that *early identification improves the likelihood that gifts will develop into talents*. When students from diverse backgrounds are identified early and attend schools and classes for gifted and talented students, they have higher achievement than those who are placed in general education classrooms with limited or no services (Borland, Schnur, & Wright, 2000; Cornell, Delcourt, Goldberg, & Bland, 1995). Therefore, identification needs to begin as early as pre-kindergarten and comprehensively address a diverse range of characteristics.

Another principle that influences identification is that *students exhibit their gifts and talents not only within a specific domain but also within an interest area* (Johnsen, 2008). For example, a student with a talent in the scientific domain may have a particular interest in penguins, specifically emperor penguins. She may not show her knowledge and skills on a standardized grade-level achievement test, but might show them through teacher or parent observations or in products from independent studies that could be included in a portfolio.

The final principle is also included in the Gifted Programming Standards—*giftedness is exhibited across all diverse groups*. Gifted students from diverse groups are underrepresented in gifted education programs (Daniels, 1998; Ford & Harris, 1999). Researchers suggest that underrepresentation is influenced by factors related to the educators involved in the identification process, specific instruments, and interpretations of assessments (Ford & Harmon, 2001; Frasier, Garcia, & Passow, 1995; Harris, Plucker, Rapp, & Martinez, 2009; Maker, 1996; Peterson & Margolin, 1997; Soto, 1997). These factors, which have a negative impact on students, are of serious concern to gifted education professionals.

Each of these principles (i.e., gifts and talents are dynamic and developmental, early identification, interest-specific gifts and talents, and diversity) is foundational to the three student outcomes within the identification standards.

Student Outcome 1: Establishing Equal Access

The first student outcome (2.1) within the assessment standard focuses on providing equal access to a comprehensive assessment system by developing environments at school and at home that encourage students to express diverse characteristics and behaviors that are associated with giftedness. The placement of students in special education, in schools that may or may not offer gifted education services, or in classrooms where teachers do not believe in gifted education should not preclude the consideration of a student for gifted programming.

To ensure that this student outcome is achieved, all educators need professional development on the characteristics of gifted and talented students. Without training, teachers are more likely to nominate children who reflect their conceptions of giftedness, such as students who are academically able (Guskin, Peng, & Simon, 1992; Hunsaker, Finley, & Frank, 1997), are from higher socioeconomic status groups (Guskin et al., 1992), and are verbal and well-mannered (Dawson, 1997; Schack & Starko, 1990; Speirs Neumeister, Adams, Pierce, Cassady, & Dixon, 2007). Students who are economically disadvantaged (Peterson & Margolin, 1997) or who are English language learners (Plata & Masten, 1998) are often excluded from the identification process.

Along with training, educators also need to develop classroom environments that differentiate for individual differences (Hertzog, 2005). Individual differences may manifest themselves in what students know and want to know (e.g., the knowledge and skills they are learning—the subject matter content), how quickly they learn the content (e.g., pacing and rate of learning), how they learn (e.g., preference for types of activities), and the environment where they learn (e.g., individual, small group, community; Johnsen, 2011a). In differentiating content, teachers might develop activities that emphasize depth, complexity, and creativity; ask higher level and open-ended questions; use above-grade level materials; develop problem- or concept-based units of study; and provide opportunities for independent research in an area of interest. In differentiating for rate of learning, teachers might use fewer drill and practice activities; preassessments to determine student mastery allowing students to accelerate in the curriculum; and self-checking rubrics so that students can pace themselves through assignments. In differentiating preference, teachers might vary the method of presentation allowing for discussion, experimentation, and demonstration; provide students with choices of assessments; and offer students choices in content, process, and product. In differentiating environment, teachers might provide independent learning activities, use flexible grouping for students with similar interests and academic abilities, arrange for a mentor to work with students in an area of interest or strength, establish multilevel learning stations or centers, and integrate community-based activities. A differentiated classroom will allow all students opportunities to show diverse talents and gifts.

Along with professional development for educators in the school setting, parents and families also need to be educated about characteristics of children with gifts and talents, how to nurture these characteristics at home, and the importance of gifted education (Johnsen, 2011b). Researchers have found that parents, particularly those from minority or lower income backgrounds, may be reticent to nominate their children for gifted education programs (Louis & Lewis, 1992; Scott, Perou, Urbano, Hogan, & Gold, 1992). Therefore, families need to understand not only characteristics but also the importance of nurturing them at home and at school. They need to be knowledgeable about school gifted education services and the identification process. Families also need to know how to support their children's interests outside of school. Those parents who have fewer financial resources may need assistance in finding afterschool and summer enrichment programs that offer scholarships (Johnsen, Feuerbacher, & Witte, 2007).

Student Outcome 2: Using and Interpreting a Variety of Assessment Evidence

The second student outcome (2.2) focuses on assessment evidence that allows for students to reveal their exceptionalities so that instructional accommodations and modifications can be provided. The evidence-based practices focus on the comprehensiveness of the identification procedures (2.2.1), the variety of assessments (2.2.2–2.2.4), interpreting multiple assessments (2.2.5), and informing and eliciting evidence from parents (2.2.6).

Comprehensive, Cohesive, and Ongoing Identification Procedures

Comprehensive procedures require that educators align assessments across grade levels and provide programming options in all domains (e.g., math, science, social studies, English/language arts, visual and performing arts). For example, if a school district has an accelerated mathematics program for students with gifts and talents, off-level assessments might be used beginning in pre-kindergarten and aligned with end-of-course exams in various mathematics and Advanced Placement (AP) courses at the secondary level. In this way, assessments would not only identify students as being advanced in mathematics but also provide information regarding instructional modifications. These assessments should also be cohesive—performance on one math assessment would predict performance on a later math assessment. Moreover, equivalent difficulty levels are important in identifying students and helping them make transitions across grade levels and math courses. With these types of procedures in place, a gifted student in math could be identified at any grade level and proceed smoothly, receiving appropriate accelerated math programming.

Along with comprehensiveness and cohesion, educators need to develop procedures for informed consent from families, committee reviews of assessment information, retention of identified students, reassessment of identified students if more information is needed regarding their strengths and weaknesses, exiting from program services, and appeals for entering and exiting gifted program services (2.2.1). Details regarding these types of procedures can be found in state resources (see Colorado Department of Education, 2004; Georgia Department of Education, 2006; Pennsylvania Department of Gifted Education, 2010; Texas Education Agency, 2009).

Variety of Assessments

The selection of assessments is dependent upon the characteristics of the students and available programming. For example, if a school offers special programming for young artists in the field of music, then the identification instruments would most likely be different from those used for identifying students with potential in the sciences (e.g., auditions vs. portfolio of science experiments). In addition, if the majority of students are from minority groups or special populations (e.g., English language learners, low income), then different types of assessments might need to be considered such as those that are nonverbal or linguistically reduced. In all cases, the Gifted Programming Standards identify the following attributes as important to selecting a variety of assessments (see 2.2.3–2.2.4).

Multiple sources. Multiple sources provide a more comprehensive view of the student's behaviors across settings. No single source of information has an opportunity to observe students at home, at school, and during afterschool activities. Sources may include teachers (special, general, and gifted education), coaches, counselors, psychologists, administrators, peers, parents and other family members, and the student him- or herself (Coleman & Cross, 2005; Johnsen, 2011a). Caution needs to be used in including one source of information multiple times. For example, a teacher might nominate a student, might evaluate a portfolio of work, and might complete observation checklists. In this case, the teacher's information would be heavily weighted during the identification procedure over other sources.

Qualitative and quantitative. Similar to a variety of sources, qualitative and quantitative information provides a broader description of students. Each type provides different information. With qualitative assessments, words are used to describe a student's strengths and weaknesses; with quantitative, numbers are used (Ryser, 2004b). Qualitative assessments provide flexibility and freedom, whereas quantitative assessments provide more consistency and are more controlled. Types of qualitative assessments include portfolios, anecdotal records, interviews, methods of learning and other dynamic assessments, past educational experiences, awards and honors, observations, and CDs or DVDs of performance. Types of quantitative assessments include norm-referenced, standardized tests (e.g., achievement, intelligence, creativity, aptitude), grades, checklists, and rating scales. Because quantitative assessments' uses are more restricted and generally have right or wrong answers, they may not represent the student's performance in more authentic settings like qualitative assessments. For example, as opposed to an achievement test, portfolios of work might be used to gather artifacts of students' products and performances in core subject areas that show their best work (Johnsen, 2008). Educators in a particular field of study who have knowledge of advanced learning and development would then review the work. Ryser (2011b) added a cautionary note to educators who assign numbers to qualitative assessments. In those cases where numbers are applied, the qualitative assessment actually becomes a quantitative assessment and loses its power in providing more information about the student.

Off-level testing. Because students with potential in academic areas may be performing above grade level, off-level testing is needed to identify their strengths. Most diagnostic tests and state-developed assessments that are required by the No Child Left Behind Act of 2001 do not have enough ceiling so that advanced students are able to show what they know and can do. Multi-grade level tests and off-level tests provide more difficult items and discriminate better among students with gifts and talents (Lupkowski-Shoplik & Assouline, 1993). In fact, because assessments have more error at the upper end of a scale, students who are gifted in a particular domain may appear to perform more poorly than students who are on grade level (Johnsen, 2011b).

Nonbiased and equitable. Because students from diverse backgrounds are underrepresented in gifted education programs, educators need to play close attention to whether or not assessments are nonbiased and equitable. Tests or assessment procedures are biased if they differentiate between members of various groups on some characteristics other than the one being measured. For example, an assessment in math might be biased if it measures reading ability more than mathematical problem solving. Similarly, a test that is highly verbal might be biased against students who are English language learners. For a test to be nonbiased, it must accurately reflect a "true difference" on what the test is measuring (e.g., students who perform better than others on a math test know more math knowledge and skills than their peers).

To reduce bias, tests need to (a) include groups in the sample that match national census data (Salvia, Ysseldyke, & Bolt, 2007), (b) show that the items discriminate equally well for each of the groups (Ryser, 2011a), (c) provide separate reliability and validity information for each group (Ryser, 2011a), and (d) describe how the content is free of bias (Johnsen & Ryser, 1994). Content bias can be reduced by using performance-based items, pantomimed instruction, practice items, untimed responses, abstract reasoning and problem solving, novel items, and nonverbal items (Castellano, 1998; Jensen, 1980; Johnsen & Ryser, 1994; Joseph & Ford, 2006; VanTassel-Baska, Feng, & Evans, 2007). In some cases, local norms may need to be developed if the school district's majority is a minority (e.g., African American, Hispanic, Native American, Asian, English language learners). In those cases, educators need to use specialists in tests and measurement and use caution when comparing local norms to national norms.

Technically adequate. Assessments need to meet the standards outlined by professional organizations in the measurement field (American Educational Research Association, American Psychological Association, & National Council on Measurement in Education, 1999). These standards relate to norming, reliability, and validity. Is the norming group representative of the national population? Is the test internally consistent and consistent over time (reliability)? Does the test actually measure what it is supposed to measure (validity)? Educators need to research the technical adequacy of instruments they use in the identification procedure and become familiar with test review resources so that they are able to make informed decisions when selecting quantitative assessments (see Robins & Jolly, 2011, and the Buros Institute of Mental Measurements [http://www.unl.edu/buros] for test reviews).

Dynamic. To determine learning potential, teachers can use dynamic assessments in the classroom where the teacher focuses on the interaction between the student and the task to understand the student's academic strengths and weaknesses (Swanson & Lussier, 2001). Forms of dynamic assessment include identifying learning potential (e.g., Budoff, 1987), testing the limits (Carlson & Wiedl, 1979), mediated assessment (Feuerstein, 1980), and assisted learning and transfer (Bransford, Delclos, Vye, Burns, & Hasselbring, 1987; Campione, Brown, Ferrara, Jones, & Steinberg, 1985). To examine abilities and discover potential, the tasks need to be novel, problem-based, and require complex strategies (Geary & Brown, 1991; Kurtz & Weinert, 1989; Scruggs & Mastropieri, 1985).

In summary, in selecting a variety of assessments, educators should consider these characteristics: sources, qualitative and quantitative information, off-level subject matter, technical qualities, and their use dynamically.

Interpreting Multiple Assessments

After gathering information from a variety of assessments, educators need to know how to interpret the data in determining the best programming options for students. A committee of professionals who have training in gifted education and in educational and psychological measurement should be involved in the decision-making process. Student Outcome 6.1 suggests that educators meet national teacher preparation standards. They also need to have an understanding of the characteristics of students from special populations and factors that might influence the recognition of their gifts and talents. When organizing the information for the committee's consideration, the following guidelines should be used (Johnsen, 2004).

Equal weighting of assessments. If both qualitative and quantitative assessments are technically adequate, the committee should consider them equally in making decisions. Sometimes more weight or importance is assigned to a single assessment, which undermines the multiple criteria process and eliminates opportunities for examining a student's relative strengths and weaknesses. For example, norm-referenced, standardized tests such as intelligence and achievement might receive more weight than qualitative assessments such as portfolios or interviews. A second way of weighting assessments is by allowing one source, such as the teacher, to provide information for several assessments such as grades, classroom checklists, and portfolios. A third way of weighting assessments is to use a specific cut-off score on a single instrument before the rest of the data are considered. For example, a student might need to perform in the top 10% on a statewide achievement test before being nominated for gifted programming, or a specific score on an intelligence test is needed before the rest of the data are considered. Fourth, one assessment's subtests might be used as separate criteria, which would weight performance on a single instrument. Therefore, unless required by state rules and regulations, all assessments, if they are technically adequate, should be considered in the decision-making process. Moreover, research suggests that qualitative assessments such as portfolios (Johnsen & Ryser, 1997) and parent nominations (Lee & Olszewski-Kubilius, 2006) relate to more quantitative measures and predict performance in gifted programs.

Comparable scores. Assessments generate different types of scores: raw scores, percentile ranks, grade equivalent scores, and standard or index scores.

Raw scores are original numeric values before they are transformed to other scores. They do not have any meaning until they are converted. For example, a student who scores 70 on a biology test may have the best or worst score depending on the performance of the rest of the class. Scores in one teacher's class may also not be the same as scores in another teacher's class. Raw scores cannot be compared with each other in a meaningful way and should never be compared when interpreting data.

Percentile ranks are derived from raw scores and show the relative rank of how a student performed in relationship to other students who took the same test. They should not be confused with percentages, which are simply the number of items that a student passed divided by the total number of items. A student who obtained a percentile rank of 90 performed better than 90% of the students who took the test. Although these scores are useful and easily understood, they cannot be averaged or otherwise operated on arithmetically because they are not interval data. Because percentiles cluster heavily around the mean, or 50th percentile, and are more sparsely distributed at the top and bottom of a normal curve, a difference between 50 and 55 represents a smaller difference than between 95 and 99. If percentile ranks are considered in decision making, they need to be converted to a standard or index score for comparison purposes.

Grade equivalent scores are generated from the mean raw score obtained for children at each grade level. Using interpolation, extrapolation, and smoothing, psychometrists then create a score for each of the raw score points. Researchers have criticized the use of these scores because the content of instruction and amount of knowledge gained varies from grade level to grade level and they are open to misinterpretation (Salvia et al., 2007). For example, a first-grade student who received a 6.8 grade equivalent score (i.e., sixth grade, eighth month) on a reading achievement test does not mean that she is reading at a sixth-grade level. It simply means that she is reading above grade level. A curriculum-based measurement is more likely to indicate the knowledge and skills she has learned. Therefore, grade-equivalent scores should not be used in making placement decisions.

Standard or index scores are derived from raw scores and are transformed into a normalized score distribution (i.e., bell-shaped curve). Depending on the unit used to describe the score's distance from the mean (e.g., standard deviation [SD]) or average performance of the group), they may be called Z-scores (mean is 1 and SD is ± 1), T-scores (mean is 50 and SD is ± 10), A-scores (mean is 500 and SD is ± 100), IQ scores (e.g., mean is 100 and SD is ± 15), and stanines (mean is 5 and SD is ± 1; see Table 4.1). Because these scores are on an equal interval scale, they are more versatile than other types of scores because they can be compared to other standard scores with the same mean and standard deviation and can be added and subtracted. For example, a score of 130 on an intelligence test with a mean of 100 and a standard deviation of 15 can be compared to other tests with the same mean and standard deviation. In Table 4.1, a percentile rank of 95, the top 5% of students who took the test, is similar

Table 4.1

Relationships Among Various Standard Scores and Percentile Ranks and Their Interpretation

Percentile Rank	Quotient	A-Score	T-Score	Z-Score	Stanine	Interpreta-tion
99	150	830	83	+3.33	9	Very
99	145	800	80	+3.00	9	Superior
99	140	770	77	+2.67	9	
99	135	730	73	+2.33	9	
98	130	700	70	+2.00	9	
97	128	680	68	+1.75	8	Superior
95	125	670	67	+1.67	8	
94	123	650	65	+1.5	8	
84	115	600	60	+1.00	7	Above
81	113	580	58	+0.75	7	Average
75	110	570	57	+0.67	6	Average
63	105	530	53	+0.33	6	
50	100	500	50	0.00	5	
37	95	470	47	-0.33	4	
25	90	430	43	-0.67	4	
16	85	400	40	-1.00	3	Below
9	80	370	37	-1.33	3	Average

to an intelligence quotient of 125, an A-Score of 670, a T-Score of 67, a Z-score of +1.67, and a stanine score of 8, all of which are in the superior range. Because standard scores are on an equal interval scale, they should never be assigned a rank order number such as those used in matrices, which makes them less versatile and open to misinterpretation.

All types of standard scores represent the performance of a group of students when compared to a norm-reference group, which may be comprised of national, state, or local samples. The comparison group needs to be considered when interpreting test scores. For example, a student whose performance is compared to the performance of *only* students nominated for the gifted program may score lower than when compared to *all* of the students in the school district. Similarly, a student who is compared to a national *gifted* sample may not perform as well as when compared to the *entire* national sample. Age may also make a difference when comparing performance. Young kindergarten children with summer birthdays may not do as well as children with fall birthdays or those who have spent an additional year in kindergarten. Whenever possible, ages should be used when comparing scores. For more accurate comparisons, local norms may need to be developed when schools have a dominant minority or income level group or whose scores differ dramatically from the nationally normed scores.

Although scores from quantitative measures can be compared using a conversion chart, qualitative information should remain descriptive.

Test error. Many factors contribute to a student's performance on a test. Some of these relate to the test itself, the test taker and his or her background, and the testing situation. Because all assessments have some error, a single test score should be viewed as an estimate of a student's actual performance. When speaking of quantitative assessments, this error is based upon the reliability and the standard deviation of the test and is called the standard error of measurement (SEM). The SEM is a way of calculating the upper and lower limits in which the student's "true score" lies. By adding and subtracting the SEM from a student's obtained score, educators can determine the likelihood that a score will fall within a particular range. For example, 68% of the time, a student's true score will likely fall within a range of plus or minus one SEM from the obtained test score; 95% of the time between plus or minus two SEMs; and 99% of the time between plus or minus approximately three SEMs. Suppose that Elena scored 115 on an intelligence test with an SEM of 5 points. One would expect that 68% of the time her true score would be within the range of 110–120 (adding and subtracting one SEM from 115); 95% of the time, within the range of 105–125 (adding and subtracting two SEMs from 115); and 99% of the time, within the range of 100–130 (adding and subtracting three SEMS from 115). In interpreting Elena's score, if she were to take the test again, she would conceivably score within the average (e.g., 100) to very superior (e.g., 130) range 99% of the time. Educators need to remember that having strict cut-off scores that are exceedingly high (e.g., 130) may eliminate students whose performance is affected by test error. Therefore, the SEM is very important when interpreting scores.

Best performance. In organizing data, the committee needs to be able to examine a student's relative strengths and weaknesses. Students don't always perform similarly across assessments or even within the same assessment because they sample different behaviors and/or different domains. Therefore, scores from each assessment should be separated to view the student's best and worst performances. The highest score is often indicative of a student's potential. Some forms that are used for organizing data, such as matrices, sum and average scores and collapse data into a single rating number. This approach does not help identify students with potential, nor does it provide information for examining a student's talent area for programming.

Description of the student. Qualitative information also needs to be examined by the committee. This information might include interviews with students, anecdotal information from the classroom or home observations, students' reflections regarding their products and performances, students' responses to teaching tasks, and clinical impressions from those who administered quantitative assessments. These assessments are important in explaining the quantitative data and in providing a more holistic view of the student.

Informing and Eliciting Evidence From Parents

In their conceptual models of giftedness, Tannenbaum (2003) and Gagné (1999) identified parents as an important environmental influence in developing their child's gifts and talents. Parental support is extremely important (Olszewski-Kubilius, 2000; Yun & Schader, 2001) in providing early exposure to the talent domain (Williams, 2003), special tutoring or learning outside of school (Filippelli & Walberg, 1997), external incentives (Filippelli & Walberg, 1997), and quality education (Subotnik, 1997). Parents need training regarding the range of characteristics within the gifted population, their role in developing their child's gifts and talents, the identification process, and the benefits for their child in participating in gifted education programming. Researchers have suggested that with training, parents may be better than teachers at identifying young children (Jacobs, 1971; Johnsen & Ryser, 1994).

Without this training, parents or guardians may be reluctant to refer their children for assessment, particularly those from minority backgrounds (Frasier et al., 1995; Scott et al., 1992) and may not understand or approve behaviors associated with giftedness (Coleman & Cross, 2005). Consequently, special populations may be underrepresented in the first phase of the identification process. To increase the representation of special populations in the referral phase, schools need to send home flyers in multiple languages to parents of all students, include information about the gifted program at school orientations and special meetings, make announcements through public media, and provide professional development for parents or guardians and others who are involved in the nominating process (Coleman, 1994; Dawson, 1997; Johnsen & Ryser, 1994; Reyes, Fletcher, & Paez, 1996; Shaklee & Viechnicki, 1995).

Because parents can offer perspectives about their child's interests and potential outside the school setting, they need to be actively involved in gathering information throughout the identification process. For example, schools need to help parents understand how to complete student nomination forms such as checklists and rating scales and also how to contribute to their student's portfolios. Parents who are educated about gifted education are a critical component to implementing nondiscriminatory identification procedures and developing quality programming.

Example Case Study

All of the data collected during the identification process may be organized into a case study format (see Figure 4.1). As can be seen in Figure 4.1, the assessment data can be organized by phases (e.g., nomination/referral, screening, and selection) although another format could be used (e.g., organizing the data by qualitative and quantitative information).

In this case, the gifted education teacher was responsible for collecting information from a variety of sources (e.g., parents, counselor, teacher, and the student; 2.2.3). Quantitative data included checklists, achievement tests, and intelligence tests and were interpreted within ranges of performance (see comments column; 2.2.2–2.2.4). Along with percentile ranks and standard scores, the school chose to insert stanine scores because they are comparable and provide a range of performance, which takes into account some of the error in the assessments. Qualitative data included comments on the checklists, an interview with Cesar, and a portfolio of his work and were interpreted using the presented evidence (2.2.5).

The committee was comprised of the general education teacher, the gifted education teacher, the special education teacher, the parents, the counselor, and the principal. All of the committee members had training in gifted education (2.2.5). Before the committee met, each of the members reviewed the evidence for Cesar. They learned that the parents had nominated their son for the gifted education program (2.2.6). The background information indicated that Cesar's first language was Spanish, and he began learning English in kindergarten in the school's bilingual program. He was a young third grader when compared to his peers, because he was born in August, which may have influenced his performance on some of the tests if they did not provide age-related norms. There did appear to be discrepancies in the perspectives of the individuals regarding Cesar's characteristics (e.g., the teacher's perspective vs. the parents' perspectives) and also in Cesar's performance on achievement subtests. His relative areas of strength appeared to be in science and math, with a strong interest in art. Upon reviewing the referral assessment data, the committee noted that Cesar had met the school district's standard, which was set at the 90th percentile or within the superior to very superior range, on the majority of the indicators, which was sufficient to recommend him for further assessment. During the screening phase, the counselor administered the nonverbal reasoning subtest of the Screening Assessment for Gifted Elementary and Middle School Students-2 (SAGES-2; Johnsen & Corn, 2001) because Cesar was an English language learner, the committee interviewed Cesar, and Cesar submitted a portfolio of his best work (2.3.1). The second phase of screening corroborated the earlier

Student: <u>Cesar Rivera</u>   D.O.B.: <u>8-30-2003</u>   ID#: <u>553</u>   Date of Review: <u>2/18/11</u>
Home School/Grade: <u>Zavala/Grade 3</u>   Language Spoken at Home: <u>Spanish</u>

I. Nomination/Referral Phase

Assessment	Score Obtained	Met Standard	Comments
Parents	99th percentile SS 135 (9th stanine)	Yes	(See checklist) Art/Science
Counselor	94th percentile SS 120 (8th stanine)	Yes	(See checklist) Likes art; doesn't like classwork
Teacher	84th percentile SS 115 (7th stanine)	No	(See checklist) Doesn't turn in homework
Achievement: Iowa Tests of Basic Skills			
Reading	75th percentile SS 110 (6th stanine)	No	Average range
Math	97th percentile SS 128 (8th stanine)	Yes	Superior range
Science	99th percentile SS 140 (9th stanine)	Yes	Very superior range
Social Studies	84th percentile SS 115 (7th stanine)	No	Above-average range

II. Screening Committee Recommendation (See committee members' signatures on back.)

The Screening Committee has reviewed this student's data and has determined that he/she:
_√_ Is recommended for additional screening.
____ Is recommended and an exception is made because _____.
____ Is not recommended for additional screening.

III. Screening Phase

Interview	Exhibits character-istics (see attached interview)	Yes	Confirmed interests in sci-ence/art; drew 3-D figures at age 4
Screening Assess-ment for Gifted Elementary/Middle School Students-2	98th percentile SS 130 (9th stanine)	Yes	Very superior score on reasoning when com-pared to gifted sample
Portfolio of Work	Exhibits character-istics (see attached artifacts)	Yes	Art and science work shows interests and aptitudes

IV. Selection Committee Recommendation (See committee members' signatures on plan.)

Cesar qualifies for services in the gifted classroom in science and math, with differentiation in the general education classroom. His aptitude in art needs to be developed through the middle school art program or with mentors. He needs Tier I support services in reading.

Figure 4.1. Example case study.

assessment evidence. His interview and portfolio showed his talents in the art and science areas, and his performance on the SAGES-2 revealed his strengths in problem solving and overall learning potential. All of this information was considered in the committee's final recommendation, which was to place him in the gifted classroom for science and math, develop his talent in art, assist the general education teacher in differentiating the curriculum, assist his parents in nurturing his talents at home, and provide further support in reading. If his relative weakness in reading continues and he is nonresponsive to special interventions, then he will be referred for a Tier 2 intervention, which incorporates intensive instruction by a reading specialist.

The case study format meets the suggested guidelines for organizing and interpreting multiple assessments: (a) both qualitative and quantitative assessments were equally weighted, (b) comparable scores were used, (c) the SEM was considered, (d) data clearly showed the best performance of the student and his relative strengths and weaknesses, and (e) descriptive information was attached to the case. All of the data provided a broad picture of the student across contexts.

Student Outcome 3: Representing Gifted Students From Diverse Backgrounds

The third student outcome within the assessment standard (2.3) focuses on the inclusion of gifted and talented students from diverse backgrounds in gifted education programming. The goal is for these students to be representative of the total school population. The underrepresentation of minority students in gifted education has been well documented (Daniels, 1998; Ford & Harris, 1999; Morris, 2002). Researchers have suggested that the following practices within the identification procedure have limited the inclusion of special populations: exclusive definitions (Passow & Frasier, 1996), test bias (Frasier et al., 1995; Ryser, 2011a), the overreliance on traditional tests (Ford & Harmon, 2001; Maker, 1996), selective referrals (Frasier et al., 1995; Peterson & Margolin, 1997), and educators' attitudes (Harris et al., 2009; Soto, 1997).

Inclusive Definitions

Narrow definitions requiring superior performance on intelligence or achievement tests (e.g., 130, or 98th percentile) may limit the number of students who are gifted, particularly those who are English language learners and those from lower income groups. Broader definitions that encompass a wider range of characteristics and include student potential similar to the federal definition of gifted and talented and use multiple assessments are more likely to identify students who exhibit their talents in a variety of ways (Passow & Frasier, 1996). For example, a cut-off score at the 90th or even the 84th percentile rank on a variety of assessments would include a more diverse group and consider measurement error. Differentiation would then need to occur within programming for students identified as "at-potential."

Test Fairness

Test fairness relates to the characteristics of the norming population, the linguistic demands of the instrument, item bias, and the test's usefulness in predicting all students' success in gifted programming (Ryser, 2011a). Although test norms primarily reflect the population of individuals who live in the United States, they may not reflect local norms. Therefore, some school districts with a greater number of individuals from minority or ethnic groups might consider establishing local norms for comparison purposes. Tests with high language demands may also create barriers for culturally and linguistically diverse students and those from economically disadvantaged backgrounds with limited experiences (Johnsen & Ryser, 1994; Reid, Udall, Romanoff, & Algozzine, 1999). To reduce these barriers, professionals have recommended the use of nonverbal or individually administered tests (Ryser, 2004a). These types of tests not only limit linguistic requirements but also reduce the amount of previous information required in responding to the items. Moreover, items that stereotype or have knowledge that may be unknown in a particular culture may be biased against certain cultural and socioeconomic groups. Most test developers have professionals review the items for gender or cultural stereotyping and analyze each item statistically (e.g., differential item functioning) to ensure that every special group has the same probability of answering the item correctly and that overall the test predicts equally well for each subgroup.

Nontraditional Tests

Although 21 states use multiple criteria for identifying students for gifted education services (Council of State Directors of Programs for the Gifted [CSDPG] & NAGC, 2009), at least one or more of the assessments need to be quantitative (e.g., intelligence and/or achievement tests), which are considered more traditional. Some researchers argue that special populations do not perform well on norm-referenced, standardized tests and have recommended alternative assessments (Callahan, Hunsaker, Adams, Moore, & Bland, 1995; Ford, 1996; Frasier et al., 1995). Recent studies have indicated that minority students do tend to perform better on nonverbal, problem-solving, and performance-based types of assessments when compared to traditional forms (Pierce et al., 2007; Reid et al., 1999; VanTassel-Baska et al., 2007; VanTassel-Baska, Johnson, & Avery, 2002).

Selective Referrals

Along with the selection of nonbiased and nontraditional assessments, educators need to be aware that bias may occur at any point in the identification process. As mentioned previously, selective referrals sometimes exclude special groups (see Student Outcome 1). Because of misconceptions, children who have disabilities, who are economically disadvantaged, or who are English language learners are referred less frequently (Harris et al., 2009; Morrison & Rizza, 2007; Peterson & Margolin, 1997; Plata & Masten, 1998). Moreover, without training and the knowledge of how to differentiate and challenge students, teachers often find it difficult to complete the required assessment forms and checklists reliably to validly refer a student for further testing. Researchers recommend extensive training of educators who are involved in the identification process. When *all* educators (i.e., general, gifted, and special education teachers; psychologists; counselors; administrators; parents) are trained about specific characteristics of gifted and talented students, they are better able to contribute to the identification process (Johnsen & Ryser, 1994; Shaklee & Viechnicki, 1995).

Educators' Attitudes

Because educators are involved in most aspects of the identification procedure, their attitudes can influence the students who are not only referred but also selected and served. In light of high-stakes testing, teachers of children from economically disadvantaged backgrounds may view their job as one of remediation rather than talent development and may not nominate students for gifted programs because they are only looking for students who are academic achievers (Johnsen & Ryser, 1994). Gifted children with disabilities also pose special problems because their disability may mask their ability or vice versa (Whitmore, 1981). With special education services focusing more often on the disability, the exceptional student's gift may go unrecognized. Other researchers have noted educators' cultural prejudice and indifference (Passow & Frasier, 1996), negative cultural perceptions toward giftedness (Morris, 2002), low teacher expectations (Alviderez & Weinstein, 1999; Johnsen & Ryser, 1994), and negative reactions toward non-English-speaking students (Soto, 1997) and lower SES students (McBee, 2006). In all of these cases, if the students' characteristics are too different from a stereotyped view of model gifted students, educators are less likely to refer and provide gifted education programming services. Extensive training is recommended to overcome negative attitudes, to help educators value multicultural perspectives (Kitano & Pedersen, 2002), and to develop environments where students are able to demonstrate their gifts and talents (Johnsen & Ryser, 1994; Weber, 1999).

In summary, more equal representation across groups is enhanced when (a) definitions are broader, (b) tests are fair to all populations in the identification process, and (c) professional development is provided for educators and parents to improve their understanding and importance of gifted education programming.

Remember that bias may enter at any point in the identification procedure: notice, referral/screening, evaluation/placement, and program participation. The Office for Civil Rights has provided guidelines that might assist educators in evaluating the fairness of their overall system and identifying areas for improvement (see Table 4.2; Trice & Shannon, 2002).

Summary

Foundational to the three NAGC student outcomes related to identification within the assessment standard are the views that (a) gifts and talents are dynamic and develop over time, (b) early identification improves the likelihood that gifts will develop into talents, (c) students exhibit their gifts and talents within interest areas, and (d) giftedness is exhibited across all diverse groups. The first student outcome addresses equal access to the identification process. To achieve this outcome, educators must learn how to differentiate their classroom environments and parents must learn how to nurture gifts and talents at home. The second outcome, which encourages the use of a variety of assessment evidence, requires the implementation of four evidence-based practices: designing a comprehensive identification procedure, using a variety of assessments, interpreting multiple assessments, and informing and eliciting evidence from parents. The final student outcome focuses on ensuring that students from diverse groups, in sufficient numbers to be representative of the total school population, are considered for services. Practices that appear to be effective in increasing the number of gifted students from special populations in gifted education programming include developing more inclusive definitions, using fair and nontraditional tests, and changing teacher and parent attitudes so that more students are included in the identification process. When all of these student outcomes are achieved, educators can be more assured that their identification procedure is effectively identifying each and every student who needs gifted education programming.

Table 4.2

Guidelines From the Office for Civil Rights

Statistical Analysis

_____ Racial/ethnic composition of the district's student enrollment.

_____ Racial/ethnic composition of student population receiving gifted services.

_____ Determine if minority students are statistically underrepresented in gifted programs.

_____ Number (%) of students by race/ethnicity referred for evaluation for gifted eligibility.

_____ Number (%) of students by race/ethnicity determined eligible for gifted services.

_____ Number (%) of students by race/ethnicity withdrawing from, or otherwise discontinuing participation in, gifted programs/services.

Notice

_____ Notice simply and clearly explains the purpose of the program, referral/screening procedures, and eligibility criteria and identifies the district's contact person.

_____ Notice is provided annually to students, parents, and guardians, in a manner designed to reach all segments of the school community.

Referral/Screening

_____ Multiple alternative referral sources, e.g., teachers, parents, etc., are, in practice, accessible to and utilized by, all segments of the school community.

_____ Teachers and other district staff involved in the referral process have been trained and/or provided guidance regarding the characteristics of giftedness.

_____ Referral/screening criteria are applied in a nondiscriminatory manner.

_____ All referral/screening criteria/guidelines are directly related to the purpose of the gifted program.

_____ Standardized tests and cut-off scores are appropriate (valid and reliable) for the purpose of screening students for gifted services.

Evaluation/Placement

_____ Eligibility criteria are applied in a nondiscriminatory manner.

_____ Eligibility criteria are consistent with the purpose and implementation of the gifted program: Eligibility is based on multiple criteria; criteria include multiple assessments; and eligibility incorporates component test scores as appropriate.

_____ Assessment instruments/measures and cut-off scores are appropriate (valid and reliable) for the purpose of identifying students for gifted services.

_____ To the extent that subjective assessment criteria are utilized, those individuals conducting the assessments have been provided guidelines and training to ensure proper evaluations.

_____ Alternative assessment instruments are utilized in appropriate circumstances.

_____ If private testing is permitted as the basis for an eligibility determination, it does not have a disparate impact on minority students, or if it does, the use of such testing is legitimately related to the successful implementation of the program and no less discriminatory alternative exists which would achieve the same objective.

Program Participation

_____ Continued eligibility standards/criteria are applied in a nondiscriminatory manner.

_____ Continued eligibility standards/criteria are consistent with the purpose and implementation of the gifted program.

_____ Implementation procedures and practices facilitate equal access for all students.

Note. Adapted from Trice and Shannon (2002).

References

Alviderez, J., & Weinstein, R. S. (1999). Early teacher perceptions and later student academic achievement. *Journal of Educational Psychology, 91,* 731–746.

American Educational Research Association, American Psychological Association, & National Council on Measurement in Education. (1999). *Standards for educational and psychological testing.* Washington, DC: American Educational Research Association.

Borland, J. H., Schnur, R., & Wright, L. (2000). Economically disadvantaged students in a school for the academically gifted: A post-positivist inquiry into individual and family adjustment. *Gifted Child Quarterly, 44,* 13–32.

Bransford, J. C., Delclos, J. R., Vye, N. J., Burns, M., & Hasselbring, T. S. (1987). State of the art and future directions. In C. S. Lidz (Ed.), *Dynamic assessment: An interactional approach to evaluating learning potential* (pp. 479–496). New York, NY: Guilford Press.

Budoff, M. (1987). The validity of learning potential assessment. In C. S. Lidz (Ed.), *Dynamic assessment: An interactional approach to evaluating learning potential* (pp. 52–81). New York, NY: Guilford Press.

Callahan, C. M., Hunsaker, S., Adams, S. M., Moore, S. D., & Bland, L. (1995). *Instruments used in the identification of gifted and talented students.* Storrs: University of Connecticut, The National Research Center on the Gifted and Talented.

Campione, J. S., Brown, A. L., Ferrara, R. A., Jones, R. S., & Steinberg, E. (1985). Breakdowns in the flexible use of information: Intelligence-related differences in transfer following equivalent learning performance. *Intelligence, 9,* 297–315.

Carlson, J. S., & Wiedl, K. H. (1979). Toward a differential testing approach: Testing the limits employing the Raven Matrices. *Intelligence, 3,* 323–344.

Castellano, J. A. (1998). *Identifying and assessing gifted and talented bilingual Hispanic students* (Report No. EDO-RC-97-9). Charleston, WV: ERIC Clearinghouse on Rural Education and Small Schools. (ERIC Document Reproduction Service No. ED423104)

Cattell, R. B. (1971). *Abilities: Their structure, growth, and action.* Boston, MA: Houghton Mifflin.

Coleman, L. J. (1994). Portfolio assessment: A key to identifying hidden talents and empowering teachers of young children. *Gifted Child Quarterly, 38,* 65–69.

Coleman, L. J., & Cross, T. L. (2005). *Being gifted in school: An introduction to development, guidance, and teaching.* Waco, TX: Prufrock Press.

Colorado Department of Education. (2004). *Gifted education guidelines and resources.* Retrieved from http://www.cde.state.co.us/gt/download/pdf/Guidelines_2nd_Edition.pdf

Cornell, D. G., Delcourt, M. A. B., Goldberg, M. D., & Bland, L. C. (1995). Achievement and self-concept of minority students in elementary school gifted programs. *Journal for the Education of the Gifted, 18,* 189–209.

Council of State Directors of Programs for the Gifted, & National Association for Gifted Children. (2009). *2008–2009 state of the states in gifted education: National policy and practice data*. Washington, DC: National Association for Gifted Children.

Daniels, V. I. (1998). Minority students in gifted and special education programs: The case for educational equity. *Journal of Special Education, 32,* 41–44.

Dawson, V. L. (1997). In search of the wild bohemian: Challenges in the identification of the creatively gifted. *Roeper Review, 19,* 148–152.

Feuerstein, R. (1980). *Instrumental enrichment: An intervention program for cognitive modifiability*. Baltimore, MD: University Park Press.

Filippelli, L. A., & Walberg, H. J. (1997). Childhood traits and conditions of eminent women scientists. *Gifted Child Quarterly, 41,* 95–103.

Ford, D. Y. (1996). Multicultural gifted education: A wake up call to the profession. *Roeper Review, 19,* 72–78.

Ford, D. Y., & Harmon, D. A. (2001). Equity and excellence: Providing access to gifted education for culturally diverse students. *Journal of Secondary Gifted Education, 12,* 141–148.

Ford, D. Y., & Harris, J. J., III. (1999). *Multicultural gifted education*. New York, NY: Teachers College Press.

Frasier, M. M., Garcia, J. H., & Passow, A. H. (1995). *A review of assessment issues in gifted education and their implications for identifying gifted minority students*. Storrs: University of Connecticut, The National Research Center on the Gifted and Talented.

Gagné, F. (1999). My convictions about the nature of abilities, gifts, and talents. *Journal for the Education of the Gifted, 22,* 109–136.

Geary, D. C., & Brown, S. C. (1991). Cognitive addition: Strategy choice and speed-of-processing difference in gifted, normal, and mathematically disabled children. *Developmental Psychology, 27,* 398–406.

Georgia Department of Education. (2006). *Resource manual for gifted education services*. Retrieved from http://www.doe.k12.ga.us/ci_iap_gifted.aspx

Guskin, S. L., Peng, C. J., & Simon, M. (1992). Do teachers react to "multiple intelligences"? Effect of teachers' stereotypes on judgments and expectancies for students with diverse patterns of giftedness/talent. *Gifted Child Quarterly, 36,* 32–37.

Harris, B., Plucker, J. A., Rapp, K. E., & Martinez, R. S. (2009). Identifying gifted and talented English language learners: A case study. *Journal for the Education of the Gifted, 32,* 368–393.

Hertzog, N. B. (2005). Equity and access: Creating general education classrooms responsive to potential giftedness. *Journal for the Education of the Gifted, 29,* 213–257.

Hunsaker, S. L., Finley, V. S., & Frank, E. L. (1997). An analysis of teacher nominations and student performance in gifted programs. *Gifted Child Quarterly, 41,* 19–24.

Jacobs, J. (1971). Effectiveness of teacher and parent identification as a function of school level. *Psychology in the Schools, 9,* 140–142.

Jensen, A. R. (1980). *Bias in mental testing*. New York, NY: Free Press.

Johnsen, S. K. (2008). Identifying gifted and talented learners. In F. Karnes & K. Stephens (Eds.), *Achieving excellence: Educating the gifted and talented* (pp. 135–153). New York, NY: Merrill Education/Prentice Hall.

Johnsen, S. K. (2011a). Making decisions about placement. In S. K. Johnsen (Ed.), *Identifying gifted students: A practical guide* (2nd ed., pp. 119–148). Waco, TX: Prufrock Press.

Johnsen, S. K. (2011b). Using standards to design identification procedures. *Tempo, 31*(2), 8–15, 33.

Johnsen, S. K., & Corn, A. L. (2001). *Screening assessment for gifted elementary and middle school students* (2nd ed.). Austin, TX: Pro-Ed.

Johnsen, S. K., Feuerbacher, S., & Witte, M. M. (2007). Increasing the retention of gifted students from low-income backgrounds in a university programs for the gifted: The UYP project. In J. VanTassel-Baska (Ed.), *Serving gifted learners beyond the traditional classroom: A guide to alternative programs and services* (pp. 55–79). Waco, TX: Prufrock Press.

Johnsen, S. K., & Ryser, G. (1994). Identification of young gifted children from lower income families. *Gifted and Talented International, 9*(2), 62–68.

Johnsen, S. K., & Ryser, G. R. (1997). The validity of portfolios in predicting performance in a gifted program. *Journal for the Education of the Gifted, 20,* 253–267.

Joseph, L., & Ford, D. Y. (2006). Nondiscriminatory assessment: Considerations for gifted education. *Gifted Child Quarterly, 50,* 42–51.

Kitano, M. K., & Pedersen, K. S. (2002). Action research and practical inquiry: Multicultural-content integration in gifted education: Lessons from the field. *Journal for the Education of the Gifted, 26,* 269–289.

Kurtz, B. E., & Weinert, F. E. (1989). Metacognition, memory performance, and causal attributions in gifted and average children. *Journal of Experimental Child Psychology, 48,* 45–61.

Lee, S., & Olszewski-Kubilius, P. (2006). Comparison between talent search students qualifying via scores on standardized tests and via parent nomination. *Roeper Review, 29,* 157–166.

Lidz, C. S. (1991). *Practitioner's guide to dynamic assessment*. New York, NY: Guilford.

Louis, B., & Lewis, M. (1992). Parental beliefs about giftedness in young children and their relation to actual ability level. *Gifted Child Quarterly, 36,* 27–31.

Lupkowski-Shoplik, A., & Assouline, S. G. (1993). Identifying mathematically talented elementary students: Using the lower level of the SSAT. *Gifted Child Quarterly, 37,* 118–123.

Maker, C. J. (1996). Identification of gifted minority students: A national problem, needed changes, and a promising solution. *Gifted Child Quarterly, 40,* 41–50.

McBee, M. T. (2006). A descriptive analysis of referral sources for gifted identification screening by race and socioeconomic status. *Journal of Secondary Gifted Education, 17,* 103–111.

McCoach, D. B., Kehle, T. J., Bray, M. A., & Siegle, D. (2001). Best practices in the identification of gifted students with learning disabilities. *Psychology in the Schools, 38,* 403–411.

Morris, J. E. (2002). African American students and gifted education. *Roeper Review, 24,* 59–53.

Morrison, W. F., & Rizza, M. G. (2007). Creating a toolkit for identifying twice-exceptional students. *Journal for the Education of the Gifted, 31,* 57–76.

National Association for Gifted Children. (2010). *NAGC Pre-K–Grade 12 gifted programming standards: A blueprint for quality gifted education programs.* Washington, DC: Author.

No Child Left Behind Act, 20 U.S.C. §6301 (2001).

Olszewski-Kubilius, P. (2000). The transition from childhood giftedness to adult creative productiveness: Psychological characteristics and social supports. *Roeper Review, 23,* 65–71.

Passow, A. H., & Frasier, M. M. (1996). Toward improving identification of talent potential among minority and disadvantaged students. *Roeper Review, 18,* 198–202.

Pennsylvania Department of Gifted Education. (2010). *Gifted guidelines.* Retrieved from http://www.portal.state.pa.us/portal/server.pt/community/gifted_education/7393/gifted_guidelines-august_2010/756695

Peterson, J. S., & Margolin, R. (1997). Naming gifted children: An example of unintended "reproduction." *Journal for the Education of the Gifted, 21,* 82–101.

Pierce, R. L., Adams, C. M., Speirs Neumeister, K. L., Cassady, J. C., Dixon, F. A., & Cross, T. L. (2007). Development of an identification procedure for a large urban school corporation: Identifying culturally diverse and academically gifted elementary students. *Roeper Review, 29,* 113–118.

Plata, M., & Masten, W. (1998). Teacher ratings of Hispanic and Anglo students on a behavior rating scale. *Roeper Review, 21,* 139–144.

Reid, C., Udall, A., Romanoff, B., & Algozzine, B. (1999). Comparison of traditional and problem solving assessment criteria. *Gifted Child Quarterly, 43,* 252–264.

Renzulli, J. (1978). What makes giftedness? Reexamining a definition. *Phi Delta Kappan, 60,* 180–184.

Reyes, E. I., Fletcher, R., & Paez, D. (1996). Developing local multidimensional screening procedures for identifying giftedness among Mexican American border population. *Roeper Review, 18,* 208–211.

Robins, J. H., & Jolly, J. L. (2011). Technical information regarding assessment. In S. K. Johnsen (Ed.), *Identifying gifted students: A practical guide* (pp. 75–118). Waco, TX: Prufrock Press.

Ryser, G. R. (2011a). Fairness in testing and nonbiased assessment. In S. K. Johnsen (Ed.), *Identifying gifted students: A practical guide* (2nd ed., pp. 63–74). Waco, TX: Prufrock Press.

Ryser, G. R. (2011b). Qualitative and quantitative approaches to assessment. In S. K. Johnsen (Ed.), *Identifying gifted students: A practical guide* (2nd ed., pp. 37–61). Waco, TX: Prufrock Press.

Salvia, J., Ysseldyke, J. E., & Bolt, S. (2007). *Assessment* (10th ed.). Boston, MA: Houghton-Mifflin.

Schack, G. A., & Starko, A. J. (1990). Identification of gifted students: An analysis of criteria preferred by preservice teachers, classroom teachers, and teachers of the gifted. *Journal for the Education of the Gifted, 13,* 346–363.

Scott, M. S., Perou, R., Urbano, R., Hogan, A., & Gold, S. (1992). The identification of giftedness: A comparison of White, Hispanic and Black families. *Gifted Child Quarterly, 36,* 131–139.

Scruggs, T., & Mastropieri, M. (1985). Spontaneous verbal elaborations in gifted and nongifted youths. *Journal for the Education of the Gifted, 9,* 1–10.

Shaklee, B. D., & Viechnicki, K. J. (1995). A qualitative approach to portfolios: The early assessment for exceptional potential model. *Journal for the Education of the Gifted, 18,* 156–170.

Soto, L. D. (1997). *Language, culture, and power: Bilingual families and the struggle for quality education.* Albany: SUNY Press.

Spearman, C. (1904). General intelligence objectively determined and measured. *American Journal of Psychology, 15,* 201–293.

Speirs Neumeister, K. L., Adams, C. M., Pierce, R. L., Cassady, J. C., & Dixon, F. A. (2007). Fourth-grade teachers' perceptions of giftedness: Implications for identifying and serving diverse gifted students. *Journal for the Education of the Gifted, 30,* 479–499.

Subotnik, R. F. (1997). Talent developed: Conversations with masters in the arts and sciences: Vladimir Feltsman: Piano virtuoso and educational innovator. *Journal for the Education of the Gifted, 20,* 306–317.

Swanson, H. L., & Lussier, C. M. (2001). A selective synthesis of the experimental literature on dynamic assessment. *Review of Educational Research, 71,* 321–363.

Tannenbaum, A. (2003). Nature and nurture of giftedness. In N. Colangelo & G. A. Davis (Eds.), *Handbook of gifted education* (3rd ed., pp. 45–59). Boston, MA: Allyn & Bacon.

Texas Education Agency. (2009). *Texas state plan for the education of gifted/talented students.* Retrieved from http://www.tea.state.tx.us/index2.aspx?id=6420

Trice, B., & Shannon, B. (2002, April). *Office for Civil Rights: Ensuring equal access to gifted education.* Paper presented at the annual meeting of the Council for Exceptional Children, New York, NY.

VanTassel-Baska, J., Feng, A. X., & Evans, B. L. (2007). Patterns of identification and performance among gifted students identified through performance tasks: A three-year analysis. *Gifted Child Quarterly, 51,* 218–231.

VanTassel-Baska, J., Johnson, D., & Avery, L. D. (2002). Using performance tasks in the identification of economically disadvantaged and minority gifted learners: Findings from Project STAR. *Gifted Child Quarterly, 46,* 110–123.

Weber, P. (1999). Mental models and the identification of young gifted students: A tale of two boys. *Roeper Review, 21,* 183–188.

Whitmore, J. (1981). Gifted children with handicapping conditions: A new frontier. *Exceptional Children, 48,* 106–114.

Williams, F. (2003). What does musical talent look like to you? And what is the role of the school and its partners in developing talent? *Gifted Education International, 17,* 272–274.

Yun, D. D., & Schader, R. (2001). Parents' reasons and motivations for supporting their child's music training. *Roeper Review, 24,* 23–25.

Chapter 5

The Curriculum Planning and Instruction Standard in Gifted Education: From Idea to Reality

by Joyce VanTassel-Baska

This chapter presents the new curriculum planning and instruction standard and provides a template for districts to examine their current curriculum work for the gifted and determine what needs to be done in order to move toward compliance. The chapter also provides examples of how to think about the macro curriculum products that are called for in the standards and the alternative assessment approaches that need to be used. Finally, the chapter focuses on the uses of the new standards for improving gifted programs and meeting the needs of gifted learners. The chapter concludes with a set of suggestions for action in implementing the new standards.

An Overview of Curriculum Planning

The nature of curriculum planning for high-ability learners requires the teacher or other educator to engage in several tasks somewhat simultaneously. Educators who take on the task must be able to do macro planning of curriculum across years of schooling, establishing a curriculum framework that extends from early primary through the late secondary years. This framework shows the scope and sequence of curriculum for the gifted at each stage of development in each core area of learning. Moreover, it illustrates well the differentiated emphases to be used consistently throughout the underlying layers of the curriculum work. At the same time, teachers must be able to adapt or create units of study to be used with gifted learners. These adaptations or new units must attend to the principles of good curriculum design, exemplary practice in the subject area, and differentiated features of a curriculum for the gifted. Additionally, strong curriculum planning involves experts from the various subject areas to serve as validators of the work.

Definition of Differentiation

In order to make appropriate changes in a curriculum for the gifted, we must be clear about the meaning of differentiation for this population. It is not just providing project work on an independent or group basis. It is not just about providing choice. Rather, it is about the careful incorporation of multiple approaches to make the curriculum more responsive to students who learn faster, deeper, and in more complex ways than their same-age peers. A useful definition might be:

> *The process of differentiation is the deliberate adaptation and modification of the curriculum, instructional processes, and assessments to respond to the needs of gifted learners.*

Necessary Curriculum Planning Documents

In the new NAGC Pre-K–Grade 12 Gifted Programming Standards, there is a major emphasis on establishing curriculum planning across levels of schooling. The documents that represent this macro planning effort include a curriculum framework that articulates goals, outcomes, strategies, activities, and assessment across the pre-K–12 levels of schooling. A second emphasis is the development of a scope and sequence that goes beyond the grade-level content standards and demonstrates reasonable outcomes for gifted learners to master at appropriate levels of learning. These documents alone would make a good starting point for meeting the new gifted education curriculum standards.

Curriculum Framework

Curriculum planning requires a team approach where ultimately a school district publicizes its differentiated plan for gifted learners to the community and holds itself accountable for fidelity of implementation. In order to do this, the team must first identify the specific goals that it wishes to pursue for these learners in grades pre-K–12. Such goals, linked to the outcomes identified in the new standards, might be:

- » to develop advanced skills and concepts in areas of aptitude at a pace consonant with capacity and readiness,
- » to develop critical and creative thinking and problem-solving methods,
- » to internalize learning for new applications and creative solutions to problems, and
- » to develop self-understanding and confidence in one's abilities.

Linked to these goals are the following student outcomes:

» Demonstrate growth commensurate with aptitude during the school year.
» Develop their abilities in their domain of talent and/or area of interest.
» Use critical and creative thinking in solving problems within their talent domain.
» Transfer advanced knowledge and skills across environments that lead to creative, productive careers in society.
» Become more self-aware from their engagement in curriculum and evidence-based instructional practices.
» Believe in their ability (i.e., self-efficacy).

If a curriculum framework can be established such as the example above, then work within each content area may proceed to provide greater specificity to the framework but to honor its intent. The curriculum framework of goals and outcomes then may be translated into activities, strategies, and resources for each subject.

Scope and Sequence

Scope and sequence development in content areas is best effected through vertical planning groups that can tackle a given subject and suggest the differences needed in outcomes for the gifted at each level. So, for example, if Advanced Placement coursework at grades 11 and 12 is desirable for gifted learners in the area of English, then what should the program of study in English/reading/language arts look like at earlier stages of development? A sample pre-K–12 scope and sequence chart is noted in Table 15.1 by grade level clusters.

Emphases Within the Curriculum Planning and Instruction Standard

Just as we can cite outcomes for gifted learners as a part of our macro planning documents, we also can recognize the importance of key features that the new standards are calling for. These features or indicators include the following:

» **Alignment with relevant content standards.** There is a need for gifted programs to ensure they are able to articulate the relationship between standards for teaching language arts, math, science, and social studies for all learners and how these standards are differentiated for the gifted.

Table 5.1
Scope and Sequence Chart

Grade level	Outcomes: Students will be able to:	Indicators	Assessment techniques	Comments
Pre-K–3	Engage in advanced reading opportunities; use writing models; develop research and communication skills	Evidence of advanced behaviors in each strand	Performance-based assessment (PBA) and/or portfolios	Use of appropriate research-based materials will enhance the capacity to demonstrate outcome behaviors.
4–5	All of the above outcomes, plus acquire linguistic competency in vocabulary, grammar, and usage	Mastery of advanced vocabulary and basic elements of grammar and usage	Pre/post assessment of skills	Apply compacting techniques to ensure appropriate-level work.
6–8	Analyze and interpret literature; design arguments in written and oral forms; research issues and present findings	Continued development of critical thinking skills in language arts	Product assessment; pre/post performance-based	Participate in writing competitions or take second language course.
9–10	Evaluate multiple texts for comparative literary elements; synthesize literary concepts and themes; create literary products of merit	Evidence of critical thinking and creative thinking abilities	Pre/post PBA, product assessment, portfolio of work	Submit to *Concord Review* or other high-quality publication outlet; take advanced coursework in second language.
11	AP language course	Performance at level of 3 or higher on AP exam	AP exam	Take AP coursework in a world language.
12	AP literature course	Performance at level 3 or higher on AP exam	AP exam	Take AP coursework in other subjects.

NAGC Pre-K–Grade 12 Gifted Education Programming Standards

In most instances, this differentiation means going beyond the grade-level content standards and providing indicators beyond proficiency.

» **Comprehensive scope and sequence of opportunities in all curriculum areas.** As described earlier, this planning effort represents the clear articulation of comprehensive offerings for gifted learners at each stage of development in each area of learning.

» **Use of acceleration techniques, including preassessment, formative assessment, and pacing.** This indicator calls for attention to developing consistent and ongoing acceleration approaches in determining the need for advancement within and across content areas. It also suggests the strong use of assessment to determine curriculum level and content. Finally, it suggests that the instructional approach of using a fast pace with gifted learners who can master the same material in half the time is a modality recognized in the instructional arsenal of teachers working with the gifted.

» **Use of differentiation strategies.** Although differentiation has become a buzz word in general education, it is important to retain its meaning in adapting curriculum for the gifted through acceleration, complexity, depth, challenge, creativity, and abstraction (VanTassel-Baska, 2003).

» **Adaptation or replacement of the core curriculum.** Although the alignment to the core curriculum suggests ways to adapt it for the gifted, it is also important to clearly show how the curriculum for the gifted is related to the core.

» **Use of culturally sensitive curriculum approaches leading to cultural competence.** Curriculum for the gifted needs to be sensitive to culturally different learners who inhabit our programs. This means that we need to select reading materials by other cultural groups, choose biographies that illustrate the contributions and role model potential of other cultural groups, and present a view of history that explores multiple perspectives, including minority viewpoints.

» **Use of inquiry-based strategies.** As the research suggests (VanTassel-Baska & Brown, 2007), inquiry techniques form the backbone of differentiated instruction and its many manifestations in problem-based learning, project-based learning, and discussion strategies like Socratic seminar and shared inquiry. The indicator also suggests the power of higher level question-asking as a specific model for enhancing inquiry in students.

» **Use of research-based materials.** The standards are clear that curriculum for the gifted is not something to be created from scratch. Rather, the curriculum materials developed over the past 20 years with federal funding under the auspices of the Jacob K. Javits Gifted and Talented Students Education Act of 1988 provide an important base for curriculum development in all of the core subject areas. These materials have been piloted, field-tested, and researched for their effectiveness with gifted learners. As such, they provide an important resource for meeting the standards in curriculum (VanTassel-Baska & Little, 2011).

» **Use of strategies that teach critical and creative thinking, research, and problem-solving skills.** Just as inquiry is an important instructional tool, so too are the higher level process skills of thinking and problem solving. It is important that districts adopt models that can be used across grade levels in order to provide a common language around these skills and make professional development more articulated.

» **Use of information technologies.** A strong curriculum for the gifted will employ an integrated technology approach in implementing learning. Many approaches to this are possible within classrooms and in tandem with special computer labs.

» **Use of metacognitive strategies.** All curriculum for the gifted should attend to the need for gifted learners to reflect on what they have learned as well as engage in serious planning, monitoring, and assessing of that learning, especially when it applies to project work and research efforts. Engaging students in such questions about their performance and activities that extend their thinking in a reflective mode all represent appropriate directions.

» **Use of community resources.** Strong curriculum for the gifted will find ways to include community opportunities, from speakers, to field trips, to key partnerships that result in mentorships and internships. Such opportunities should be available for gifted learners at various stages of development.

» **Career development.** One of the best researched areas of intervention for the gifted, career development provides a focus on the future for gifted learners and their families at critical stages of development. It is an exploration of interests, aptitudes, and values across the years in school, culminating in actual experiences that model what it means to work in a given career.

» **Talent development in areas of aptitude and interest in various domains (cognitive, affective, aesthetic).** This standard indicator suggests that schools document ways they are engaging gifted learners in multiple domains that develop the whole student. Arts opportunities, affective development options, and cognitive means all provide a rich array of gifted programming.

Case Example: Acceleration as a Necessary But Not Sufficient Differentiation Feature

Let's use the acceleration strategy to illustrate the way that differentiation can work for gifted learners in schools. We know that preassessment is an important approach to find the functional level of a student and move forward with the curriculum based on results. We also know we can ask gifted learners to do fewer problems or activities in order to master a core standard. Moreover, at the secondary level, we know that a course of study can be compressed to focus on essential learnings at a higher level of organization around higher level skills and concepts. An example of a carefully structured activity in the mathematics strand of statistics demonstrates the use of preassessment, followed by a project-based set of options, followed by reflection about what has been learned and how to extend that learning. It illustrates further the use of acceleration, complexity, depth, challenge, and creativity, all key features to showcase differentiated activities.

Phase I

» Pretest students' knowledge and skills of statistics.
» Group students by results of the pretest in groups of four. Provide streamlined instruction for the top group.
» Provide task demands for the top group, using a problem-solving approach.

Phase II

» Assignment of task demand to the top group:
◇ Use statistics (i.e., mean, median, mode, frequencies, and percentages) to analyze one of the following data sets, prepare graphs to illustrate your understanding of the data, and present findings in a presentation for your school.
» Data set options for Phase II:
◇ health care expenses for people in each decade of life from 10–90 years for the years 2006–2008,
◇ auto sales in the U.S. by car type across 10 years compared to world sales for those same car makes, or

◇ ten-year trends in salary for different sectors of the U.S. economy for 2000–2010.

Phase III

» *Follow-up questions:*
  ◇ What would you predict would be the trend for your data over the next 5 years?
  ◇ How would you estimate it?
  ◇ What factors would influence it?
» *Product assessment:* Assess the following dimensions of the project work on a 1–5 scale, 5 being high:
  ◇ appropriate use of statistical analysis,
  ◇ articulation of trends, and
  ◇ logical consistency of predictions.
» *Performance-based assessment (in-class response):* Using the following dataset of 10-year career trends in the U.S., analyze patterns of meaning by using appropriate statistics. What fields would be most open? What ones would be most closed? What is the evidence to support your choices? Graph your prediction of trends over the next 3 years. What is the evidence to support your prediction?
  ◇ *Rubric dimensions:* patterns of meaning identified, evidence presented for choices, and quality of prediction graph.
» *Portfolio assessment (one-week response):* Select three new datasets that capture trends across 10-year periods and use statistics to analyze them for patterns. Make predictions about the next 3-year periods. Graph your results. Write a journal entry that reflects on the value of using existing datasets to understand societal trends.
  ◇ *Rubric dimensions:* quality of analysis, evidence for predictions, and depth of written reflection

Review of Research Supporting the Curriculum Standards

The curriculum planning and instruction standard may be parsed into three parts. The first section addresses the macro planning tasks that must be completed in order to proceed with a district-wide planning effort in gifted education. The second part addresses core instructional strategies seen as crucial in implementing the standard. Finally, the third part suggests supportive approaches and structures that must be in place for successful implementation. The following section of this chapter reviews the literature supporting the importance of these elements in designing and implementing differentiated curriculum for the gifted.

Macro Planning

The research on macro planning approaches to curriculum for the gifted has been available to use for more than 30 years, yet many districts do not use the approach, as it requires the involvement of many district personnel in different roles to carry it out. VanTassel-Baska (2003) has noted the importance of using curriculum design as a basis for all curriculum work with the gifted, modifying the structure to accommodate the characteristics and needs of the population. VanTassel-Baska and Stambaugh (2006) illustrated the ways such modification might work in different subject areas at different stages of development. Design products include both a curriculum framework and scope and sequence charts for each subject area. VanTassel-Baska and Little (2011) illustrated the application of the differentiated design model as it has been used in The College of William and Mary curriculum units of study over the past 20 years. The resulting units have demonstrated ongoing and sustained learning gains for both gifted and promising learners in the subject areas of language arts (VanTassel-Baska, Zuo, Avery, & Little, 2002), science (VanTassel-Baska, Bass, Ries, Poland, & Avery, 1998), and social studies (Little, Feng, VanTassel-Baska, Rogers, & Avery, 2007). Each of these studies employed pre- and postassessments to calibrate the nature and extent of advanced learning as well as to decide on grouping and instructional considerations during implementation. These studies and others using a systematic framework (e.g., Gavin et al., 2007) attest to the power of macro planning curriculum, using a predetermined model for organization and structure. These developed units of study also provide a basis for district-wide curriculum implementation or modeling for further curriculum development in the common core areas of learning.

Instructional Strategies

There is a large and emergent body of literature on the use of specific strategies in working effectively with the gifted. Perhaps the strongest literature base exists for the use of inquiry-based approaches (VanTassel-Baska & Brown, 2007). However, other models have also been researched and found effective. Emphases on critical and creative thinking are well supported by current research as well as older studies. Problem-solving approaches and models also have been found effective. The use of research skills to individualize curriculum and instruction for the gifted has gained much support within the field over the years, with several models organized to allow gifted students greater autonomy in learning (Betts, 2004; Reis & Renzulli, 2009). Moreover, the literature on the use of faster pacing and advanced curriculum is well supported by the 80 years of acceleration literature that includes longitudinal studies supporting the use of such strategies.

Supportive Structures

The use of appropriate integrative technologies suggests that curriculum for the gifted may be provided in ways that increase depth and complexity in implementation (Besnoy, 2006). For example, students may use their laptop technology to explore a real-world problem online, conversing with an expert on some aspect of the problem, obtaining an online video of the reporting of the problem in the media, and studying a three-dimensional model of the underlying aspects of the problem.

Moreover, the inclusion of a culturally relevant curriculum also enhances the learning of gifted students, especially if it is multicultural in orientation and takes into account the backgrounds of the learning group to be taught (Ford, 2006; Kitano & Espinosa, 1995). The use of literature written by authors from different cultural groups, the inclusion of minority group perspectives on historical events, and the use of biographies and autobiographies of luminaries from different cultural groups all provide curriculum approaches for such inclusion. The use of differentiation strategies and resources within gifted programs also accommodates diverse interests and needs of students from underrepresented groups. Career development opportunities such as mentorships and internships further the enhancement of diverse talent in a district, as such options emphasize the real-life connections between schooling and a student's future aspirations and level of education and work.

The use of metacognitive strategies also enhances learning for the gifted, whether it is emphasizing reflection on learning in general or in more deliberate forms such as planning, monitoring, and assessing one's learning with regularity. To ensure such an emphasis, it should be woven into the fabric of the instructional system. For example, students may be asked to reflect on their increased understanding and application of the concepts they are learning that have relevance for multiple disciplines. How does understanding systems in science enhance your understanding and application of the concept to economics policy in the United States? How does the concept of change have meaning for you personally?

The standards also call for an emphasis on talent development in discrete areas of curriculum of interest to gifted learners. The domains of cognitive, affective, aesthetic, social, and leadership are stressed as they provide a balance in the opportunities afforded gifted learners. These curriculum areas have a long history of support within the literature of the field. They suggest that school districts may want to integrate these areas for purpose of curriculum planning or to treat them as separate areas for emphasis and delivery of instruction. Thus, specialized arts curriculum for the gifted might represent a separate scope and sequence as well as a leadership curriculum. Social and affective curriculum might be viewed as a separate strand to be addressed differentially at each stage of development, although several curriculum models provide avenues for inclusion of these strands within a common core curriculum.

Two Curriculum Models That Respond to the Demands of the Gifted Programming Standards

Although new curriculum may be designed using the standards as the basis, it may be more prudent to consider existing models that have already designed curriculum that employs the features discussed thus far in this chapter. Two such models are discussed in respect to the features employed and the extent to which they are responsive to the new national standard for curriculum planning and instruction.

Parallel Curriculum Model

The Parallel Curriculum Model (PCM) is a model for curriculum planning based on the composite work of Tomlinson et al. (2008). The heuristic model employs four dimensions, or parallels, that can be used singly or in combination. The parallels are the core curriculum, the curriculum of connections, the curriculum of practice, and the curriculum of identity. PCM assumes that the core curriculum is the basis for all other curricula and it should be combined with any or all of the three other parallels. It is the foundational curriculum that is defined by a given discipline. National, state, and/or local school districts' standards should be reflected in this dimension and are used as the basis for understanding relevant subjects within and across grade levels. The second parallel, the curriculum of connections, supports students in discovering the interconnectedness among and between disciplines of knowledge. It builds from the core curriculum and has students exploring those connections for both intra- and interdisciplinary studies. The third parallel, the curriculum of practice, also derives from the core curriculum. Its purpose is to extend students' understandings and skills in a discipline through application and promote student expertise as a practitioner of a given discipline. The last parallel, the curriculum of identity, serves to help students think about themselves within the context of a particular discipline; to see how a particular discipline relates to their own lives. The curriculum of identity uses curriculum as a catalyst for self-definition and self-understanding. The authors suggest that the level of intellectual demand in employing all elements of the Parallel Curriculum Model should be matched to student needs. Units have been developed based on the model for use across content areas K–12 (Tomlinson et al., 2006).

Integrated Curriculum Model

The VanTassel-Baska (1986) Integrated Curriculum Model (ICM) was developed specifically for high-ability learners, based on research evidence of what works with the gifted in classroom contexts. It has three dimensions: (a) advanced content, (b) high-level process and product work, and (c) intra- and interdisciplinary concept development and understanding. VanTassel-Baska, with funding from the Jacob K. Javits Gifted and Talented Students Program, used the ICM to develop specific curriculum frameworks and underlying units of study in language arts, social studies, and science. The model was designed to demonstrate a way to use the content standards but go beyond them, using differentiation practices for the gifted.

The content dimension is the first component of the model and represents, in the unit development process, a total alignment with national and state standards. However, it also represents the use of appropriate advanced content that goes beyond the standards, often calibrating unit activities or reading choices to what typical students can do at higher grade levels in the content area. In addition to being aligned with standards, the content dimension was designed to represent the most exemplary curriculum in that subject area by using the research-based pedagogical practices that are effective and national reports emanating from the various subject areas. Thus, the content of the standards is the core area for beginning the differentiation process with respect to acceleration, adding complexity and depth, incorporating creativity demands, and increasing the challenge level.

The process-product dimension of the ICM focuses on the importance of designing curriculum that incorporates higher level processing skills as a part of the challenge for students. Units of study systematically use a reasoning model, a research model, or a problem-solving model to ensure that students can manipulate these thinking skills within specific subject areas. In some instances, like science and literature, the subject area already incorporates higher level thought in the use of the scientific research model and the study of literary elements that move from the concrete elements of character, plot, and setting to the abstract elements of theme, motivation, and structure. As students manipulate these skills, they are encouraged to generate a meaningful product that demonstrates their capacity to apply these higher level skills effectively. In most units of study, the product or series of products are research-oriented.

The third dimension of the model emphasizes the use of a higher level macro concept that has meaning within and across subject areas and provides an interdisciplinary pathway to bind the curriculum together. It is the integrative glue that allows the model to be cohesive in design and implementation. The concepts used in the unit development process were those identified by scientists as the most critical for today's students to understand—concepts like change, systems, models, and scale. These concepts and their underlying generalizations guide the learning of specific content and amplify the use of higher level skills and processes. Students continue to apply these concepts to their learning across subject areas and across grades, and to see ways they apply to their own lives.

The ICM was conceived to be integrative in design and implementation, whereas the PCM has deliberately put the components on parallel tracks. They also diverge with respect to the treatment of affective development. In the PCM, the affective emphasis in the curriculum is a separate focus with respect to identity development and other aspects of affective development. In the ICM, the affective emphasis is woven into the fabric of the design by the use of activities, questions, and assessments that stress student reflection and establishing personal relevance of the curriculum for one's life. By choosing books for discussion that employ gifted characters who face problems and issues similar to those of gifted students, the ICM curriculum also promotes affective understanding in the context of the real world. Both models employ multiple approaches and opportunities for social learning through collaborative project work and discussion.

Assessing Student Outcomes

Differentiating the assessment approaches in curriculum for the gifted is an essential part of the new standards, both in assessment and curriculum elements. Why is such differentiation required? Because typical assessment, usually defined as results on the state assessment test, is not sufficiently advanced to assess real learning of gifted students. Even though most state tests contain an "advanced level," it is not discriminating enough to discern the level of performance of gifted learners within a given domain. Moreover, there is often a misalignment between what is tested and what is taught in programs for the gifted. Often these tests, for example, do not assess higher level thinking or problem solving, both key features of such programs. Thus, a differentiated approach to assessment is required that employs a combination of the following approaches:

» *Preassessment:* the use of assessments to understand what gifted learners already know before a unit of study begins in order to calibrate the appropriate level for curriculum intervention. These assessments may be end-of-year or semester tests on the current year curriculum in common core areas like spelling, vocabulary, math skills and concepts, and science concepts.

» *Off-level assessment:* the use of achievement tests and ability-aptitude measures at one or two grade levels above recommended use to provide sufficient ceiling for gifted student performance. These tests then allow teachers to effectively discriminate gifted performance in a domain (e.g., identify what a gifted student does and does not know).

» *Portfolio assessment:* the use of a collection of student work over time to make judgments about growth gains in one or more areas.

» *Performance-based assessment:* the use of products or extended activities within or across domains to demonstrate higher level thinking and problem solving of gifted students.

» *Pre/post assessment of thinking:* the use of an assessment that directly assesses the elevation of critical or creative thinking skills in gifted learners.

Research in gifted education indicates that curriculum-embedded performance-based assessments are reliable measures of student learning (Moon, Brighton, Callahan, & Robinson, 2005) and provide a means to assess higher level thinking in content areas (VanTassel-Baska, Johnson, & Avery, 2002). Pre- and postexperiment concept maps have provided a valid and reliable measure for assessing changes in conceptual understanding (Nafiz, 2008). Curriculum-embedded science performance-based assessments were found to foster critical thinking with middle grades gifted students (Tali Tal & Miedijensky, 2005). Further, VanTassel-Baska et al. (2002) developed a process to construct valid and reliable measures of performance where the performance measures have also been found to be successful at identifying typically underserved populations of gifted students (VanTassel-Baska, Feng, & de Brux, 2007; VanTassel-Baska, Feng, & Evans, 2007).

Product-based assessments have proved useful in demonstrating gifted students' inventive qualities in constructing and implementing Type III activities

(Renzulli & Callahan, 2008), and portfolio approaches have been employed as especially useful tools in schools for the gifted where integrative learning is stressed (Johnsen & Johnson, 2007). Off-level assessment has been most strongly applied in the talent search literature, not only to identify advanced-level functioning, but also to assess outcomes of learning using College Board achievement tests with younger populations. The use of Advanced Placement (AP) exams represent an off-level assessment approach, calibrated to first-year college. The International Baccalaureate (IB) program and Talent Searches also use a similar off-level approach (Olszewski-Kubilius & Kulieke, 2008).

All of these assessment approaches are viable ways to gain insight into gifted student learning as a result of using a differentiated curriculum and instructional template. Choosing a suitable approach may depend on several factors such as availability of tests, familiarity with the approach, desire to create performance-based tools, or relevance to the nature of the curriculum outcomes selected for the program.

How Might the Curriculum Planning and Instruction Standards Be Employed?

Most gifted programs will not be starting from scratch in using the new curriculum standards. Thus, there is a need to think about how to go about the process of alignment to the standard, including the student outcomes and evidence-based practices. In the area of curriculum planning and instruction, there are several ways they might be employed. A few ideas follow:

- » *Create coherent macro curriculum documents.* The task of creating such documents constitutes the heart of curriculum development work in a school district and sets the stage for the nature of the programs to unfold.
- » *Design new curriculum.* The curriculum planning and instruction standards may call for new curriculum to be developed in order to close a gap revealed by the discrepancy analysis. This may take the form of units or syllabi that respond to need areas.
- » *Revise existing curriculum.* Sometimes districts have curriculum in place that needs to be upgraded for alignment and differentiation.
- » *Provide exemplars of differentiated curriculum.* Educators from general and special education backgrounds need to have a sense of what a differentiated curriculum for the gifted looks like. The macro documents meet that need very well.
- » *Train teachers in differentiated curriculum, instruction, and assessment.* Curriculum development is always followed by professional develop-

ment of educators responsible for implementing it. In this way, assurance of fidelity of implementation is made.

Recommendations for Getting Started

» Do a gap analysis of current curriculum and revisions needed. Work with a district team to determine priorities across a 3-year period, as changes cannot be done quickly. The following Yes/No checklist may be a good place to start the analysis:

_____ Y/N: Alignment with relevant content standards?
_____ Y/N: Comprehensive scope and sequence of opportunities in common core curriculum areas?
_____ Y/N: Use of acceleration techniques, including preassessment, formative assessment, and pacing?
_____ Y/N: Use of differentiation strategies?
_____ Y/N: Adaptation or replacement of the core curriculum?
_____ Y/N: Use of culturally sensitive curriculum approaches leading to cultural competence?
_____ Y/N: Use of inquiry-based strategies?
_____ Y/N: Use of research-based materials?
_____ Y/N: Use of strategies that teach critical and creative thinking, research, and problem-solving skills?
_____ Y/N: Use of information technologies?
_____ Y/N: Use of metacognitive strategies?
_____ Y/N: Use of community resources?
_____ Y/N: Career development emphases?
_____ Y/N: Talent development in areas of aptitude and interest in various domains (cognitive, affective, aesthetic)?

» Tackle the big-picture items first. Most districts will need to engage in developing a curriculum framework, designing scope and sequence charts in common core areas, and aligning the gifted curriculum with the common core. Consequently, these tasks should be undertaken as a first priority as they provide the frame for other modifications to be made.

» Develop a vertical planning task force that can undertake the curriculum changes most efficiently and effectively. By engaging teachers from relevant grade-level clusters, gifted education staff, and administrators relevant to the curriculum in the district, progress can be made on the macro tasks.

» Integrate the needed changes into the School Improvement Plan (SIP) model so that the gifted curriculum receives appropriate attention within a school setting and so that general and special educators have an understanding of the differentiation features required for gifted learners that go beyond the simple feature of choice.

» Disseminate the macro documents through various professional development venues, including webinars, school-based workshops, and faculty discussions at relevant meetings. The sessions may be conducted by different members of the vertical planning team as appropriate. Provide educators with the knowledge, skills, and concepts in order to implement the changes effectively.

» Monitor the progress of implementation through using school-based instructional specialists, mentor teachers, peer coaches, and administrative staff as appropriate. Trying out new practices precedes changing attitudes to institutionalize change (Guskey, 2000); thus, the monitoring of such changes is crucial to gauging what needs to be done next.

» Assess student outcomes for value-added benefits of the changes. As is suggested by the new standards, student assessment tactics must be changed in order to understand authentic learning of the gifted. The coordinator of gifted education programming or whoever is designated in charge of the program must see this piece as a critical part of the role of managing the program.

» Develop workshops for parents on the changes made in the gifted curriculum, instruction, and assessment features of programming. Celebrate the changes through a family night that emphasizes the strategies used and the student products that have resulted. In this way, the approaches can be diffused into the homes of gifted learners where strategies and projects can be replicated in home settings.

These steps must be viewed as action steps to be implemented across a multi-year period lest the tasks be seen as overwhelming. Some of them, like program monitoring and assessment, however, should be undertaken annually.

Conclusion

This chapter has presented several ideas for implementing the new curriculum standards at pre-K–12 levels. It has provided models for incorporating curriculum planning tools such as a curriculum framework and scope and sequence on which to build a sound curriculum base. It has also provided the research support for the suggestions made along with ideas for implementation. The work needed to meet these standards is ongoing as school districts recognize the primacy of a strong curriculum in building a powerful program emphasis for gifted education. The effort, however, is worth it in regard to the importance of the enterprise for our best learners.

References

Besnoy, K. (2006). How do I do that? Integrating web sites into the gifted education classroom. *Gifted Child Today, 29*(1), 28–34.

Betts, G. (2004). Fostering autonomous learners through levels of differentiation. *Roeper Review, 26,* 190–191.

Ford, D. Y. (2006). Creating culturally responsive classrooms for gifted students. *Understanding Our Gifted, 19*(1), 10–14.

Gavin, M. K., Casa, T. M., Adelson, J. L., Carroll, S. R., Sheffield, L. J., & Spinelli, A. M. (2007). Project M3: Mentoring mathematical minds—a research-based curriculum for talented elementary students. *Journal for the Education of the Gifted, 18,*566–585.

Guskey, T. R. (2000). *Evaluating professional development.* Thousand Oaks, CA: Corwin Press.

Johnsen, S. K., & Johnson, K. (2007). *Independent study program* (2nd ed.). Waco, TX: Prufrock Press.

Kitano, M. K., & Espinosa, R. (1995). Language diversity and giftedness: Working with gifted English language learners. *Journal for the Education of the Gifted, 18,* 234–254.

Little, C., Feng, A., VanTassel-Baska, J., Rogers, K., & Avery, L. (2007). A study of curriculum effectiveness in social studies. *Gifted Child Quarterly, 51,* 272–284.

Moon, T., Brighton, C. M., Callahan, C. M., & Robinson, A. (2005). Development of authentic assessments for the middle school classroom. *Journal of Secondary Gifted Education, 16,* 119–133.

Nafiz, K. (2008). A student-centered approach: Assessing the changes in prospective science teachers' conceptual understanding by concept mapping in a general chemistry classroom laboratory research. *Science Education, 38,* 91–110.

Olszewski-Kubilius, P., & Kulieke, M. J. (2008). Using off-level testing and assessment for gifted and talented students. In J. VanTassel-Baska (Ed.), *Alternative assessments with gifted and talented students* (pp. 89–106). Waco, TX: Prufrock Press.

Reis, S. M., & Renzulli, J. S. (2009). The Schoolwide Enrichment Model: A focus on students' strengths and interests. In J. S. Renzulli, E. J. Gubbins, K. S. McMillen, R. D. Eckert, & C. A. Little (Eds.), *Systems and models for developing programs for the gifted and talented* (2nd ed., pp. 323–352). Mansfield Center, CT: Creative Learning Press.

Renzulli, J. S., & Callahan, C. (2008) Product assessment. In J. VanTassel-Baska (Ed.), *Alternative assessments with gifted and talented students* (pp. 259–283). Waco, TX: Prufrock Press.

Tali Tal, R., & Miedijensky, S. (2005). A model of alternative embedded assessment in a pull-out enrichment program for the gifted. *Gifted Education International, 20,* 166–186.

Title V, Part D. [Jacob K. Javits Gifted and Talented Students Education Act of 1988], Elementary and Secondary Education Act of 1988 (2002), 20 U.S.C. sec. 7253 et seq.

Tomlinson, C. A., Kaplan, S. N., Purcell, J. H., Leppien, J. H., Burns, D. E., & Strickland, C. A. (Eds.). (2006). *The parallel curriculum in the classroom, Book 2: Units for application across the content areas, K–12.* Thousand Oaks, CA: Corwin Press.

Tomlinson, C. A., Kaplan, S. N., Renzulli, J. S., Purcell, J. K., Burns, D. E., Strickland, C. A., & Imbeau, M. B. (2008). *The parallel curriculum: A design to develop learner potential and challenge advanced learners.* Thousand Oaks, CA: Corwin Press.

VanTassel-Baska, J. (1986). Effective curriculum and instructional models for talented students. *Gifted Child Quarterly, 30,* 164–169.

VanTassel-Baska, J. (2003). *Curriculum planning and instructional design for gifted learners.* Denver, CO: Love.

VanTassel-Baska, J., Bass, G., Ries, R., Poland, D., & Avery, L. (1998). A national study of science curriculum effectiveness with high ability students. *Gifted Child Quarterly, 42,* 200–211.

VanTassel-Baska, J., & Brown, E. (2007). Towards best practice: An analysis of the efficacy of curriculum models in gifted education. *Gifted Child Quarterly, 51,* 342–358.

VanTassel-Baska, J., Feng, A., & de Brux, E. (2007). A longitudinal study of identification and performance profiles of Project STAR performance task-identified gifted students. *Journal for the Education of the Gifted, 31,* 7–34.

VanTassel-Baska, J., Feng, A., & Evans, B. (2007). Patterns of identification and performance among gifted students identified through performance tasks: A three-year analysis. *Gifted Child Quarterly, 51,* 218–231.

VanTassel-Baska, J., Johnson, D., & Avery, L. D. (2002). Using performance tasks in the identification of economically disadvantaged and minority gifted learners: Findings from Project STAR. *Gifted Child Quarterly, 46,* 110–123.

VanTassel-Baska, J., & Little, C. (Eds.). (2011). *Content-based curriculum for gifted learners* (2nd ed.). Waco, TX: Prufrock Press.

VanTassel-Baska, J., & Stambaugh, T. (2006). *Comprehensive curriculum for gifted learners* (3rd ed.). Boston, MA: Allyn & Bacon.

VanTassel-Baska, J., Zuo, L., Avery, L., & Little, C. (2002). A curriculum study of gifted-student learning in the language arts. *Gifted Child Quarterly, 46,* 30–43.

Chapter 6
Instructional Strategies for Differentiation Within the Classroom

by Julia Link Roberts

The *NAGC Pre-K–Grade 12 Gifted Programming Standards: A Blueprint for Quality Gifted Education Programs* (National Association for Gifted Children [NAGC], 2010) will guide educators at the classroom, school, and school district levels as they plan and implement best practices in teaching children with gifts and talents. A blueprint provides the plan, but it takes specialists to complete the structure. Likewise, it takes special educators, general educators, and gifted educators to create a learning environment and implement strategies that will facilitate learning among all students, including those with gifts and talents. These standards focus on student outcomes. They guide classroom teachers in tandem with special teachers of music, art, and physical education; gifted resource teachers; special education teachers; counselors; librarians; and principals on strategies to implement quality gifted education programming or services in classrooms, schools, and school districts.

All educators have the opportunity to develop the talents of all children, and the phrase *all children* includes young people who are gifted and talented as well as every other child. So often the phrase "all children" is used with no reference to gifted children. In fact, the phrase is sometimes used to exclude gifted children with a comment such as "No, this practice is for *all* children," implying that all children must be able to benefit from that particular lesson or content in the same way at the same time. These new standards do not exclude any children but rather focus attention on ensuring that all children will make continuous progress and develop their potentials. The Gifted Programming Standards highlight the need to see that children with gifts and talents have opportunities to develop their potential to the highest levels just as it is expected will happen with all other children. It is apparent that a one-size-fits-all philosophy will not work, as children have different needs, interests, and levels of readiness that must be addressed if each child is to make continuous progress. Differentiation strategies must be implemented if all children are to learn throughout each year in grades pre-K–12.

The focus of this chapter is on instructional strategies for differentiation in classrooms. These instructional strategies are found in each of the Gifted Programming Standards rather than just in one particular standard, as various standards and components of standards relate to differentiation. These standards include planning for differentiation, preassessing to determine how to proceed to ensure that everyone is learning on an ongoing basis, and implementing learning experiences to match interests, learning preferences, and readiness. Differentiation can focus on enrichment as well as on acceleration. The goal of differentiation is to produce young people who love to learn and are on the way to becoming lifelong learners.

Teamwork: Educators Working Together to Implement Standards

5.2 Coordinated Services. Students with gifts and talents demonstrate progress as a result of the shared commitment and coordinated services of gifted education, general education, special education, and related professional services, such as school counselors, school psychologists, and social workers. (NAGC, 2010, p. 12)

Student Outcome 5.2 highlights the importance of educators working together toward the goal of offering quality gifted education services. Educators across a school or district need to coordinate programming and services for gifted children. Educators in leadership positions must understand the needs of gifted children and be knowledgeable about strategies that allow these young people to have the learning ceiling removed so they can soar in their learning. It is always easier to implement strategies when there is support and direction from leadership within a school or district, preferably support at both levels. If the school is big enough to have instructional leaders in various content areas, it is important for the content leaders to be knowledgeable of strategies that will best address the needs of all children, including those who are gifted and talented.

Implementing the new standards in a classroom has a lot to do with the school administrators' understanding of gifted education. With leaders in the school who understand the needs of children with gifts and talents, a teacher has an optimal situation in which to implement the Gifted Programming Standards. However, if that is not the case, teachers (e.g., general education, special education, specialists) can implement the standards in their own classrooms. Hopefully, other educators will see the benefits and join in implementing the standards in their classrooms as well.

Educators as Talent Scouts

3.3. Talent Development. Students with gifts and talents develop their abilities in their domain of talent and/or area of interest. (NAGC, 2010, p. 10)

Educators must see themselves as talent scouts. Talents need opportunities for coaching and teaching in academics just as they do in sports. In his study of talent development, Bloom (1985) reported,

> strong evidence that no matter what the initial characteristics (or gifts) of the individuals, unless there is a long and intensive process of encouragement, nurturance, education, and training, the individuals will not attain extreme levels of capability in these particular fields. (p. 3)

Teachers must have the knowledge, skills, and dispositions to develop the talents and potential of all children, including those children who are advanced and those with the capability of moving at a fast pace and learning at complex levels. Not doing so limits the possibilities of talent development for the young person.

> No matter how precocious one is at age ten or eleven, if the individual doesn't stay with the talent development process over many years, he or she will soon be outdistanced by others who do continue. A long-term commitment to the talent field and an increasing passion for talent development are essential if the individual is to attain the highest level of capability in the field. (Bloom, 1985, p. 538)

Continuous Progress as the Instructional Goal

2.5. Evaluation of Programming. Students identified with gifts and talents demonstrate important learning progress as a result of programming and services. (NAGC, 2010, p. 9)

2.5.2 Educators ensure that the assessment of the progress of students with gifts and talents uses multiple indicators that measure mastery of content, higher level thinking skills, achievement in specific program areas, and affective growth. (NAGC, 2010, p. 9)

All students, including advanced learners, benefit from learning experiences that allow them to make continuous progress in classrooms. A classroom teacher who focuses on grade-level learning or proficiency will not create learning experiences that facilitate all children making a year's academic growth for each year in school. In fact, it is possible that advanced learners make little or no growth in such a classroom. The executive summary of *High-Achieving Students in the Era of NCLB* (Loveless, Farkas, & Duffett, 2008) stated: "While the nation's lowest-achieving students made rapid gains from 2000 to 2007, the performance of top students was languid" (p. 2). Loveless (2008) found that "the achievement gap between high and low achievers narrowed during the NCLB era (2000–2007)," but "the narrowing of the gap during the NCLB era is largely due to a significant improvement in the performance of low achievers and smaller gains by high achievers" (p. 23). Gifted children can actually make greater gains than one year's achievement growth if the teacher implements best practices for differentiating experiences by removing the learning ceiling. Less than a year's growth for any student in grades K–12 should not be tolerated.

Mind the (Other) Gap! (Plucker, Burroughs, & Song, 2010) also reports that the excellence gap is obvious in the United States, with small percentages reaching the advanced levels in mathematics and reading. In fact, this report coined the term the "excellence gap" (p. i): "The comparatively small percentage of students scoring at the highest level on achievement tests suggests that children with advanced academic potential are being under-served, with potentially serious consequences for the long-term economic competitiveness of the U.S." (Plucker et al., 2010, p. 1). *Mind the (Other) Gap!* highlights the very low numbers of children from various ethnic and racial groups and from low-income families as well as English Language Learners who are scoring at the advanced levels on the National Assessment of Educational Progress (NAEP) tests.

Barriers to continuous progress are numerous and exist in many classrooms and schools:

>> The current emphasis on proficiency overshadows goals for excellence. Proficiency is not an appropriate goal for children who are already there or beyond.

>> Teachers have few models and limited, if any, experience with differentiation.

>> Myths continue to persist about children who are gifted and talented. Two of these harmful myths are that all children are gifted and that gifted children will be fine without any help.

>> The belief that you cannot be fair and equal at the same time also gets in the way of all children having opportunities to learn what they are ready and capable of learning.

The Gifted Programming Standards need to be used in ways to counter these barriers and allow all children, including those who are gifted and talented, to make learning gains on an ongoing basis.

Promoting Self-Understanding

1.2. Self-Understanding. Students with gifts and talents possess a developmentally appropriate understanding of how they learn and grow; they recognize the influences of their beliefs, traditions, and values on their learning behavior. (NAGC, 2010, p. 8)

4.1.4. Educators provide feedback that focuses on effort, on evidence of potential to meet high standards, and on mistakes as learning opportunities. (NAGC, 2010, p. 11)

Students who are gifted and talented need to make continuous learning progress just as every other child does. Without appropriate academic challenge, students develop incorrect ideas about being smart, often thinking that smart equates with easy. Quite the contrary, students who are highly capable need to link success to hard work and lack of success to lack of effort. Young people need to understand that working hard on academic tasks will build an independent, capable learner. They need to realize that perseverance is essential if they are going to do well in postsecondary opportunities and later in careers. Teachers need to understand that it hurts advanced learners when they are not challenged to work hard on meaningful tasks. The myth that you don't need to worry about gifted kids, as they will make it on their own, is just that—a myth.

Dweck (2006) described two ways that individuals view intelligence. One mindset is that intelligence is fixed, and the other mindset views the growth potential in intelligence, where growth is the result of effort. A person with a growth mindset equates success with working hard to reach a goal and failure to do as well as expected with failing to put forth adequate effort. Teachers who differentiate effectively focus feedback on effort rather than on being smart.

Effective Differentiation

The purpose of differentiation is to provide appropriately challenging learning experiences so that young people enjoy learning and become independent learners. Differentiation that is effective in meeting the goals of challenge and enjoyment is guided by the answers to four questions:

1. *Planning Question*—What do I want students to know, understand, and be able to do?
2. *Preassessment Question*—Who already knows, understands, and/or can use the content or demonstrate the skill?
3. *Differentiation Question*—What can I do for him, her, or them so they can make continuous progress and extend their learning? (Roberts & Inman, 2009b, p. 9)
4. *Ongoing Assessment Question*—What have students learned?

These four questions must be answered in sequential order if differentiation is to provide clear opportunities for ongoing learning.

Planning as the Starting Point for Effective Differentiation

3.1. Curriculum Planning. Students with gifts and talents demonstrate growth commensurate with aptitude during the school year. (NAGC, 2010, p. 10)

The planning question initiates differentiation as the teacher decides the learning goals for the unit. Until planning has been done, any attempt to differentiate cannot be evaluated because no measurement bar has been established that would determine what the student already knew when the unit began. Answering the question "What do I want students to know, understand, or be able to do?" will precede preassessment and the implementation of learning experiences when differentiation is effective.

Preassessment as the Step to Follow Planning

Once planning has been completed, the next question to be answered is: Who already knows, understands, and/or can use the content or demonstrate the skill?

2.2. Identification. Each student reveals his or her exceptionalities or potential through assessment evidence so that appropriate instructional accommodations and modifications can be provided. (NAGC, 2010, p. 9)

Although the root of the word differentiation is *different*, simply providing different learning experiences for children in a class does not make differentiation effective. Differentiating learning experiences without data is whimsical and cannot be defended. Data provide information to guide the teacher in planning challenging learning for all students. It does not necessarily follow that a child who is gifted in one area will be gifted in others, although he or she may be.

Contrary to the assumptions that some teachers make, preassessing students to determine what they already know and can do in relation to the objectives in the planned unit or lesson actually saves time. Teachers may find that no one in the class knows much about the topic or concept; however, they may also discover one or even several students know quite a bit about the topic. This information establishes the starting points for all students, including advanced students. Knowing what the students already know and are able to do can save valuable teaching/learning time by not requiring a student or students to spend time on information they already know about the topic or concept; they can study more complex content on the same topic or concept. In this way, when discussions of the topic or concept occur, all students contribute ideas, and no one is held back in terms of learning.

Preassessment provides information to allow the teacher to match learning experiences to what students know and are able to do. The assessment gathers data about the students' readiness to begin a new unit of study in relation to the content, their abilities to cognitively process the content, and the experiences they have with the required product or choice of products assigned during the unit. Preassessment comes in many forms, and different forms of preassessment can be used, depending on the one the teacher deems most appropriate for the unit. It may be an end-of-the previous-unit test if the learning from one unit to another is sequential. Another possibility is a 5-minute writing on the concept or completing a mind map on the topic to be studied. Another possibility is a T-W-H Chart (What do you **think** about the topic? What do you **want** to know about the topic? **How** do you want to learn about the topic?; Roberts & Boggess, 2011).

> 2.4.4. Educators use and interpret qualitative and quantitative assessment information to develop a profile of the strengths and weaknesses of each student with gifts and talents to plan appropriate intervention. (NAGC, 2010, p. 9)

Other types of preassessments help the teacher discern interests of the students in relationship to the topic or their learning preferences. The more the teacher knows about the student, the better the match between the learner and the learning experiences. That match is the true test of differentiation and makes differentiation effective.

The teacher must learn as much as possible about each student in order to ensure that all students are learning on an ongoing basis. Matching the learning experience to the student's knowledge and skills about a topic or concept is essential. Using information or data as the basis for instructional decisions makes differentiation effective.

Matching Learner Needs and Extending Learning

The third question to answer when differentiating is: What can I do for him, her, or them so they can make continuous progress and extend their learning?

> 3.1.3. Educators adapt, modify, or replace the core or standard curriculum to meet the needs of students with gifts and talents and those with special needs such as twice-exceptional, highly gifted, and English language learners. (NAGC, 2010, p. 10)

Effective differentiation focuses on learning experiences that are matched to the students based on their interests, learning preferences, and readiness to learn a specific content. Differentiation requires teachers to adapt, modify, or replace curriculum if they have information that indicates a student or students already know or can do the knowledge or skills within the objectives. Differentiation does not require that the students who need differentiation do assignments that everyone else does, just in case the student has "missed a skill," and then also engage in the differentiated learning experiences. Rather it means that the students will study the same concept or topic but do so at a different pace and/or at a more complex level. *Adapt*, *modify*, and *replace* are the key words describing what the teachers do when they differentiate the curriculum in effective ways. Assessment data signal what content and processes should be adapted, modified, or replaced in order to allow for continuous progress.

The important step after gathering preassessment data is to do something with the information and not just file it. Preassessment data must be used to inform decisions about instruction. That information can include readiness, learning preferences, and interests. The teacher must determine what the data tell about how the students need to be grouped for instruction as well as how the learning experiences can be differentiated to ensure that all students are challenged to learn new information about the topic or concept and to hone their skills in doing so. Chappuis, Stiggins, Arter, and Chappuis (2005) emphasized that educators must use assessment *for* learning rather than only considering assessment *of* learning. Assessment for learning is just exactly what formative assessment is all about.

Other groups of children for whom differentiation is needed are English language learners and twice-exceptional learners, those with gifts and disabilities. These groups benefit from modifications in the curriculum to ensure that they have every opportunity to make continuous progress. These children need differentiated learning opportunities that match their abilities, readiness, and learning preferences yet accommodate their disability or language difference while focusing on strengths and allowing learning to continue on an ongoing basis. Neither twice-exceptional learners nor English language learners will be at a disadvantage in a classroom with teachers who implement effective differentiation strategies. For both of these groups of students, it is important to concentrate on strengths while building up areas of need.

Highly gifted learners, as mentioned in Evidence-Based Practice 3.1.3, require differentiated learning opportunities. These young people need opportunities to make continuous progress even though they may be reading or understanding mathematics several grade levels above their age-mates. Their questions are usually advanced, as is their level of understanding of the content. Contrary to mythology, these children need to be learning continually because they will not make it on their own. Neither should they need to be doing peer tutoring or biding their time while others are studying new concepts. Instead, highly gifted learners should also have ongoing opportunities to engage in learning experiences in which teachers have adapted, modified, and replaced core or standard content to ensure continuous progress. After all, children and young people go to school to learn each day. In the Gifted Children's Bill of Rights, NAGC (2008) enumerated one of the rights as being "to learn something new every day." Students with gifts and talents—including those who are twice-exceptional, highly gifted, or English language learners with gifts and talents—deserve the opportunity to make continuous progress.

> 3.1.5. Educators use a balanced assessment system, including preassessment and formative assessment, to identify students' needs, develop differentiated education plans, and adjust plans based on continual progress monitoring. (NAGC, 2010, p. 10)

It has long has been expected that educators make modifications in the learning experiences for students who need additional time to learn a concept or need modifications to make the content more basic to facilitate learning. Making modifications in the curriculum to differentiate learning should happen for all children who are exceptional, including those with learning problems and with gifts and talents. The end goal for all children is for each to make continuous progress, which requires a differentiated curriculum.

Effective differentiation is intentional. Teachers must expect to differentiate and plan from the beginning to do so. Consequently, they will see differentiation as the way to plan for and teach a class of students rather than as a burden or something extra to do. Often the range of reading abilities in a classroom spans several grades, posing an impossible situation when the text is a major resource and is too difficult for some students and too basic for others. Even in a class of advanced learners, all students will not be at the same place in all content areas, nor will they have the identical interests or preferred ways of learning. Consequently, differentiation is a must if each student in the class is to experience continuous learning.

Assessments That Measure Learning Progress

2.4. Learning Progress and Outcomes. Students with gifts and talents demonstrate advanced and complex learning as a result of using multiple, appropriate, and ongoing assessments. (NAGC, 2010, p. 9)

2.4.1. Educators use differentiated pre- and post- performance-based assessments to measure the progress of students with gifts and talents. (NAGC, 2010, p. 9)

Progress assessments include formative, ongoing, and summative instruments. They present an ongoing picture of student learning. Assessment can make differentiation learner-centered, and the results are worth the effort. Black and William's (1998) landmark review found that focused efforts to improve student learning based on formative assessment provided gains greater than one-half standard deviation, which would be "equivalent to raising the achievement of the average student to the 65th percentile" (p. 18).

Progress assessments could be equated with the tasting process as the chef is preparing his special soup. The chef's intended outcome is a delicious soup. In order to reach that goal, he wants to know if the soup needs additional seasoning or other ingredients in order to reach its full taste potential. Likewise, the teacher sets learning goals. She wants to know what the students already know and are able to do before the unit of study begins, and then she checks on how much has been learned at various points of time in the teaching of the unit. She uses various types of assessments to determine what the student or students have learned in relation to the unit's goal. The summative assessment for the culinary expert is the soup that is served to family or guests. At that point, the tasting phase is over, and the final product is on the table, hopefully, to be enjoyed by the diners. In teaching, formative assessments help the teacher make instructional decisions that tailor the learning experiences to what the students know and are able to do, but the summative assessment is the final one where students show what they have learned about a particular concept or topic and skills they have mastered in the course of the unit. The summative assessment is the end product—the bowl of soup for the chef and what students have learned.

Strategies and Tools for Differentiating

3.3.1. Educators select, adapt, and use a repertoire of instructional strategies and materials that differentiate for students with gifts and talents and that respond to diversity. (NAGC, 2010, p. 10)

Differentiation in the classroom can involve content, process, and product.
» The content is what the teacher plans for the students to learn.
» The process is what the teacher wants the students to do cognitively.
» The product is how the teacher wants the students to demonstrate what they have learned.

Figure 6.1 shows the relationship of content, process, and product as they combine to create a learning experience.

Differentiating Content to Add Challenge and Complexity

3.1.4. Educators design differentiated curricula that incorporate advanced, conceptually challenging, in-depth, distinctive, and complex content for students with gifts and talents. (NAGC, 2010, p. 10)

Content can be both basic and complex. Complex content includes issues and problems related to the concept or topic being studied. When preassessment results tell the teacher that the students already know the basic information, progressing to complex content is in order. Teachers are never limited by lack of content, as most topics taught in pre-K to grade 12 may be extended beyond what is typically taught in elementary, middle, and high school classrooms.

Teachers need to be knowledgeable in the content or at least be interested learners in the content areas they teach. It is difficult for teachers to show enthusiasm for a content area or discipline that they do not like. It is also difficult to make the content interesting if teachers do not have depth of knowledge,

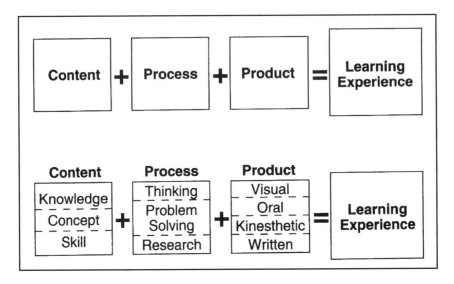

Figure 6.1. Learning experiences. From "Writing Units That Remove the Learning Ceiling," by J. L. Roberts and R. A. Roberts in *Methods and Materials for Teaching the Gifted* (3rd ed., p. 199), by F. A. Karnes and S. M. Beans (Eds.), 2009, Waco, TX: Prufrock Press. Copyright 2009 by Prufrock Press. Reprinted with permission.

and it is a challenge for them to differentiate in a content area in which their knowledge is limited. It is all too apparent to students if teachers do not love the content or lack depth in their knowledge in a particular area they teach.

Content must be significant; indeed, it must be worth learning. Gardner (1993) stated, "Schools should try to educate for understanding, which I define as having a sufficient grasp of concepts, principles, or skills so that [students] can bring [their understandings] to bear on new problems and situations" (p. 21). The content is often more engaging when the learning experiences involve the students through inquiry or problem-solving approaches. Content coupled with process engages students in high-level thinking.

Strategies That Build on Unique Characteristics

1.6. Cognitive and Affective Growth. Students with gifts and talents benefit from meaningful and challenging learning activities addressing their unique characteristics. (NAGC, 2010, p. 8)

Learning experiences for all students need to be meaningful and challenging. Meaningful learning experiences are ones to which students can relate, while challenging ones require the students to stretch to acquire the knowledge or skills. In order to provide meaningful and challenging learning activities for all students, differentiation of content, process, product, and assessment is essential. Combining basic or complex content, lower and higher level processes, and a variety of authentic products allows all young people to have meaningful and challenging learning experiences.

Various characteristics of children with gifts and talents create the potential for high-level learning, but the learning experiences must encourage those characteristics if these children are to thrive in the learning environment. One example of a characteristic that must be accommodated to foster high-level learning is inquisitiveness. All children ask questions, but the number of gifted children's questions can be irritating to teachers and to parents. These exceptional children learn at a faster pace and a more complex level than many children. Differentiated learning experiences can address the needs of these children with gifts and talents by addressing the pace and complexity as well as providing curriculum that encourages posing and answering questions.

What constitutes challenging content differs among students, even for students of the same age. Grouping by age reveals a wide range of interests as well as a variety of learning preferences and levels of readiness. The content needs to be planned for the students' zones of proximal development (Vygotsky, 1980). The zone of proximal development presents a challenge that requires each student to stretch to reach the learning goal, which is possible to reach through perseverance.

Differentiation requires teachers to use a repertoire of strategies and multiple resources in order to ensure that all students learn what they need to learn and advance at a pace that is commensurate with their abilities.

Differentiating Process to Prepare Thinkers and Independent Learners

3.4. Instructional Strategies. Students with gifts and talents become independent investigators. (NAGC, 2010, p. 10)

3.4.1. Educators use critical-thinking strategies to meet the needs of students with gifts and talents. (NAGC, 2010, p. 10)

3.4.2. Educators use creative-thinking strategies to meet the needs of students with gifts and talents. (NAGC, 2010, p. 10)

3.4.3. Educators use problem-solving model strategies to meet the needs of students with gifts and talents. (NAGC, 2010, p. 10)

3.4.4. Educators use inquiry models to meet the needs of students with gifts and talents. (NAGC, 2010, p. 10)

4.5. Communication Competence. Students with gifts and talents develop competence in interpersonal and technical communication skills. They demonstrate advanced oral and written skills, balanced biliteracy or multiliteracy, and creative expression. They display fluency with technologies that support effective communication. (NAGC, 2010, p. 11)

Process focuses on what a person does cognitively. It includes many skills that allow students to think at high levels and communicate in myriad ways. Process must always elevate the content, so students need to be engaged in asking questions, thinking about content from different perspectives, and creating possible solutions to issues and problems. Process must move beyond basic knowledge, although such knowledge is necessary in order to engage in higher level thinking about that particular content. Integrating concepts and big ideas from various disciplines can start early through interdisciplinary studies that focus on a universal theme.

The buzz in education is to develop 21st-century learners. Among other skills, creative and critical thinking skills are included under the umbrella of 21st-century skills. All children should be taught to think creatively and critically. These skills can be combined with content in all learning experiences. It is important to move beyond the right-answer questions—who, what, when, and where—just as soon as basic information is learned. Inquiry and problem-based learning are great ways to develop young people who are comfortable and expert at thinking creatively and critically. "Rather than just talking to students about thinking, teachers must actively engage students in thinking in areas such as the writing process, scientific experimentation, reading comprehension and analysis, computation, and study skills" (Robinson, Shore, & Enersen, 2007, p. 106).

Of course, there is a close tie between content and process.

Memory is probably essential to all other higher-level cognitive skills. One cannot analyze, create, or apply knowledge without first having the knowledge to analyze, create, or use. But memory for an impressive knowledge base seems like a beginning rather than an end. (Sternberg, 2008, p. 63)

Basic knowledge is the starting point rather than the destination for learning.

Critical and creative thinking are encouraged with a variety of strategies. Problem-based learning can be used in all content areas. Inquiry teaching changes the pace of learning and adds to its depth. It is important to teach young people to think like an historian, a scientist, or a mathematician. Research can begin early in a child's school career and become more sophisticated as the child moves through school. Problem-based learning, inquiry, and independent learning projects build inquisitive learners, ones who can think critically and creatively as well as solve problems.

Products Engage Learners and Add Authenticity

2.4.2. Educators use differentiated product-based assessments to measure the progress of students with gifts and talents. (NAGC, 2010, p. 9)

Products provide an effective way to address learner strengths and passions. Many times, teachers care about the students understanding the content but not necessarily how the students present the content. In those cases where presentations can vary, teachers frequently offer a choice of products for students to demonstrate what they have learned. Usually young people give their best efforts when they work on products that allow them to combine their talents and interests with content that they are expected to learn. It is likely that working on a product that engages students in their preferred way of learning or a talent area can motivate them in learning something they may not even have realized they were interested in learning. The product can motivate students to work hard on their projects, which is a win-win for the teacher and the student.

Numerous products can be assigned in all content areas. Figure 6.2 provides a list of possible products (Roberts & Inman, 2009a). Products can be categorized in various ways. Roberts and Inman (2009a) used kinesthetic, oral, technological, visual, and written to categorize products. Karnes and Stephens (2009) specifed visual, oral, performance, written, and multicategorical as the categories for products. Curry and Samara (1991) offered four categories for products: kinesthetic, oral, visual, and written. The important consideration for teachers is not which categories they use for products but that they offer variety in order to match the interests, talents, and learning preferences of their students. This opportunity to select and create products can be the key to motivating even underachieving or less than highly motivated learners.

Teachers are more inclined to offer choice of products if they have assessment rubrics ready to use. The Developing and Assessing Product Tool (DAP Tool; Roberts & Inman, 2009a) provides a protocol to use with all products.

Advertisement/PSA (print)	Game	Photo
Advertisement (radio)	Graph	Photo Essay
Advertisement (television)	Graphic Organizer	Plan
Audiotape	Greeting Card	Play
Biography	Illustrated Story	Podcast
Blog	Illustration	Poem
Blueprint	Interview (live)	Political Cartoon
Book	Interview (recorded)	Poster
Book Cover	Interview (written)	PowerPoint Presentation
Bulletin Board	Invention	Project
Cartoon	Lesson	PSA (radio)
Case Study	Letter (business)	PSA (television)
Chart	Letter (friendly)	Puppet
Choral Reading	Letter to Editor	Puppet Show
Collage	Mask	Questionnaire
Collection	Matrix	Research Report
Column	Mentorship	Review
Computer Graphic	Mime	Science Fair Project
Computer Program	Mock Trial (attorney)	Sculpture
Costume	Mock Trial (defendant)	Scrapbook
Dance	Mock Trial (judge)	Script
Debate	Mock Trial (plaintiff)	Service-Learning Project
Demonstration	Model	Skit
Diagram	Monologue	Song
Dialogue	Movie	Speech (oral)
Diary/Journal	Mural	Speech (written)
Diorama	Museum Exhibit	Story
Document-Based Question	Musical	Story Telling
Documentary	Newscast	Survey
Dramatic Presentation	Newsletter	Technical Report
Drawing	Newspaper Article	Timeline
Editorial	Open Response	Venn Diagram
Essay	Oral Report/Presentation	Video Game
Exhibit/Display	Outline	Web Page
Experiment	Painting	Wiki
Feature Article	Pamphlet/Brochure	Written Report

Figure 6.2. Product list. From *Assessing Differentiated Student Products* (p. 10), by J. L. Roberts and T. F. Inman, 2009, Waco, TX: Prufrock Press. Copyright 2009 by Prufrock Press. Reprinted with permission.

Consistent in form and vocabulary, four components are common across all DAP Tools: Content, Presentation, Creativity, and Reflection. Certain aspects of every product are essential to assess, whether it is an interview, an experiment, a podcast, or an essay. Students must have an accurate level of understanding of the content that goes beyond a surface understanding (i.e., Content). They must also put something of their own personalities into the product itself and into the way they approach the content (i.e., Creativity). Students also should think about the impact the learning process has had on them (i.e., Reflection). Because these three components are common to all products, they are the same on all DAP Tools. Only the Presentation component changes from product to product as the essentials of an oral report differ from the essentials of a technical report, podcast, poster, or model. Each DAP Tool has three versions or tiers ranging from less to more sophisticated so that teachers can differentiate the expectations for students who have different levels of experience with a specific product (e.g., some students have never produced a PowerPoint presentation while others have had successful experiences doing so).

A major step in developing talent with products is to show students what excellent products look like. They need models to emulate. Rubrics can set goals for students developing products, as can DAP Tools. Likewise, it is illuminating for students to see products that professionals use in their careers. These models can inspire students to work harder, as they realize that their products have real-life uses.

Differentiated learning experiences need to be equally or nearly equally engaging to all learners in the class. All learning tasks must be respectful. Giving one student or a cluster of students a worksheet at the same time that others have something very engaging to do is not a satisfactory way to differentiate. All learning experiences need to engage the intellect or be minds-on learning experiences. Learning experiences can be both hands-on and minds-on some of the time, but never should the classroom activities be solely hands-on. Focusing on hands-on learning without engaging student thinking presents missed learning opportunities. Minds-on learning experiences require the students to think about what they learned and later reflect on what questions the learning experience prompted and what follow-up learning they would enjoy doing.

Multiple Resources Enhance Differentiation

3.6. Resources. Students with gifts and talents benefit from gifted education programming that provides a variety of high quality resources and materials. (NAGC, 2010, p. 10)

3.6.1. Teachers and administrators demonstrate familiarity with sources for high quality resources and materials that are appropriate for learners with gifts and talents. (NAGC, 2010, p. 10)

3.3.2. Educators use school and community resources that support differentiation. (NAGC, 2010, p. 10)

For teachers to remove the learning ceiling through differentiation, multiple resources that support differentiated learning opportunities are a must.

Reading materials need to be available so that students who read at any level can access information about the topic being studied at an appropriately challenging reading level. Technological resources are both motivating for young people and useful in terms of developing skills needed to continue to access information that will support their inquiries and aid them in solving problems in the classroom. Technology also can stay up-to-date in ways that print resources cannot.

Resources also must include human resources. As teachers plan differentiated learning experiences, they need to consider individuals who may bring their expertise to the classroom. For example, a local specialist on solar energy would be a wonderful resource in a classroom in which students are engaged in a problem-based unit on sources of energy. An architect or engineer would have experiences to share on the usefulness and the importance of developing spatial skills or in demonstrating the importance of using models in their careers. Resources do not always present themselves, so educators must be aware of various careers that are practiced in the community and be ready with invitations when they see the match between learning about a particular topic or concept and the human resources that are available in the area.

Teachers and administrators also must be familiar with sources for high-quality resources and materials to match the potential level of young people with gifts and talents. They need to know where to find resources that have been developed for advanced learners and understand how to use them. Grade-level resources are not motivating for children who are beyond that point in their learning on a particular topic.

Evidence-Based Programming Options

5.1. Variety of Programming. Students with gifts and talents participate in a variety of evidence-based programming options that enhance performance in cognitive and affective areas. (NAGC, 2010, p. 12)

Acceleration as a Form of Differentiation

5.1.1. Educators regularly use multiple alternative approaches to accelerate learning. (NAGC, 2010, p. 12)

Colangelo, Assouline, and Gross (2004) described acceleration "as an intervention that moves students through an educational program at rates faster, or at younger ages, than is typical. It means matching the level, complexity, and pace of the curriculum to the readiness and motivation of the student" (p. i). Their two-volume report listed 18 types of acceleration. These different types of acceleration can be divided into subject-based acceleration options (subject-matter acceleration and curriculum compacting) and acceleration based on timing—when a student has the opportunity to move ahead (e.g., start school earlier than age-mates, take Advanced Placement classes that are college-level courses).

Numerous benefits come from any type of acceleration if decisions to accelerate are made carefully. One benefit is that acceleration options do not add additional education costs. Differentiation can occur in a school as teachers communicate and collaborate to allow students to move from one classroom to another in order to receive appropriate instruction. One student or several students may need accelerated opportunities in reading and/or mathematics but need grade-level instruction the rest of the day. Such decisions to accelerate can be set up on a trial basis to ensure that the match between the child and the level of instruction is appropriate. The most important benefit from all types of acceleration is that the young people have opportunities to make continuous progress—to learn on an ongoing basis.

Differentiating With Enrichment

5.1.2. Educators regularly use enrichment options to extend and deepen learning opportunities within and outside of the school setting. (NAGC, 2010, p. 12)

Renzulli (2008) enumerated a range of potential enrichment resources: virtual field trips, real field trips, creativity training, critical thinking, projects and independent study, contests and competitions, websites, fiction books, nonfiction books, how-to books, summer programs, online classes and activities, research skills, videos, and DVDs (p. 279). Resources such as these may add enrichment opportunities in classrooms or through extracurricular experiences within the school or the community. Students may engage in some of them independently. All of these additional learning opportunities can enrich learning.

Enrichment opportunities can be infused throughout classroom experiences, help to remove the ceiling, and make learning appealing. Integrating creative and critical thinking into instruction enriches learning for all students, although the type of enrichment may vary between students based on previous experiences, levels of readiness, and a wide variety of interests.

1.4.2. Educators identify out-of-school learning opportunities that match students' abilities and interests. (NAGC, 2010, p. 8)

Although some of the enrichment experiences will be available beyond the classroom, young people may not ever hear about opportunities unless teachers tell them about the possibilities. For example, an English teacher would know which students are outstanding writers and who might enjoy participating in a writing contest; the art teacher would announce to the class about a poster contest and perhaps encourage budding artists to give the contest a try. Teachers might also provide information about Saturday and summer opportunities that would be of high interest to the young people and sponsor extracurricular activities, especially in their own content areas. These experiences deepen understanding in a content area and put the students in contact with others who are their idea-mates rather than just their age-mates. During follow-up conversations, educators might share information about scholarships and financial aid that would make it possible for young people to participate in a variety of enrichment activities, particularly those who could not do so without financial assistance. No enrichment opportunity is an opportunity for children who do not know the opportunity exists.

Differentiating by Grouping for Instructional Purposes

1.3.1. Educators provide a variety of research-based grouping practices for students with gifts and talents that allow them to interact with individuals of various gifts, talents, abilities, and strengths. (NAGC, 2010, p. 8)

5.1.3. Educators regularly use multiple forms of grouping, including clusters, resource rooms, special classes, or special schools. (NAGC, 2010, p. 12)

Grouping for instructional purposes takes many forms, some of which are flexible and some of which are in place for the year. The reason to group must always tie to instruction. Grouping may be done in various ways, but must always have a reason. Sometimes the instructional purpose may be to group students by interests. For example, implementing this type of grouping might involve putting together students who are interested in arts, economics, or politics of the 1920s in U.S. history. At other times, students might be grouped within a class by those who already know the basic information about cells, those who know some of it, and those who have little background or understanding of the basics of cells. "Flexible grouping of students within elementary classrooms promotes achievement, especially in mathematics and reading. The achievement effects are positive for high-ability students, as well as average and low-achieving students" (Robinson et al., 2007, p. 123).

Special programming placements can enhance learning for children with interest and readiness to learn in a particular area. For example, a magnet program one day a week can build expertise in science and mathematics or the arts. Students may be clustered in classrooms with teachers who are knowledgeable about differentiation strategies to ensure that differentiation occurs, or they may learn in self-contained classrooms where students learn with other gifted and talented peers throughout the school day. Students may receive services through pull-out classes, where gifted and talented students are grouped for a portion of the day or a portion of the week. It is very important to ensure that children from all backgrounds have opportunities to qualify for all placement options. The key for all decisions is to find children with interest and advanced ability in order for them to be appropriately challenged and to have time to spend with idea-peers.

Policies and Procedures Put Best Practice in Place

5.6. Policies and Procedures. Students with gifts and talents participate in regular and gifted education programs that are guided by clear policies and procedures that provide for their advanced learning needs (e.g., early entrance, acceleration, credit in lieu of enrollment). (NAGC, 2010, p. 12)

Policies open up possibilities for accommodating the needs of advanced learners in myriad ways. Each policy has the intent of ensuring that young people who are advanced learners make continuous learning progress. Such policies pave the way for implementing strategies that allow children to learn at readiness levels that are more advanced than their age-mates (e.g., a kindergarten student who is learning third- or fourth-grade math knowledge and skills), to take courses that might not be offered at a particular grade level (e.g., an AP class in the eighth or ninth grade), and to remove barriers to learning. Policies set precedents, so that parents and educators do not need to have continuing conversations about a particular student's needs.

Some policies, however, can complicate the flexibility in education options for advanced students. For example, a policy might specify that students must have 4 years of high school English. This policy would establish a barrier to early graduation, even for a young person for whom that would be appropriate. A more flexible example might be to simply have a list of courses that students would need to take during high school. For younger students, another policy might limit children from entering kindergarten if their birthday comes even a day after a deadline in spite of their readiness to do so. A policy that would lift that deadline for students who are ready to start school would include the opportunity to demonstrate readiness.

Instilling Lifelong Learning

6.3. Lifelong Learners. Students develop their gifts and talents as a result of educators who are life-long learners . . . (NAGC, 2010, p. 13)

The goal of schooling must be to produce lifelong learners. After all, the time comes when students graduate from their formal schooling and move into careers. The earlier in their school experiences that young people pique their interests and acquire and perfect their abilities, the better for their future. A few students will emerge as self-motivated learners, but others will need opportunities to develop as independent learners.

Differentiated learning experiences can prepare students in becoming independent learners. A variety of strategies that differentiate the content, process, products, and assessments will engage students in learning, which is essential to developing lifelong learners. Ongoing opportunities for learning in an area of interest enhance enthusiasm for continued learning about that topic or area of study.

Conclusions

Differentiation is essential for ensuring that children and young people are learning on an ongoing basis. The purpose of differentiation is to provide appropriately challenging learning experiences to reach the end goal—young people enjoying learning and becoming independent learners. Planning and preassessment results guide the teacher in matching instructional strategies to the interests, readiness levels, and learning preferences of students, which are key considerations in implementing effective and appropriate differentiation.

It would be easy to assume that the standard(s) affecting the differentiation of instructional strategies in the classroom would be one or two of the six standards, but such an assumption is incorrect. All six standards impact learning in the classroom, so they must be considered in combination. Just as it takes all educators working together to implement quality gifted education services, all standards must be addressed if programming is to be implemented at a level needed for learners with gifts and talents. Educators need to know the standards and work with colleagues to fully implement them. The Gifted Programming Standards can help educators as they collaborate with other educators and families. When everyone knows the guiding principles (i.e., the standards), it enhances the opportunities of implementing them in providing quality gifted programming for young people throughout their school careers.

References

Black, P., & William, D. (1998) Assessment and classroom learning. *Assessment and Education: Principles, Policy and Practice, 5*(1). Retrieved from http://web.ebsco host.com/ehost/detail?sid=0e9c73f7-d011-4084-a39f-104773c5818b%40sessio nmgr104&vid=5&hid=111&bdata=JnNpdGU9ZWhvc3QtbGl2ZQ%3d%3d# db=aph&AN=725610

Bloom, B. S. (1985). (Ed.). *Developing talent in young people*. New York, NY: Ballantine.

Chappuis, S., Stiggins, R. J., Arter, J., & Chappuis, J. (2005). *Assessment for learning: An action guide for school leaders*. Portland, OR: Educational Testing Service.

Colangelo, N., Assouline, S. G., & Gross, M. U. M. (2004). *A nation deceived: How schools hold back America's brightest students* (Vol. 1). Iowa City: The University of Iowa, The Connie Belin & Jacqueline N. Blank International Center for Gifted Education and Talent Development.

Curry, J., & Samara, J. (1991). *Product guide kit: The curriculum project*. Austin, TX: Curriculum Project.

Dweck, C. S. (2006). *Mindset: The new psychology of success*. Philadelphia, PA: Psychology Press.

Gardner, H. W. (1993). Educating for understanding. *The American School Board Journal, 180*(7), 20–24.

Karnes. F. A., & Stephens, K. R. (2009). *The ultimate guide for student product development and evaluation* (2nd ed.). Waco, TX: Prufrock Press.

Loveless, T. (2008). Analysis of NAEP data. In T. Loveless, S. Farkas, & A. Duffett (Eds.), *High-achieving students in the era of NCLB* (pp. 13–48). Washington, DC: Thomas B. Fordham Institute.

Loveless, T., Farkas, S., & Duffett, A. (Eds.). (2008). *High-achieving students in the era of NCLB*. Washington, DC: Thomas B. Fordham Institute.

National Association for Gifted Children. (2008). *Gifted children's bill of rights*. Retrieved from http://www.nagc.org/uploadedFiles/PHP/Bill%20of%20Rights. pdf

National Association for Gifted Children. (2010). *NAGC pre-K–grade 12 gifted programming standards: A blueprint for quality gifted education programs*. Washington, DC: Author.

Plucker, J. A., Burroughs, N., & Song, R. (2010). *Mind the (other) gap! The growing excellence gap in K–12 education*. Retrieved from http://ceep.indiana.edu/mind thegap

Renzulli, J. S. (2008). A practical approach for developing the gifts and talents of all students. In B. Z. Presseisen (Ed.), *Teaching for intelligence* (2nd ed., pp. 245–287). Thousand Oaks, CA: Corwin Press.

Roberts, J. L., & Boggess, J. R. (2011). *The teacher's survival guide: Gifted education.* Waco, TX: Prufrock Press.

Roberts, J. L., & Inman, T. F. (2009a). *Assessing differentiated student products: A protocol for development and evaluation.* Waco, TX: Prufrock Press.

Roberts, J. L., & Inman, T. F. (2009b). *Strategies for differentiating instruction: Best practices for the classroom* (2nd ed.). Waco, TX: Prufrock Press.

Robinson, A., Shore, B. M., & Enersen, D. L. (2007). *Best practices in gifted education: An evidence-based guide.* Waco, TX: Prufrock Press.

Sternberg, R. J. (2008). Schools should nurture wisdom. In B. Z. Presseisen (Ed.), *Teaching for intelligence* (2nd ed., pp. 61–88). Thousand Oaks, CA: Corwin Press.

Vygotsky, L. (1980). *Society of the mind.* Cambridge, MA: Harvard University Press.

Chapter 7

Programming Models and Program Design

by Cheryll M. Adams,
Chrystyna V. Mursky,
and Bill Keilty

Educators are aware of empirical evidence regarding (a) the cognitive, creative, and affective development of learners with gifts and talents, and (b) programming that meets their concomitant needs. Educators use this expertise systematically and collaboratively to develop, implement, and effectively manage comprehensive services for students with a variety of gifts and talents to ensure specific student outcomes. (National Association for Gifted Children [NAGC], 2010b, p. 12)

Introduction

According to the NAGC Pre-K–Grade 12 Gifted Programming Standards (2010b), "programming refers to a continuum of services that address students with gifts and talents' needs in all settings" (p. 12). This definition is supported by professionals in the field of gifted education who advocate for a continuum of services rather than a single program to meet the needs of students with gifts and talents (Callahan, 2009; Renzulli & Reis, 2008; Rogers, 2001, 2006; Tomlinson, 2009; Treffinger, Young, Nassab, & Wittig, 2004). To ensure that this continuum of services is in place and appropriately implemented, policies and procedures to guide and sustain the necessary service components must be developed. In order for gifted education to be considered a vital and critical component of pre-K–12 education, the services that are developed must be aligned with both general education and special education. Thus, educators must have the necessary knowledge and skills to choose appropriate programming options such as acceleration and enrichment, provide varied grouping arrangements (e.g., cluster grouping, special classes), and offer individualized learning options (e.g., independent study, mentorships) to increase students' performance academically as well as socially and emotionally (Johnsen, Van-Tassel-Baska, & Robinson, 2008). Through the use of technology to enhance performance or increase access to additional learning opportunities and collaboration with persons within the family, school, and community, the diverse learning needs of these students have a better chance of being met. Although there are a number of services that can be provided for little additional cost to the district (Adams, 2009; Gentry & Mann, 2008; Tomlinson, 2003), some districts cite lack of funding as a reason for not providing services to these students. Even the most well-conceived and appropriately designed range of services cannot be implemented without the continued support of administrators and policymakers who determine the level of funding and resources that are allocated to students with gifts and talents.

Despite many years of research, including a landmark study by The National Research Center on the Gifted and Talented (Delcourt, Cornell, & Goldberg, 2007; Delcourt, Loyd, Cornell, & Goldberg, 1994), we have yet to determine programming or services that allow all academically gifted students to reach their full potential. At one time, schools may have had specific programming such as self-contained classes or a resource room, but over the last several years, programming for gifted learners has been frequently eliminated in favor of an inclusionary model that places all students in the general education classroom. Reasons for this phenomenon include a lack of funding and an appropriate infrastructure for gifted services (VanTassel-Baska, 2006) as well as the passing of the No Child Left Behind Act (2001) and its policies that focus on struggling learners and not those who are above proficiency (Scot, Callahan, & Urquhart, 2009). Thus, default programming has often become differentiation in the general education classroom rather than a continuum of services. Without a deep understanding of differentiation, particularly with respect to gifted learners, educators may only provide minimal services at best to these students.

The purpose of this chapter, then, is to provide information that will allow school personnel to make appropriate choices for programming for gifted students. These choices are predicated on educators' awareness of empirical evidence to guide their understanding of gifted students' cognitive, affective, and creative development. Understanding the development of students with gifts and talents is the foundation necessary for choosing appropriate programming options and services. By using Standard 5 to focus on evidence-based practices and the corresponding student outcomes, educators can make informed choices to select programming that meets the specific learning needs of their students.

Program Design

Standard 5 specifically addresses these questions:

» Is a properly funded continuum of services provided that offers a variety of programming and learning options that are collaboratively developed and implemented and that enhance student performance in cognitive and affective areas?

» Has a system been put in place, including articulated policies and procedures, that allows for educators to develop multiyear plans, plan and coordinate programming and services with the school's professional service providers, and communicate with family and community members to meet student needs and program goals?

These guiding questions imply that the programming options selected are viable, effective, thoughtfully considered, and proactively designed with advanced learner needs in mind. Merely providing programming or a set of services for students with gifts and talents does not indicate the quality of that programming. Too often, programming may be operating as a patch to cover weak general education programming (Tomlinson, 2009) or an add-on that does not align with the general education curriculum (Robinson, 2009; VanTassel-Baska, 2009). Before any discussion of various types of services or programming options can occur, we must first look at the criteria for exemplary programming.

Effective programming and services have the following clearly articulated elements: a philosophy, goals, a definition, an identification plan, coherent curriculum, scope and sequence, a professional development plan, and an evaluation plan (Purcell & Eckert, 2006; Tomlinson, 2009). Furthermore, the services are aligned with the general curriculum; there is administrative support, oversight by qualified personnel, and communication among all stakeholders (Adams, 2009; Tomlinson, 2009). When all of these elements are in place and working effectively, the cognitive and affective needs of students with gifts and talents can be met. Evidence of students' needs being met includes yearly growth in cognitive and affective areas commensurate with their abilities through a variety of programming options that allow them to progress without administrative barriers.

Philosophy

The philosophy gives a broad overview of the vision for programming. It may be helpful to think of this as a "This we believe" statement about students who are gifted and talented and the manner in which a continuum of services may be provided for them. It is in this statement that the alignment to special education and general education can be initially affirmed. For example, we believe that all students require a program of study that provides choice, challenge, and a response to their individual needs. This statement implies that the needs of *all* children, including the gifted and talented, will be met and their learning strengths and limitations will be considered. The next statement may be one that addresses gifted students specifically, such as: There are some students whose performance or potential for performance exceeds what is generally expected at their grade level. The Low Country Community School District believes that these students need to be offered a continuum of services that meet their academic, social, and emotional needs. Other statements may further address particular beliefs of the school district.

Goals

Goals are the road maps for programming; without a clear idea of the outcomes of the services provided, we won't know when (or if) we have succeeded. High-quality goals must be aligned with best practices in the field, valid and worthy of attaining, comprehensive, and clear (Adams, 2006). For example, let's look at this goal: All gifted students in the Low Country Community School District will reach their full potential. When measured against the above criteria, this goal has little evidence of alignment, is lacking in validity, provides little guidance in how the programming would be developed, and is neither measurable nor unambiguous. In contrast, the following goal is more closely aligned with the criteria for high-quality programming goals: Gifted students demonstrate progress as a result of programming that provides a variety of appropriate types and levels of acceleration and enrichment that are based on students' learning needs in grades K–12.

Definition

There is currently no universal definition of giftedness, but we do have many definitions that identify this population based on particular behaviors, habits of mind, potential, and/or facility for learning. Some theorists ascribe to a more conservative definition (e.g., Stanley, 1980; Terman, 1922) and some to a more liberal one (e.g., Gagné, 1995; Renzulli, 1986). NAGC (2010a) convened a task force to redefine giftedness for the 21st century. Note that this definition has a student outcome component:

Gifted individuals are those who demonstrate outstanding levels of aptitude (defined as an exceptional ability to reason and learn) or competence (documented performance or achievement in top 10% or rarer) in one or more domains. Domains include any structured area of activity with its own symbol system (e.g., mathematics, music, language) and/or set of sensorimotor skills (e.g., painting, dance, sports). (NAGC, 2010a, para. 4)

It is vital that an appropriate definition be chosen that adequately describes the group for whom the programming is being designed. If the definition puts an emphasis on cognitive skills and programming aimed at visual and performing arts is designed, then we have a mismatch between the programming options and the students who will be provided those options.

Identification Plan

Once a definition has been selected, the school must provide a clearly articulated plan to determine who is eligible for services based on that definition. If the definition focuses on mathematics and language arts, for example, then the instruments chosen will be those that identify students who are gifted in mathematics and language arts, and the programming options will focus on those two content areas. Selecting appropriate instruments that provide both quantitative and qualitative data, ensuring that all students have an opportunity to demonstrate their gifts and talents, recognizing potential as well as performance, determining placement options, and providing procedures for due process are critical issues that must be considered when designing an identification plan. (See Chapter 4 for a complete discussion of these issues.)

Curriculum, Professional Development, and Evaluation

Ludicrous as it may seem, a number of schools and districts spend time carefully crafting a gifted education program's philosophy and goals, choosing a research-based definition, and selecting appropriate instruments for identification only to place identified students in the general education classroom using the same curriculum that all other students of that grade use. Teachers assigned to provide an appropriately differentiated curriculum that addresses advanced learner needs do not necessarily possess the knowledge and skills crucial for this task. Furthermore, there may be no evaluation plan in place, no plans for evaluations, and/or no consideration that evaluation is an important component of programming. Issues and outcomes related to curriculum, professional development, and evaluation are discussed in detail in other chapters in this volume; we make mention of them here to underscore their importance as vital pieces of comprehensive programming for gifted learners.

Evidence-Based Programming Options

To meet the advanced learning needs of students with gifts and talents, schools must choose programming options that have amassed a body of empirical evidence suggesting they are appropriate for this population and result in students making gains commensurate with their abilities. There are other popular options that have practice-based evidence of effectiveness, generally through action research. This chapter will examine both bodies of evidence of effectiveness with students with gifts and talents. It should be noted that the responsibility of developing and implementing gifted programming options for gifted students is best undertaken by qualified personnel who have the appropriate knowledge and skills to accomplish these tasks effectively.

Acceleration

Students with gifts and talents may need their classwork or performance level adjusted to a degree that dramatically affects the pace of their instruction resulting in acceleration. According to VanTassel-Baska (2005), "Acceleration assumes that different students of the same age are at different levels of learning within and across learning areas, thus necessitating diagnosis of learning level and prescription of curriculum at a level slightly above it" (p. 91). In general, the flexibility needed to allow a third-grade student to accelerate into middle school math, for example, has not had strong support in schools. The Templeton Report, *A Nation Deceived*, compiled by Colangelo, Assouline, and Gross (2004), sought to change negative attitudes and beliefs about acceleration by providing empirical evidence about 18 different forms of acceleration going far beyond grade skipping and clearly setting the record straight on the advantages of each in an easily understood manner.

Despite the publicity surrounding the Templeton Report and the extensive research support, many school administrators still discourage the use of acceleration as a programming option. An often-mentioned reason for not accelerating students is the long-held belief about the certainty of social and emotional problems for students who have been subject skipped. Because having an acceleration policy is key to any set of programming options, teachers, administrators, and other school personnel would benefit from reading the report and designing a policy based on the *Guidelines for Developing an Academic Acceleration Policy* (Institute for Research and Policy on Acceleration, 2009).

We will examine two forms of acceleration that offer schools fairly inexpensive, viable programming options for students with gifts and talents.

Subject-based acceleration. Subject-based acceleration, or subject skipping, is most often employed when students have demonstrated outstanding growth in and understanding of the curriculum for their grade levels. Providing enrichment and extension activities for these students no longer results in progress commensurate with their abilities. Accelerating these students may simply involve placing them in the particular subject or performance area at the next grade or level. Other forms of subject acceleration include taking advanced classes through precollegiate talent search sites, independent learning programs, or distance education programs. Although subject-based acceleration that occurs within the school generally does not involve additional expense, classes at Talent Search sites, independent study involving an outside source, and distance learning may require out-of pocket expenses on the part of the student's family, the school, or both.

Much of the research on subject-based acceleration focuses on mathematics instruction (Lubinski & Benbow, 2006; Swiatek & Lupkowski-Shoplik, 2003) rather than other areas, although this should not preclude choosing acceleration as an option for those students whose performance in another area requires it. The effect size for subject acceleration in Rogers's (1991) study of acceleration and grouping management strategies was .59 across 21 studies; that is, the students gained about 6 months additional educational growth per academic year. One important caveat: Once subject acceleration has been implemented, it is too late to worry about what happens the next year and in the future! A discussion about having a fourth-grade student take fifth-grade science needs to include a thoughtful conversation about the student the next year when, as a fifth grader, she may have to be transported to the middle school for sixth-grade science.

Grade-based acceleration. Grade-based acceleration, or grade skipping, involves taking classes generally a year or more ahead of age-mates. Early entrance to school (e.g., entering first grade when age-mates are entering kindergarten) and early entrance to college (e.g., skipping the senior year and proceeding to college after grade 11) are included. In its simplest form, grade acceleration entails moving from one grade to another but skipping the grade between the two (e.g. completing grade 2 and entering grade 4 the next year rather than grade 3). Gifted students whose achievement measures indicate they are performing several years above their grade-level peers are good candidates for grade skipping, but researchers encourage choosing grade skipping as an option as early in the child's school career as possible (Coleman & Cross, 2005; Rogers, 2001).

Grade skipping, including early entrance to school and college, has a positive effect on achievement with an effect size for academic achievement for early entrance into school of .49. For grade-skipping, the effect size is 1.00 compared to students' same-age peers. Compared to their older peers, the effect size is .56, and for early admission to college, it is .35 (Rogers, 2007). Because the students join an already intact class and thus no additional materials or teachers are needed, this form of acceleration is cost effective.

Enrichment

Enrichment may be defined as "modifications a teacher makes to go above and beyond the regular curriculum for a student or cluster of students who need advanced learning opportunities" (Roberts, 2005, p. 6). When students have mastered the grade-level material and acceleration is not a viable option, the teacher may choose to offer options for them to study the topic in more depth or breadth or at a more complex level while other students needing more practice continue to work with the general education or grade-level curriculum. The key to providing appropriate enrichment options is predicated on the view that the activities have substance, are meaningful and respectful, and provide a level of challenge commensurate with the student's ability.

In his study of grouping, Kulik (1992) reported significant learning gains for students when they were ability grouped and when the curriculum was adjusted to reflect the performance level of the students. Similarly, Rogers (1991) found an effect size of .65 when students were grouped by ability in a pull-out program using a curriculum extension approach. Clearly, enrichment is supported by empirical research, but one must not forget that in these studies enrichment extended and complemented the general education curriculum. According to Adams and Boswell (2012), "Simply having students engage in an exciting project such as making a piñata is best situated within a discussion of cultures whose celebrations include piñatas, the science involved in making papier-mâché, or the origins of papier-mâché" (p. 44). Hence, enrichment must be carefully planned and clearly articulated so that students can enhance their performance through higher level critical and creative thinking skills as they complete the activities.

Differentiation

Differentiation is a mindset that takes into account the variety of learner needs and characteristics that students bring to the classroom (Tomlinson, 2001). In response to these characteristics and needs, teachers modify the content, process, product, learning environment, and affect to meet the needs of all learners, including gifted learners. The emphasis is on developmentally appropriate lessons that provide students with choice and a moderate challenge. A fundamental principle is that students should not be required to continually repeat something they have already learned. Instead, the teacher employs a variety of instructional strategies that are engaging, meaningful, and worthy of the time students spend completing these activities.

Differentiation is perhaps the most widely employed programming option because it does not require that students be pulled into a resource room, special class, or special school. Students with gifts and talents are placed in the general education classroom with their age-mates. The teacher must constantly assess students to determine where they are academically, socially, and emotionally to select suitable materials to advance their learning. Based on this knowledge, the teacher modifies one or more aspects according to the student's interest, learning profile, or readiness level for the task. Much of the evidence we have about differentiation is based on observational data or action research from practitioners (Adams & Pierce, 2006; Renzulli & Reis, 2008; Tomlinson, 2001, 2003, 2009) or about particular strategies (Gavin, Casa, Adelson, Carroll, & Sheffield, 2009; Pierce et al., 2011). Although differentiation is quite popular as a programming option, many schools that choose this option have great difficulty putting it into practice appropriately. Implementing differentiation runs the whole gamut from providing individual spelling lists or novels based on reading levels to constantly arranging and rearranging students into flexible configurations based on the teacher's data from continuous assessments using exit cards, informal dialog, observation, and formal testing. For differentiation to be a viable and effective programming option, teachers and administrators must embrace it wholly, and administrators must ensure that teachers have proper training and support to consistently put it into practice.

Individual Options

Mentorships, internships, and independent study are options that may be selected on a case-by-case basis for individual students who need these opportunities to enhance their learning or refine their knowledge and skills in a particular area of study. For example, a student may want to pursue a particular subject such as the nest-building habits of the cerulean warbler. Generally, a topic like this is beyond the realm of expertise of the regular classroom teacher. A field study might be arranged with a university professor who has a similar research interest. Internships for students who want an opportunity to acquire real-world experience in a particular field such as medicine or accounting may be arranged with members of the community who work in the field of interest. Independent studies are often completed in the classroom or resource room under the guidance of the teacher. Many teachers and students may see independent study as simply writing a research paper, but according to Johnsen and Johnson (2007), "Independent studies may be used for solving community problems; uncovering new questions; writing histories; and, most importantly, helping a student create a lifelong love affair with learning" (p. 379). For a meaningful independent study experience, both the teacher and the students must set out a clear plan with checkpoints along the way, particularly for younger students. Just assigning the topic and sending students off to work on their own until the due date is neither appropriate nor effective as an alternative to regular assignments. No matter which individual option is presented to students as a learning option, it is vital that a study plan be developed so that all those involved know the expectations and responsibilities involved.

Grouping Options

One of the first empirical studies that looked at students in a variety of grouping options was undertaken by Delcourt et al. (1994). Focusing on achievement, the study compared students enrolled in gifted programs (special school, separate class, pull-out, within-class), high-achieving students from districts in which no program was available at the designated grade levels, and nongifted students in regular classrooms. Several recommendations from this study are worth noting:

» Decisions about programming implementation should be based on research about learning outcomes for specific program types (i.e., special school, separate class, pull-out, within-class).

» Gifted children who were provided specific programming options performed better than their gifted peers not in programs. Specifically, children in special schools, separate class programs, and pull-out programs for the gifted showed substantially higher levels of achievement than both their gifted peers not in programs and those attending within-class programs.

» Students from the separate class program scored at the highest levels of achievement.

In the qualitative extension of this study, Delcourt and Evans (1994) sought to determine what attributes separated the exemplary programs from the rest. Regardless of the overall results about a particular programming option, to be effective, the school district using the model must demonstrate effectiveness in the following areas: leadership, atmosphere and environment, communication, curriculum and instruction, and attention to student needs. Thus, there is not one programming option that works for all students with gifts and talents; instead, student outcomes are dependent on both the match to the student's needs and the quality of implementation of the programming option.

Cluster Grouping

Cluster grouping is a widely recommended and frequently used strategy for meeting the needs of high-achieving students in the regular classroom. Originally, clustering was the intentional placement of 4–10 identified gifted students in a heterogeneous classroom with a teacher who possessed both desire and expertise in working with gifted children. Many variations in the total number within the cluster appear in the literature (Gentry & Mann, 2008; Rogers, 2001) and practice. The students in the cluster are then provided appropriate materials and learning experiences beyond what is offered in the general education curriculum to enhance their performance in the cognitive, creative, and/or affective areas.

The rationale underlying this programming model suggests that it provides opportunities for gifted students to interact with intellectual peers on a full-time basis and expedites the classroom teacher's capacity to address the needs of a group of gifted students. Cluster grouping presents a cost-effective option, and evidence suggests it improves achievement across all levels by allowing students not identified as academically gifted to emerge as leaders and achievers in nonclustered classrooms (Brulles, 2005; Delcourt & Evans, 1994; Gentry & Owen, 1999; Rogers, 1991).

Several misconceptions may impact whether school districts choose cluster grouping, because it is sometimes confused with tracking students and the negativity surrounding this practice. Teachers may also believe that clustering gifted learners in several classes diminishes learning opportunities for students in nonclustered classrooms, although research indicates the opposite (Gentry & Owen, 1999; Schuler, 1997). Additionally, some hold the view that cluster grouping only benefits elementary students, even though there are several schools successfully using clustering at the middle school level.

There are challenges to the effective use of clustering, including the need to provide ongoing professional development to support cluster teachers; otherwise, the academic challenge in a cluster classroom is no greater than in a nonclustered classroom (Kulik, 1992; Kulik & Kulik, 1992; Loveless, 2008; Rogers, 1991; Tieso, 2005). Moreover, without an appropriate level of challenge for the cluster, cluster grouping becomes camouflage for no gifted program at all. When designed and implemented with fidelity, cluster grouping can simultaneously address the needs of gifted students *and* the needs of other students (Gentry & MacDougall, 2010).

Self-Contained Classes

Self-contained classes are used to group students with gifts and talents into a separate class at a particular grade (Rogers, 2001). In this grouping arrangement, students' learning activities are planned to be qualitatively different from the regular grade-level instruction. The implications are that these classes would have learning experiences that would not be appropriate for less able students and would use materials that provide a higher level of depth and complexity. When students with gifts and talents are placed in self-contained classrooms simply to have them in one place without changing what actually occurs differently in that classroom, educators should not expect them to make academic gains commensurate with their abilities. It is not just the configuration that makes the difference; it is what happens in the configuration that allows gains to be made. Generally, there is no need for an additional teacher or classroom because students are pulled from all of the other classrooms at that grade level. The additional expense comes from the need to purchase specialized materials that are not being used by other students at that grade.

Special Schools

The most expensive grouping option is the special school configuration. Because of the expense involved in creating a separate school, many special schools that currently exist are laboratory schools connected to a university, state-supported residential or day schools, or private schools. In addition to all of the expenses incurred in the day-to-day maintenance of a building, teaching staff must be hired, materials must be ordered, and, in the case of a residential program, students must have dormitory space, residence counselors must be hired, and a plan for dealing with students who are high school age and living away from home must be developed. Some schools currently focus on particular content areas such as the performing arts or science and mathematics. Despite the expense involved in setting up and maintaining a special school, there are decided advantages of such an arrangement. Students with gifts and talents spend the majority of their day surrounded by other such students; students have access to curriculum and instruction that is not available in their regular school; and teachers generally are content specialists with advanced degrees.

For students who want a challenge that is above what is generally offered in a regular classroom, a special school may be a viable choice (Kolloff, 2003).

Pull-Out/Resource Room

Pull-out programs have been the mainstay of gifted education, particularly at the elementary level, for years, although many are being eliminated due to the current state of the economy. The expense comes from the need for an additional teacher and a separate classroom or place for the program to be housed. Exemplary programs of this type are carefully aligned to the regular curriculum and extend it vertically or horizontally. A good example would be a third-grade pull-out program for math. When the third-grade class has math, those identified as high ability in math would go to the resource room and work on math at a higher level of depth and complexity than the regular class. Conversely, pulling out the gifted students to go to the resource room and work on critical thinking puzzles without a context that is centered in a content area is not a good use of anyone's time. Often, pull-out programs are difficult to schedule around the activities of several classrooms at the same grade level. Thirty minutes once a week will not greatly affect the learning needs of these students with gifts and talents, thus the pull-out program needs to extend over a significant amount of time each week. The onus for meeting these students' needs when they are not in the resource room falls on the classroom teacher. Educators also do not want to insist students make up all of the work that was missed when they were pulled out. In addition, starting new material or providing a special treat such as a video or an extra recess when students who are gifted are out of the room receiving services is not appropriate.

Delivery of Services

It's clear that there are a variety of effective, evidence-based programming options that will support students with gifts and talents. Two questions emerge as educators examine these choices. First, how do educators select appropriate strategies? Second, how do educators ensure consistent implementation of programming? Standard 5 provides guidance on these matters.

There are five critical components to providing a systematic and continuous delivery of services:

- » comprehensive and coordinated services (5.5 and 5.2),
- » collaboration in schools and with families (5.3),
- » career and talent development pathways (5.7),
- » policies and procedures (5.6), and
- » resources (5.4).

Comprehensive and Coordinated Services

Historically, instruction for students with gifts and talents has been relegated to a gifted specialist down the hall a few times a week. Landrum (2001) noted that this type of service delivery model has potential limitations because it tends to

> operate separately from the regular education programs and serve students on a limited basis. Further, in a traditional service delivery model, the content and focus of the program activities seldom endure any relationship to the general education core curricula or programs of studies, which limits transfer of learning for students. (p. 457)

Educators have recently questioned whether a more comprehensive approach to programming would better support cognitive and affective growth. Cox, Daniel, and Boston (1985) agreed with this notion, contending that students with gifts and talents need school services that address their needs every hour of the school week. Perhaps spurred by recent budgetary challenges, schools have begun to examine how they can develop and deliver thoughtful, multiyear programming for students in new ways. There appear to be two key ideas schools take into consideration when designing comprehensive service systems for students with gifts and talents. The first is defining and providing direction to the curriculum. The second is supporting effective collaboration.

Defining and directing the curriculum. Coleman and Southern (2006) pointed out: "Academic growth and high achievement demand children have experiences in challenging curriculum" (p. 36). Schools must define what this curriculum looks like before they can develop a comprehensive system to deliver services. The Florida Department of Education's (2007) *Frameworks for K–12 Gifted Learners* provides an example. The document defines a challenging, rigorous curriculum, identifying seven goals that are important for students with gifts and talents to accomplish by graduation. They include critically examining knowledge; conducting research; solving real-world problems; assuming leadership roles; and setting and achieving personal, academic, and career goals.

But, according to Coleman and Southern (2006), asking students "to learn again and again what they already know is like asking a child to stay behind" (p. 36). This implies that there must also be direction to the curriculum. VanTassel-Baska (1989) suggested that

> Districts should develop a scope and sequence chart for the gifted that reflects the content adaptations to be made from kindergarten through

12th grade, the progressive development of higher level skills and concepts, the complex ideas students are expected to integrate, and the sophistication of products anticipated. (p. 15)

In other words, it's important to delineate in what sequence students will acquire knowledge and skills so that they are continually learning and growing rather than stagnating. A couple examples serve to illustrate this at both a state level and at a local level.

The Common Core State Standards (CCSS) in English Language Arts and Mathematics were recently designed and have been adopted by 48 states. They are benchmarked—each standard is mapped so educators can guide students in acquiring increasingly complex knowledge and skills from kindergarten through 12th grade. Although these standards were developed with typical grade-level expectations in mind, they may hold promise for student with gifts and talents. Because the CCSS provide progressions across grades, they could remove the ceiling that often now exists for high-ability students. Educators can see what learning comes next, even if it means going beyond grade level. In addition, the CCSS offer opportunities to connect what high-ability students are doing with the core curriculum, thus addressing Landrum's (2001) concern about limiting transfer of learning. The CCSS were not developed specifically for students with gifts and talents, but Connecticut's Wallingford Public Schools' (2000) Gifted and Talented Program Scope and Sequence was. This document outlines a K–8 sequence for developing the following: creative thinking, analytical/critical thinking, problem solving/decision making, self-awareness and self-management, group interaction, and exploration and presentation.

Collaboration. It's evident that beginning with a clear definition of and direction for student learning is important. Once this is established, then educators must determine how the curriculum can be delivered to best match a student's needs. Making these decisions is effectively accomplished using a coordinated approach. This means there is a shared commitment among gifted educators, general educators, special educators, and related professionals (such as school counselors, school psychologists, and social workers) to provide service. Leonard and Leonard (2003) noted: "Building organizational capacity through collegial interaction in schools has become prominent in much of the literature on education reform and school improvement" (para. 2). Ward and Landrum (1994) explained that this is because collaboration is flexible, effective, and efficient. NAGC expanded on the benefits of collegiality. The organization noted:

Collaborative environments foster communication, cooperation, and shared responsibility for gifted and general education students among all school staff, and encourages [*sic*] communication and cooperation among educators. Through collaborative efforts, teachers share their expertise and insights as they plan for their students, regardless of the nature of the program in which they specialize. Collaboration enhances trust and understanding among fields of education, helps promote connections between services in all education fields, helps develop more positive attitudes toward gifted education, and increases opportunities for students. (NAGC, 1998, para. 5)

Collaboration among staff often plays a prominent role in Response to Intervention (RtI) frameworks, the most common systems model currently used, which may hold promise for meeting the needs of students with gifts and talents. Although not a programming option, RtI provides a system for educators to make decisions about which programming opportunities will help students to continue to develop. Collaboration occurs in both making these decisions and in actual service delivery. Examples from two states, Montana and Wisconsin, and from Oak Hills School District in Ohio demonstrate how collaboration is incorporated into RtI. The Montana Office of Public Instruction (2009) included collaboration as one of the eight nonnegotiable essential components of RtI (see Figure 7.1). It noted that ongoing collaboration among educators is part of an interrelated process, as reflected in their motto of "all educators for **all** students."

The Wisconsin Department of Public Instruction also highlighted collaboration in its visual representation of RtI (see Figure 7.2). It is one of three key components, along with high-quality instruction and balanced assessment, of an effective RtI system.

Finally, Oak Hills School District in Ohio acknowledges the importance of collaboration in its RtI framework (see Figure 7.3). It believes that systems-level capacity and support (i.e., comprehensive and coordinated services) are created when a collaborative problem-solving process involving administrators, school psychologists, school counselors, general education teachers, special education teachers, gifted intervention specialists, related service staff, and parents is used to meet student needs.

As evident in the Oak Hills model, collaboration is not limited to school staff. It also includes families and the community. Olszewski-Kubilius and Grant (1994) pointed out, "The greater the number of links among the worlds of home and school and the other microsystems, the more powerful they are in influencing individual development" (p. 186). They referred to these as social networks and added that they contain:

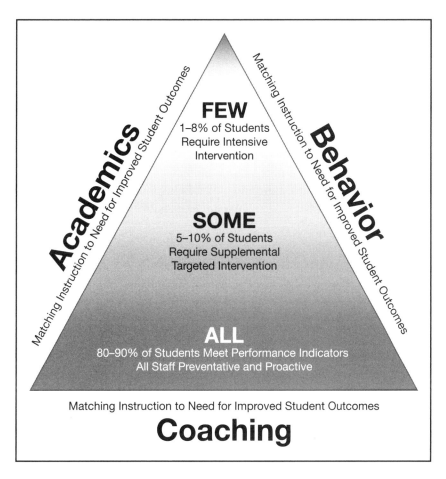

Inside the triangle:

FEW
1–8% of Students
Require Intensive
Intervention

SOME
5–10% of Students
Require Supplemental
Targeted Intervention

ALL
80–90% of Students Meet Performance Indicators
All Staff Preventative and Proactive

Left side: Academics — Matching Instruction to Need for Improved Student Outcomes

Right side: Behavior — Matching Instruction to Need for Improved Student Outcomes

Matching Instruction to Need for Improved Student Outcomes
Coaching

Figure 7.1. Montana's three tiers of instruction. From Montana Office of Public Instruction (2009).

> teachers, parents, extended family members, coaches, church and community leaders, and friends who sustain the child's physical and emotional well-being. Optimal social networks give children contacts with different individuals in different roles who could attend to particular abilities and skills and provide specialized relationships and support. (Olszewski-Kubilius & Grant, 1994, p. 188)

Colorado's RtI framework (see Figure 7.4) emphasizes the importance of collaboration with family and community. It

> is surrounded by "Family and Community" to illustrate the understanding that the education of the child goes beyond the walls of our schools into the homes and communities of our students and to

Figure 7.2. Wisconsin's visual representation of RtI. From Wisconsin Department of Public Instruction (2010).

emphasize the importance of partnerships with family and community to support student success. (Colorado Department of Education, n.d.a., para. 2)

Parents and other family members often can provide unique perspectives on the abilities of their children. They frequently recognize and nurture talent at an early age before students even enter school. Community institutions and organizations can provide support in the form of supplemental services such as educational programs, youth groups, and psychological services. For these reasons, educators should engage families and the community in identifying student needs, planning and evaluating programming opportunities, and advocating for students.

Career and Talent Development Pathways

Collaboration to support growth in academic and affective domains is incomplete without considering how students' strengths, interests, and values might contribute to developing their talent areas and to making career decisions. Teachers are important partners in helping students decide on career pathways because they convey attitudes and provide content-specific informa-

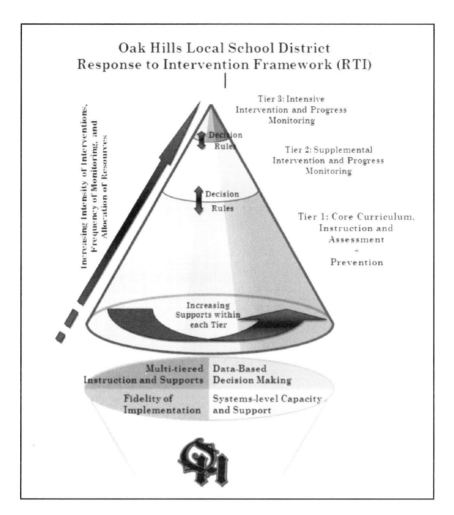

Figure 7.3. Oak Hills School District's RtI framework. From Oak Hills School Disctrict (n.d.).

tion (Coleman & Cross, 2005). School counselors, though, often play a critical role in this area because they are already active in facilitating career exploration and college searches and applications.

Wood (2009) suggested, however, that students with gifts and talents may have unique needs to consider. She noted that they often wonder "how their talent fits with a future career and how they make decisions in light of their many abilities and the diverse options and choices open to them" (Wood, 2009, p. 34). Students may need help narrowing their interests. Wood argued:

> a priority for school counselors is to help gifted students understand
> that career planning is a life-long process and is an extension of their

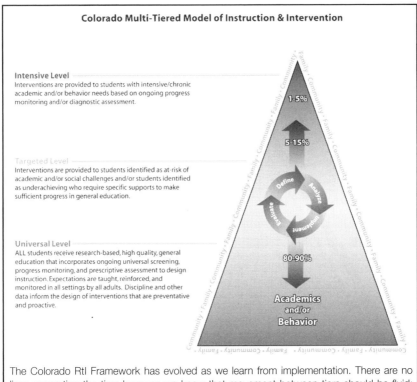

Figure 7.4. Colorado multi-tiered model of instruction and intervention. From Colorado Department of Education (n.d.b.).

individual identities, encompassing not only academics, but also an interaction of values, talent, personality, social trends, and lifestyle . . . School counselors can facilitate this process by providing gifted students with information through multiple written and online sources, and the application of that information through the use of decision-making models, cost-benefit analyses, self-reflection, and value and career inventories. (p. 34)

Wood (2009) noted that counselors might consider using small groups, individual counseling, or classroom guidance activities to provide this information. The author encouraged professionals to be proactive in their outreach to high-performing students, as they sometimes have the misconception that school counselors are there to serve those with problems. Greene (2006) added that counselors should also be aware that they might need to adjust the timing, pace, complexity, and intensity of the activities to better suit the advanced cognitive levels and/or unique internal and external issues of students with gifts and talents.

Schools should also consider mentorships, internships, and vocational programming as part of their approach to career and talent development. Maxwell (2007) reported that a variety of qualitative and case studies supports the value and success of mentorship programs, including the impact on gifted women. Mentorships, shadowing, internships, and volunteering provide opportunities for students to connect with role models, resulting in multiple benefits. These include exposure to career options and opportunities to develop an advanced or expert level of knowledge or skill. For schools without easy access to mentors, biographies of people in areas of student interest can fill the gap (Greene, 2006; Maxwell, 2007).

Policies and Procedures

To provide a comprehensive, coordinated delivery of services and thus promote student growth, schools must have clear policies and procedures in place to guide gifted education. In fact, Brown, Avery, and VanTassel-Baska (2003) pointed out that strong policy is a basic foundation of comprehensive gifted program development. They found that the policy for identifying students' needs is often strong, but that policies related to curriculum, program, and service provisions often need strengthening. As a result, they suggested giving particular attention to these areas, including details on grouping arrangements, differentiation methods, and options for acceleration, with special attention to counseling and guidance services. The authors added that specific policies regarding weighted grades, Advanced Placement (AP), testing out of standards, and dual enrollment are also relevant to include.

Resources

Although policy helps ensure a seamless delivery of services, it also "creates the rules and standards by which scarce resources are allocated to meet almost unlimited social needs" (Gallagher, 1994, p. 337). Educational institutions are not exempted from this competition for resources. The current reform movement focuses on bringing all students to a minimal level of proficiency and uses high-stakes testing and standards-based accountability systems to achieve that goal. In the minds of many, this concentrates resources to remediate those that are "falling behind" and takes away the ability to "'do the right thing' by gifted students" (Scot et al., 2009, p. 50). Students with gifts and talents have specialized needs. In order to support their continued cognitive, creative, and affective growth, adequate resources must be provided. This includes staff time, funds, and administrative support.

Two Programming Examples

Levels of Services Model

Over the past decade, some school districts have turned their attention to a model that clarifies the variety of options open to students through gifted programming and serves as a communication tool to the public. The Levels of Service Model (LoS) (Treffinger et al., 2004), grounded in the idea of talent development, integrates gifted services with the entire school population (see Figure 7.5).

For example, Pleasant View School District, an inner-ring suburban district of 4,800 students, is one such district that has used the LoS model. Located in a state where state funding goes with the student, Pleasant View must compete with neighboring districts for that available revenue by offering comprehensive programs for gifted students. Using the LoS model, district personnel were able to clearly detail programming options and provide the public with an understandable graphic representing the program's complexity (see Figure 7.6).

Level One. Level One services address all students. During the past 3 years, the Pleasant View leadership embarked on a journey to personalize learning for all students. The initial step was to implement district-wide professional development focused on differentiated instruction. All staff were released from their classrooms and duties to attend 2 days of training on practices employed in a differentiated classroom. Additional personalized professional development is provided with late start or early release days. Other professional development opportunities include developing differentiated activities through the Professional Development Learning Academy scheduled during after-school hours during which teachers are developing a growing data bank of differentiated learning activities following a lesson plan template provided as a guide.

Level Two. Level Two provides for many students but not all. Honors classes begin in middle school. Specific criteria have been developed to guide teachers in differentiating the Honors classes from the regular classes. Pace and depth of learning is the focus for the teachers as they implement the learning experiences. AP coursework is available through 12 course offerings. Many

Level I. Services for ALL Students
Providing foundational skills and tools "Discovering and Building"
Level II. Services for MANY Students Engaging and verifying interests "Curious and Exploring"
Level III. Services for SOME Students Meeting the need for alternative opportunities "Enthusiastic and Performing"
Level IV. Services for a FEW Students Responding to blossoming expertise and the need for highly individualized services "Passionate and Soaring"

Figure 7.5. Levels of Service model.

Level I. Services for ALL Students
Differentiation, Critical and Creative Thinking
Level II. Services for MANY Students Honors Classes, AP Classes, CIS Classes
Level III. Services for SOME Students Acceleration, Clustering, AP Classes, CIS Classes, Proactive Counseling
Level IV. Services for a FEW Students Early Entrance to Kindergarten, Cluster Program, Proactive Counseling, Early Graduation, Credit for Prior Learning, Mentor Connection, Lighthouse Program

Figure 7.6. Model school district: Specific Levels of Service model.

students experience a similar pathway beginning the ninth-grade year with AP Human Geography and Honors classes across language arts and the sciences. Each year, more AP options are open to students, including AP Physics, AP Chemistry, AP Calculus, and AP English Literature and Language. College in the Schools (CIS) is a college-level course taught by approved local staff. Spanish IV CIS is offered to students interested in expanding their depth of learning and earning college credit from a local university.

Level Three. Level Three provides opportunities for some students. Clustering begins in second grade. Teachers are supported by a gifted services coordinator who plans regular professional development to support the teachers in providing the "instead of's." Those learning experiences planned are differentiated in nature. Typically 3–10 students are placed in the cluster. This arrangement provides a targeted group and an opportunity for like minds to interact.

Accelerated math begins in middle school and provides a fast-paced experience to allow some students to meet their high school requirements prior to entering high school and opens the door for advanced math classes in their future. AP Calculus AB and BC along with AP Statistics provide additional options. An Honors science class is offered in the middle school and the pathway continues through high school with Honors Biology, Honors Physics, and Honors Chemistry, followed by AP Biology, AP Physics, and AP Chemistry.

Proactive counseling begins in the middle school focused on skill building, leadership training, and relationship building. Students meet with the gifted resources teacher. At the high school, the identified gifted students continue to meet in small groups and as individuals with the gifted services coordinator. Guidance in course selection, college application assistance, and support for negotiating with teachers is part of the experience.

Level Four. Level Four provides opportunities for a few students. In the spring, district staff open up screening for students whose families are considering early entrance to kindergarten. Through multiple screenings, a small number of students are recognized as gifted and are enrolled in kindergarten early. The cluster program may or may not serve those students, but typically those entered early require accelerated and enriched programming options throughout their school experience.

Acceleration is part of the experience for a few individuals. Grade skipping, concurrent enrollment, and telescoping have been employed. Each year, a handful of middle school students are bussed to the high school for advanced math. Credit for prior learning can be attained through communication and assessment. Students have earned credit through this process in world language, math, and the social sciences. Curriculum-based assessment, formative assessments, and teacher evaluations are combined to determine effectiveness of the intervention and to determine further actions.

The Lighthouse Program

The Lighthouse Program, a school within the school in Minnesota, serves as an example of another model that attempts to match its practices with the 2010 NAGC Pre-K–Grade 12 Gifted Programming Standards.

Origins. The Lighthouse Program emerged from demands of parents who had given up on public and private school and were no longer willing or felt capable of meeting their gifted children's needs in a homeschool setting. Highly gifted students are an underserved population. They are underserved by the school calendar that says students must be 5 years old to start school in September. They are underserved by grade-level assigned curriculum that targets the middle. They are underserved by the preservice teacher preparation training that ignores the nature and needs of the highly gifted (Colangelo et al., 2004).

Program structure. A significant design element of the program is the lack of designated grade levels. The Lighthouse Program accepts the natural curiosity of young minds and nurtures it through curriculum, instruction, and assessment that better supports the intrinsic nature of the learner. Grade level is determined by accomplishment, not age. Advancement is dependent on meeting high expectations, but the rate in which the goals are reached is dependent on the nature of the student. Content is grounded in essential concepts and evolves from students' questions. Assessments in this program evolve from the tasks students undertake. Feedback on performance is specific and informative and provides direction for future learning. Students are self-directed, immersed in an environment rich in resources; the purpose of each task is clearly articulated.

The application process. As the program grew, staff formalized an identification process to delineate the kind of students who were good candidates and to describe the nature of the program. The first step is for families to meet with the program director to gain a deeper understanding of the workings of the Lighthouse Program and tour the facility. Following the meeting, the parents wishing to continue the application process would schedule a day for their child to spend in the Lighthouse Program. If the families choose to then continue the process, an interview date is scheduled for the candidate to share with the selection team a portfolio that reflects him or her as a learner. It allows the selection team to rely on multiple criteria to inform their decision making (see 2.1.1–2.3.3).

The multiage setting. This multiage setting has observable benefits: Big kids model for little kids. Little kids inspire big kids. Students are connected with their intellectual peers. For example, an 8-year-old student's initial presentation is part of the Book Challenge he has chosen. He tells the story using a free downloaded animation tool called Scratch. In his audience are 12–15-year-olds. They provide their feedback to the presenter, but they are also planning their next presentation. Five days later and over the next 2 weeks that follow, the student shares performances in which Scratch is employed to progressively more complex levels.

The cognitive domain. At the core of the curriculum is a focus on depth, complexity, and choice (VanTassel-Baska, 1989, 2005). Inquiry learning, which begins with the students' questions, is grounded in student choice. That complex, trans-disciplinary learning demands the application of critical and creative thinking skills. Students are expected to write daily and to read. The opportunity to work with experts, learn their practices, and apply that learning to new challenges provides the framework and motivation. The Lighthouse Program imbeds competitions as part of the daily experience. Kids are expected to participate in at least one competition per year. They choose from History Day, Inventors' Fair, Destination Imagination, Future Problem Solving Program, Robotics League, Young Authors, and Stock Market Game, among others. The students have been successful in a number of the events (see 3.5, 4.2, 4.5).

The affective domain. At the beginning of the school year, the Lighthouse Program community attends an off-campus, 3-day, 2-night experience focused on building community and providing physically challenging experiences focused on leadership skills, self-concept, and self-esteem. Ongoing small-group and one-on-one conferences are a daily event. Often, parents and facilitators complete a Lighthouse Program Personal Plan (LP3). The LP3 meeting provides the student, parents, and facilitators a commonly understood learning plan for the student (see 4.1.1–4.1.5, 4.2.1–4.3.3).

The physical domain. Physical education is part of the daily experience throughout the school year. The Lighthouse Program has partnered with a physical education teacher who serves the program 2 hours daily. Kids are grouped by size and ability (see 4.2.1–4.3.3).

Program evaluation. Program evaluation has been frequent and ongoing (see 2.5.1–2.6.3). The selection process has been monitored and revised, curriculum has been improved, and various aspects of the program have been enhanced as a result. Staff members continue to examine resources employed to carry out their work.

Programming for gifted students comes in a variety of options. No one program can serve the differences recognized in gifted populations, and programs can look comprehensive and strong on paper. In the end, the fidelity to the model is best measured by what occurs in each classroom. Teachers are challenged every day to meet the needs of all students. Ongoing professional development and teachers' commitment to serving these students are critical to successful implementation any programming option.

Table 7.1 presents a partially completed example of an assessment tool used to assist schools and school personnel to evaluate the degree to which their programs and programming options adhere to the standards. The chart allows those who are completing it to choose ways to more closely align to the standards while identifying avenues for improvement. The determining factor is that desired student outcomes are evident.

Conclusion

Standard 5, Programming, of the NAGC Pre-K–Grade 12 Gifted Programming Standards underscores the need for educators to use empirical evidence when seeking to understand the cognitive, affective, and creative needs of learners with gifts and talents. Understanding these needs from a student outcomes perspective allows educators to match learner needs with appropriate programming options. No matter which practice educators may choose to use for a specific learner or group of learners, teachers must keep in mind that no one practice works for every student. Some learners may need multiple accommodations, and others may just need a few simple modifications to the general curriculum for challenging, meaningful learning to occur. To enhance student outcomes at a level commensurate to their needs, some learners may need access to material at a faster pace or at a higher level of complexity. Others may require in-school and out-of-school enrichment opportunities or specific individualized internships or mentorships. In summary, to ensure that specific, measurable student outcomes are attained, educators must have expertise in gathering these data and systematically using them in collaboration with other educators, parents, and community members to "develop, implement, and effectively manage comprehensive services for students with a variety of gifts and talents" (NAGC, 2010, p. 12).

Table 7.1

Assessment Tool: Standard 5: Programming

Description: Educators are aware of empirical evidence regarding (a) the cognitive, creative, and affective development of learners with gifts and talents and (b) programming that meets their concomitant needs. Educators use this expertise systematically and collaboratively to develop, implement, and effectively manage comprehensive services for students with a variety of gifts and talents to ensure specific student outcomes.

Student Outcomes	Evidence-Based Practice	Current Evidence of Compliance	Evidence of Desired Student Outcomes	Areas for Improvement
5.1. Variety of Programming. Students with gifts and talents participate in a variety of evidence-based programming options that enhance performance in cognitive and affective areas.	5.1.1. Educators regularly use multiple alternative approaches to accelerate learning.	There is an acceleration policy that allows grade skipping and subject skipping.	Twenty percent of all identified students have been accelerated by early entrance to kindergarten, subject skipping, or grade skipping. All accelerated students are making appropriate progress as evidenced by out-of-level testing.	Revisit and refine acceleration policy to include other forms of acceleration.
	5.1.2. Educators regularly use enrichment options to extend and deepen learning opportunities within and outside of the school setting.	There are afterschool, summer, and Saturday enrichment classes; 75% of teachers in grades 3–8 enrich the curriculum on a daily basis.	Seventy percent of all identified students in pre-K–12 participate in afterschool, Saturday, or summer enrichment.	Provide opportunities for all teachers to gain the knowledge and skills necessary for enrichment to occur pre-K–12; administration needs to set the tone that enrichment is expected at all levels and provide support for teachers as they seek to meet this expectation.
	5.1.3. Educators regularly use multiple forms of grouping, including clusters, resource rooms, special classes, or special schools.	Cluster grouping occurs at pre-K–5; resource room is available pre-K–12 for self-selected projects and is staffed during school hours.	Only 20% of students in the cluster groups are making appropriate academic progress; only grades 3–5 teachers provide a differentiated curriculum to those in the clusters.	Teachers with cluster groups need training to gain the knowledge and skills necessary to work with cluster groups.
	5.1.4. Educators regularly use individualized learning options such as mentorships, internships, online courses, and independent study.	Teachers in 7–12 offer individualized learning options.	All students in individualized options are progressing commensurate to their needs as evidenced by journals, performance assessments, and evaluations by supervisors.	Individualized options opportunities need to be arranged for all grade levels.
	5.1.5. Educators regularly use current technologies, including online learning options and assistive technologies to enhance access to high-level programming.	All students in pre-K–12 have laptop computers; other technology is available.	There is no evidence that technology is being used; no assessments have been used to document progress. Two students are taking an advanced class online. There is no measure of their progress.	Teachers need opportunities to gain the knowledge and skills necessary to enable them to provide access to current technologies to enhance advanced learning. They need information about opportunities for advanced online learning and how course credit can be earned.
	5.1.6. Administrators demonstrate support for gifted programs through equitable allocation of resources and demonstrated willingness to ensure that learners with gifts and talents receive appropriate educational services.	A grant is provided by the state for funding for gifted services based on the number of identified students. The majority of the money is used for the coordinator's salary.	All students identified as gifted are not making appropriate progress; there are deficiencies in the provisions of services.	The administration needs to seek ways and means to provide for the coordinator's salary from another source and consider using the grant to provided materials and training that will enhance the performance of advanced students pre-K–12.

NAGC Pre-K–Grade 12 Gifted Education Programming Standards

Student Outcomes	Evidence-Based Practice	Current Evidence of Compliance	Evidence of Desired Student Outcomes	Areas for Improvement
5.2. Coordinated Services. Students with gifts and talents demonstrate progress as a result of the shared commitment and coordinated services of gifted education, general education, special education, and related professional services, such as school counselors, school psychologists, and social workers.	5.2.1. Educators in gifted, general, and special education programs, as well as those in specialized areas, collaboratively plan, develop, and implement services for learners with gifts and talents.			
5.3. Collaboration. Students with gifts and talents' learning is enhanced by regular collaboration among families, community, and the school.	5.3.1. Educators regularly engage families and community members for planning, programming, evaluating, and advocating.			
5.4. Resources. Students with gifts and talents participate in gifted education programming that is adequately funded to meet student needs and program goals.	5.4.1. Administrators track expenditures at the school level to verify appropriate and sufficient funding for gifted programming and services.			
5.5. Comprehensiveness. Students with gifts and talents develop their potential through comprehensive, aligned programming and services.	5.5.1. Educators develop thoughtful, multi-year program plans in relevant student talent areas, pre-K-12.			
5.6. Policies and Procedures. Students with gifts and talents participate in regular and gifted education programs that are guided by clear policies and procedures that provide for their advanced learning needs (e.g., early entrance, acceleration, credit in lieu of enrollment).	5.6.1. Educators create policies and procedures to guide and sustain all components of the program, including assessment, identification, acceleration practices, and grouping practices, that is built on an evidence-based foundation in gifted education.			
5.7. Career Pathways. Students with gifts and talents identify future career goals and the talent development pathways to reach those goals.	5.7.1. Educators provide professional guidance and counseling for individual student strengths, interests, and values. 5.7.2. Educators facilitate mentorships, internships, and vocational programming experiences that match student interests and aptitudes.			

References

Adams, C. M. (2006). Articulating gifted education program goals. In J. Purcell & R. Eckert (Eds.), *Designing services and programs for high ability learners: A guidebook for gifted education* (pp. 62–72). Thousand Oaks, CA: Corwin Press.

Adams, C. M. (2009). Waiting for Santa Clause. *Gifted Child Quarterly, 53,* 272–273.

Adams, C. M., & Boswell, C. A. (2012). *Effective practices for gifted students from underserved populations.* Waco, TX: Prufrock Press.

Adams, C. M., & Pierce, R. L. (2006). *Differentiating instruction: A practical guide to tiering lessons in the elementary grades.* Waco, TX: Prufrock Press.

Brown, E., Avery, L., & VanTassel-Baska, J. (2003). *Gifted policy analysis study for the Ohio Department of Education.* Williamsburg, VA: The Center for Gifted Education.

Brulles, D. (2005). *An examination and critical analysis of cluster grouping gifted students in an elementary school* (Unpublished doctoral dissertation). Arizona State University, Phoenix, AZ.

Callahan, C. M. (2009). A family of identification myths: Your sample must be the same as the population. There is a "silver bullet" in identification. There must be "winners" and "losers" in identification and programming. *Gifted Child Quarterly, 53,* 239–241.

Colangelo, N., Assouline, S. G., & Gross, M. U. M. (2004). *A nation deceived: How schools hold back America's brightest students* (Vol. 1). Iowa City: The University of Iowa, The Connie Belin & Jacqueline N. Blank International Center for Gifted Education and Talent Development.

Coleman, L., & Cross, T. L. (2005). *Being gifted in school: An introduction to development, guidance, and teaching.* Waco, TX: Prufrock Press.

Coleman, L. J., & Southern, W. T. (2006). Bringing the potential of underserved children to the threshold of talent development. *Gifted Child Today, 29*(3), 35–39.

Colorado Department of Education. (n.d.a.). *Learn about RtI.* Retrieved from http://www.cde.state.co.us/RtI/LearnAboutRtI.htm

Colorado Department of Education. (n.d.b.). *Response to intervention: A framework for educational reform.* Retrieved from http://www.cde.state.co.us/RtI/downloads/PowerPoint/LeadershipTraining.ppt

Cox, J., Daniel, N., & Boston, B. O. (1985). *Educating able learners: Programs and promising practices.* Austin: University of Texas.

Delcourt, M. A. B., Cornell, D. G., & Goldberg, M. D. (2007). Cognitive and affective learning outcomes of gifted elementary school students. *Gifted Child Quarterly, 51,* 359–381.

Delcourt, M. A. B., & Evans, K. (1994). *Qualitative extension of the learning outcomes study* (Report No. RM94110). Storrs: University of Connecticut, The National Research Center on the Gifted and Talented.

Delcourt, M. A. B., Loyd, B. H., Cornell, D. G., & Goldberg, M. D. (1994). *Evaluation of the effects of programming arrangements on student learning outcomes.* Storrs: University of Connecticut, The National Research Center on the Gifted and Talented.

Florida Department of Education. (2007). *Florida's frameworks for K–12 gifted learners.* Retrieved from http://etc.usf.edu/flstandards/sss/frameworks.pdf

Gagné, F. (1995). From giftedness to talent: A developmental model and its impact on the language of the field. *Roeper Review, 18,* 103–111.

Gallagher, J. J. (1994). *Policy designed for diversity: New initiatives for children with disabilities.* In D. Bryant & M. Graham (Eds.), *Implementing early interventions* (pp. 336–350). New York, NY: Guilford.

Gavin, M. K., Casa, T. M., Adelson, J. L., Carroll, S. R., & Sheffield, L. J. (2009). The impact of advanced curriculum on the achievement of mathematically promising elementary students. *Gifted Child Quarterly, 53,* 188–202.

Gentry, M., & MacDougall, J. (2010). Total school cluster grouping: Model, research, and practice. In J. S. Renzulli (Ed.), *Systems and models in gifted education* (2nd ed.). Mansfield Center, CT: Creative Learning Press.

Gentry, M., & Mann, R. L. (2008). *Total school cluster grouping & differentiation: A comprehensive, research-based plan for raising student achievement & improving teacher practices.* Mansfield Center, CT: Creative Learning Press.

Gentry, M., & Owen, S. V. (1999). An investigation of total school flexible cluster grouping on identification, achievement, and classroom practices. *Gifted Child Quarterly, 43,* 224–243.

Greene, M. J. (2006). Helping build lives: Career and life development of gifted and talented students. *Professional School Counseling, 10,* 34–42.

Institute for Research and Policy on Acceleration. (2009). *Guidelines for developing an academic acceleration policy.* Iowa City, IA: Author.

Johnsen, S. K., & Johnson, K. (2007). *Independent study program* (2nd ed.). Waco, TX: Prufrock Press.

Johnsen, S. K., VanTassel-Baska, J. L., & Robinson, A. (2008). *Using the national gifted education standards for university preparation programs.* Thousand Oaks, CA: Corwin Press.

Kolloff, P. B. (2003). State-supported residential high schools. In N. Colangelo & G. A. Davis (Eds.), *Handbook of gifted education* (3rd ed., pp. 238–246). Boston, MA: Allyn & Bacon.

Kulik, J. A. (1992). *An analysis of the research on ability grouping: Historical and contemporary perspectives.* Storrs: University of Connecticut, The National Research Center on the Gifted and Talented.

Kulik, J. A., & Kulik, C.-L. C. (1992). Meta-analytic findings on grouping programs. *Gifted Child Quarterly, 36,* 73–77.

Landrum, M. S. (2001). Resource consultation and collaboration in gifted education. *Psychology in the Schools, 38,* 457–466.

Leonard, L., & Leonard, P. (2003). The continuing trouble with collaboration: Teachers talk. *Current Issues in Education*, *6*(15). Retrieved from http://cie.ed.asu.edu/volume6/number1

Loveless, T. (2008). *High-achieving students in the era of No Child Left Behind*. Retrieved from http://www.brookings.edu/reports/2008/0618_nclb_loveless.aspx

Lubinski, D., & Benbow, C. P. (2006). Study of Mathematically Precocious Youth after 35 years: Uncovering antecedents for the development of math-science expertise. *Perspectives on Psychological Science, 1,* 316–345.

Maxwell, M. (2007). Career counseling is personal counseling: A constructivist approach to nurturing the development of gifted female adolescents. *Career Development Quarterly, 55,* 206–224.

Montana Office of Public Instruction. (2009). *Response to intervention and gifted and talented education.* Retrieved from http://www.opi.mt.gov/PDF/Gifted/RtI_GTFramework.pdf

National Association for Gifted Children. (1998). *Position statement: Collaboration between gifted and general education programs.* Retrieved from http://nagc.org/index.aspx?id=462

National Association for Gifted Children. (2010a). *About NAGC positions.* Retrieved from http://www.nagc.org/uploadedFiles/About_NAGC/Redefining%20Giftedness%20for%20a%20New%20Century.pdf

National Association for Gifted Children. (2010b). *NAGC pre-K–grade 12 gifted programming standards: A blueprint for quality gifted education.* Washington, DC: Author.

No Child Left Behind Act, 20 U.S.C. §6301 (2001).

Oak Hills School District. (n.d.). *Oak Hills Local School District Response to Intervention framework (RTI).* Unpublished manuscript.

Olszewski-Kubilius, P., & Grant, B. (1994). Social support systems and the disadvantaged gifted: A framework for developing programs and services. *Roeper Review, 17,* 186–191.

Pierce, R. L., Cassady, J. C., Adams, C. M., Speirs Neumeister, K. L., Dixon, F. A., & Cross, T. L. (2011). The effects of clustering and curriculum development on gifted learners' math achievement. *Journal for the Education of the Gifted, 34,* 569–694.

Purcell, J. H., & Eckert, R. D. (2006). *Designing services and programs for high ability students.* Thousand Oaks, CA: Corwin Press.

Renzulli, J. S. (1986). The three-ring conception of giftedness: A developmental model for creative productivity. In R. J. Sternberg & J. Davidson (Eds.), *Conceptions of giftedness* (pp. 53–92). New York, NY: Cambridge University Press.

Renzulli, J. S. & Reis, S. M. (2008). *Enriching curriculum for all students* (2nd ed.). Thousand Oaks, CA: Corwin Press.

Roberts, J. L. (2005). *Enrichment opportunities for gifted learners.* Waco, TX: Prufrock Press.

Robinson, A. (2009). Examining the ostrich: Gifted services do not cure a sick program. *Gifted Child Quarterly, 53,* 259–261.

Rogers, K. (1991). *The relationship of grouping practices to the education of the gifted and talented learner.* Storrs: University of Connecticut, The National Research Center on the Gifted and Talented.

Rogers, K. (2001). *Re-forming gifted education: How parents and teachers can match the program to the child.* Scottsdale, AZ: Gifted Psychology Press.

Rogers, K. B. (2006). *A menu of options for grouping gifted students.* Waco, TX: Prufrock Press.

Rogers, K. B. (2007). Lessons learned about educating the gifted and talented: A synthesis of research on educational practice. *Gifted Child Quarterly, 51,* 382–396.

Schuler, P. (1997, Winter). Cluster grouping coast to coast. *The National Research Center on the Gifted and Talented Newsletter.* Retrieved from http://www.gifted.uconn.edu/nrcgt/newsletter/winter97/wintr974.html

Scot, T. P., Callahan, C. M., & Urquhart, J. (2009). Paint-by-number teachers and cookie-cutter students: The unintended effects of high-stakes testing on the education of gifted students. *Roeper Review, 31,* 40–52.

Stanley, J. C. (1980). On educating the gifted. *Educational Researcher, 9*(3), 8–13.

Swiatek, M., & Lupkowski-Shoplik, A. (2003). Elementary and middle school student participation in gifted programs: Are gifted students underserved? *Gifted Child Quarterly, 47,* 118–130.

Terman, L. M. (1922). A new approach to the study of genius. *Psychological Review, 29,* 310–318.

Tieso, C. L. (2005). The effects of grouping practices and curricular adjustments on achievement. *Journal for the Education of the Gifted, 29,* 60–89.

Tomlinson, C. A. (2001). *How to differentiate instruction in mixed ability classrooms* (2nd ed.). Alexandria, VA: ASCD.

Tomlinson, C. A. (2003). *Fulfilling the promise of the differentiated classroom.* Alexandria, VA: ASCD.

Tomlinson, C. A. (2009). The "patch on" approach to programming is effective. *Gifted Child Quarterly, 53,* 254–256.

Treffinger, D. J., Young, G. C., Nassab, C. A., & Wittig, C. (2004). *Talent development: The levels of service approach.* Waco, TX: Prufrock Press.

VanTassel-Baska, J. (1989). Appropriate curriculum for gifted learners. *Educational Leadership, 46*(6), 13–15.

VanTassel-Baska, J. (2005). Gifted programs and services: What are the nonnegotiables? *Theory Into Practice, 44,* 90–97.

VanTassel-Baska, J. (2006). A content analysis of evaluation findings across 20 gifted programs: A clarion call for enhanced gifted program development. *Gifted Child Quarterly, 50,* 199–210.

VanTassel-Baska, J. (2009). Gifted programs should stick out like a sore thumb. *Gifted Child Quarterly, 53,* 266–268.

Wallingford Public Schools. (2000). *Gifted and talented program scope and sequence.* Retrieved from http://www.wallingford.k12.ct.us/uploaded/Curriculum/Gifted_and_Talented_S_&_S_K-12.pdf

Ward, S. B., & Landrum, M. S. (1994). Resource consultation: An alternative service delivery model for gifted education. *Roeper Review, 16,* 276–279.

Wisconsin Department of Public Instruction. (2010). *Wisconsin Response to Intervention: A guiding document.* Retrieved from http://dpi.wi.gov/rti/index.html

Wood, S. (2009). Counseling concerns of gifted and talented adolescents: Implications for school counselors. *Journal of School Counseling, 7,* 1–47.

Chapter 8
The Professional Development Standard in Gifted Education: Creating Priorities

by Sandra N. Kaplan

There are many arguments for and against provisions for teacher training or professional development. The issues appear to center on the attributes that affect the quality of professional development. These attributes have been articulated clearly by Hawley and Valli (1999): coordinating professional development goals and student performance outcomes; integrating professional development into the total school operation; providing collaborative problem solving; defining multiple outcomes for students, including theoretical understandings; providing continuous and ongoing experiences; and ensuring comprehension of the change process. This chapter addresses these characteristics by introducing and discussing the philosophy, purposes, and procedures that need to be considered to plan and implement professional development in gifted education.

Professional Development as a Catalyst for Change: Purposes, Perspectives, Theories, and Research

Professional development serves multiple goals for teachers to affect changes in three areas: their beliefs and attitudes, their classroom practices, and the learning outcomes of their students (Guskey, 2002). Hargreaves (1994) identified a set of factors that foster educational change: listening to teachers' voices, establishing trust for collaborative working conditions, forming structures that enhance the culture to promote interaction and learning, and developing the relationship between purposes and processes for change. Descriptions of teachers as change-makers characterize them as dynamic teachers who draw on specific skills and can organize, inform, collaborate, work for collective action, catalyze, negotiate, and advocate: they are lifelong learners (Rallis & Rossman, 1995). In the *Status Report on Teacher Development in the United States and*

Abroad (Darling-Hammond, Wei, Andree, Richardson, & Orphanos, 2009), the authors defined one of the key findings of their study to include the importance of professional development and stated: "collaborative approaches to professional learning can promote school change that extends beyond individual classrooms" (p. 5).

Changes in teachers' perceptions of giftedness, changes in the social, emotional, and educational demands of the gifted; and changes in classroom environments and practices for the gifted have been the basis for planning and defining the anticipated outcomes of professional development in gifted education. The rationale for differential education for the gifted has also been the rationale to educate teachers to recognize, promote, and sustain the needs for change to educate the gifted. Educating teachers to value these changes requires professional development that acknowledges what constitutes these changes and programs aimed at initiating these changes. Instituting changes requires the skills to understand and respond to opposition, the information to juxtapose new and exciting ideas without compromising either idea, and the realization that changes in practice are dependent on changes in one's dispositions. A single change resulting from educational experiences in gifted education should have a ripple effect on general education in order to directly garner support for gifted education and to indirectly render alternatives for all teachers to accept and apply what was learned in professional development for the gifted to all students. Change as an outcome of professional development must be juxtaposed with a range of educational purposes for professional development.

The purposes for professional development are often clearer to articulate than are the many and varied interpretations of what constitutes appropriate professional development experiences designed to attain these goals. Darling-Hammond and her colleagues (2009) identified the attributes of effective professional learning experiences for teachers as ongoing; connected to practice; focused on student learning; related to specific curriculum content; aligned to school improvement, priorities, and goals; and building strong working relationships. Borko (2004) acknowledged the failure of professional development to achieve its goals and addressed using multiple conceptual perspectives and multiple units of analysis of a situative perspective to identify the key elements of professional development systems and the means by which they can be studied. Elements of a system include (a) the professional development program, (b) teachers who are the learners, (c) facilitators guiding teachers to construct knowledge and practice, and (d) the context in which the professional development takes place (see Figure 8.1).

In an analysis of research describing successful professional development, Hill (2007) recognized the importance of an extensive time frame devoted to

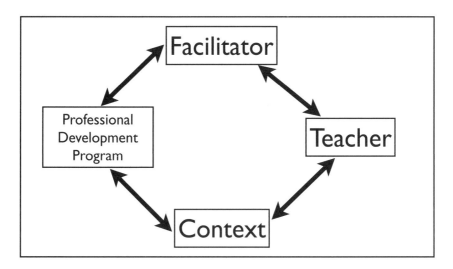

Figure 8.1. Key elements of a professional development system.

the teacher learning experiences, subject-matter-specific instruction and student learning, alignment with and support of school improvement goals, and efforts and emphasis on a scholarly collective community as essential variables to develop professional learning opportunities for teachers. Darling-Hammond and McLaughlin (1995, as cited in National College for School Leadership, 2003) presented the need to focus in-service training on opportunities for teachers to "share what they know, discuss what they want to learn, [and] connect new concepts and strategies to their own unique contexts" (p. 1). Sustained supported opportunities for teacher inquiry, collaboration, reflection, and experimentation connected to the real work of teachers and their students were advocated as the ingredients of effective professional development. Rashid (2000) proposed the specific objective to configure professional development in the same framework as the school-as-community model so that learning opportunities would reflect the total collection of all teachers and their specific needs as educators, provide a key teacher strategy or address individual teachers' needs, allow the teacher to become an action researcher, and use teacher-generated curriculum materials to enhance participants' motivation and "reduce the gap" between trainer and practitioner that can emerge in professional development experiences. In addition, peer pre- and postprofessional development observations and conferences were suggested to support the teachers' transfer of learning from the professional development experience to their classrooms.

Implications from theory and research regarding professional development align with Standard 6: Professional Development of the 2010 NAGC Pre-K–Grade 12 Gifted Programming Standards (see Table 8.1).

Table 8.1
*Key Elements of Professional Development and Their Alignment With the NAGC
Professional Development Standards*

Key Elements of Professional Development From Theory and Research	Examples of Key Elements From the NAGC Professional Development Standards
Ongoing system of professional development experience.	6.1.1: Educators systematically participate in an ongoing, research-supported professional development . . .
Professional development focused on student learning.	6.1.2: . . . addressing environments and instructional activities that encourage students to express diverse characteristics and behaviors that are associated with giftedness. 6.1.5: . . . awareness of organizations and publications relevant to gifted education to promote learning for students with gifts and talents.
Provide a variety of contexts for professional development.	6.3.3: . . . use multiple modes of professional development delivery . . .
Teacher who are learners.	6.3: . . . educators who are life-long learners participating in ongoing professional development . . .
Alignment with school improvement goals.	6.1.3: . . . addressing key issues such as anti-intellectualism and trends in gifted education . . .
Collaboration and collegial support.	6.1.4: Administrators provide human and material resources needed for professional development . . .
Connection to real world of teachers and their classrooms.	6.3.2: . . . [include] regular follow-up, and . . . [seek] evidence of impact on student learning and teacher practice.

Historical Background: Professional Development and Gifted Education

Understanding the historic evolution of professional development for gifted education provides the background to reinforce the importance of teacher training for the present and future. Teacher education as preparation to teach gifted students is a recognized long-standing historic concern in gifted education. In his 1972 report to the Congress of the United States, Marland articulated the mandatory equation between successful programs for the gifted and specialized preparation of teachers for the gifted.

The National/State Leadership Framing Institute on the Gifted and Talented, a federally funded grant established in the 1970s, was charged with promoting education for gifted and talented students by providing professional development for state and local agencies and disseminating publications to support educating teachers and administrators about gifted education. The agency has been credited with stimulating a national awareness and concern for informing educators of the critical needs of the gifted and the teachers who educate them. Provisions for training included national conferences, summer institutes, and workshops that also became the models for other agencies to emulate. Primary features of these training experiences were the balance between current status and perceived proposals for ideal conditions for gifted education and gifted students, presentations of the collective views of current experts in the field, and articulation of the roles anticipated of educators who would be deemed responsible for educating the gifted within classrooms, schools, districts, and state institutions.

Gallagher (1975) discussed the need to emphasize content and pedagogical issues appropriate for continuously providing in-service training opportunities to teachers, consultants, and supervisors of gifted program. "Gifted children have a right to be educated by teachers who are specifically qualified to teach them" (Tannenbaum, 1983, p. 464). Interestingly, this statement parallels the No Child Left Behind Act requirement for highly qualified teachers in general education. In the publication *National Excellence: A Case for Developing America's Talent* (U.S. Department of Education, 1993), the urgency to recognize the education of gifted students is explained. The concomitant emphasis on teacher development noted: "teachers must receive better training in how to teach high level curricula. They need support for providing instruction that challenges all students sufficiently. This will benefit not only students with outstanding talent, but children at every academic level" (U.S. Department of Education, 1993, p. 3).

Expectations to become qualified to teach gifted students center on determining the population that should be educated to teach these students and are predicated on answering the following questions: (a) Should all teachers be expected to acquire the competencies to teach gifted students? (b) What competencies are best aligned to teachers teaching gifted students in different types of environments: homogeneous versus heterogeneous classrooms, pullout or special day classes, and/or within-school and out-of-school programs? and (c) What types of training programs (in-service and/or pre-service) are most appropriate to facilitate the requirements of the various populations of teachers assigned directly or indirectly to teach gifted students? Clark (2008) described the range of experiences for teachers to gain the competencies pertinent to their roles as educators of the gifted: from state- and district-sponsored workshops and conferences, to extensive university courses that award a certificate or degree.

Teachers as Learners: Developing Expertise in Gifted Education

Terminology related to gifted education has obscured the outcomes from training teachers throughout the years. For example, the proliferation of the concept of differentiation as a term applicable to addressing the individual needs of all students has provided the impetus to expand the need for general education teachers to understand and receive training in the education of the gifted. However, the terms *differentiated* and *different curriculum for the gifted* have been assumed to be interchangeable. There is sufficient evidence to recognize that a major outcome of professional development is to clarify the meaning of vocabulary associated with both curriculum and instruction for gifted students. The current introduction of Response to Intervention (RtI) also confounds the issue of terminology and its relationship to train teachers. Historically, even the term gifted has resulted in a lack of clarity among teachers educated in the area of gifted education. The use of language patterns in training is fundamental to providing a comprehensive understanding of gifted education.

The introduction of teachers to the foundational knowledge of gifted education might parallel the information related to *How People Learn* (Donovan, Bransford, & Pellegrino, 2000). Based on differences between expert and novice learners, the authors suggested the importance of organizing information to teach a body of knowledge: use "big ideas" and important concepts to guide understanding in a domain, present "conditionalized" or contextualized information, encourage fluent recognition to problems in the domain, utilize appropriate pedagogical strategies to facilitate understanding of the information, and apply the ability to monitor one's own level of understanding (metacognition). Donovan et al. (2000) further explained the concept of adaptive expertise as individuals who are able to approach new experiences with flexibility and can become lifelong learners. As educators plan the professional development related to gifted education, references to developing teachers as experts could guide decisions about how the basic content or foundations of gifted education can be organized and presented. Table 8.2 is an example of how defining expertise can be used to teach some of the major concepts in a professional development plan for gifted education.

Table 8.2
Defining Expertise to Provide Essential Knowledge

Developing Expertise	Providing Essential Knowledge of Gifted Education
Address "big ideas" and major concepts to introduce basic knowledge in the domain: different versus differentiation.	• Define the characteristics of the gifted. • Demonstrate the differences between regular or basic and differentiated curriculum.
Conduct a debate to facilitate problem solving: What do schools value: the development of intelligence?	• Relate the definitions of intellectualism and intelligence to the goals of gifted education, identification procedures, and the development of differentiated curriculum.
Encourage teachers to become experts.	• Initiate teachers' opportunities to engage in self-selected topic for independent study within a given domain such as identification, curriculum development, program design, and the like.

Preconceptions teachers bring to new learning have ramifications for their achievement. Regardless of the reasons underlying a teacher's participation in professional development, each individual attends the event with preconceptions of giftedness, gifted students, and their learning needs. The range of these conceptions can be professionally and/or personally rooted. For example, the belief that teaching gifted learners is easier or more difficult than teaching other types of learners can inhibit realistic understandings of the nature of giftedness and the role of teachers of the gifted. Presentations that cause participants to confront the prior knowledge they bring to the professional development experience can eliminate or correct misconceptions and allow a foundation for new learning to be built.

Figure 8.2 is a part of a presentation aimed at confronting some of conventional as well as more idiosyncratic portrayals of gifted students. The purpose is to activate the discourse enabling teachers to address their reactions to the behaviors of gifted students.

The use of vignettes also provides a stimulus for teachers to acknowledge their preconceptions and the ramifications of these preconceptions to perceive themselves as teachers of the gifted and their gifted students as learners. Vignettes also reveal the role a teacher must assume to respond effectively to the manifestations of the attributes of gifted students that are referenced in the classic literature describing the gifted and giftedness (see Figure 8.3).

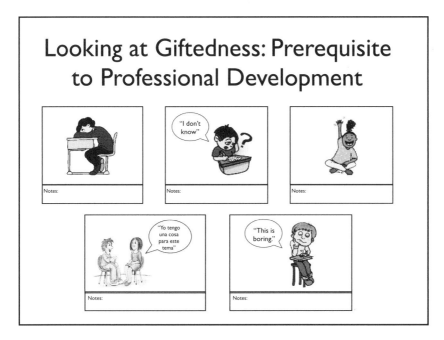

Figure 8.2. Discussing giftedness.

Belinda's Case File	
The teacher carefully reads the full title "gifted" describing Belinda's needs, interests, and abilities.	

Needs	Social adjustment to peers who are gifted to reduce competitiveness with classmates
Interests	• Favors artistic endeavors • Enjoys social studies, specifically Native American history
Abilities	99% math, at grade level in reading

A review of Belinda's behavior in class revealed her constant arrogance with peers. "I can't believe you cannot do that," is a common retort to peers.

Teacher assistance is rebuffed with a shrug and comment: "I do not need your help."

Math work is incomplete and messy. Student complains work is too easy—boring.

Figure 8.3. Using vignettes to define giftedness.

Problems of Practice

The need for professional development has not been questioned; however, the effects of professional development have been questioned. Guskey (1986) stated that disorder, conflict, and criticism historically have characterized staff development. As efforts directed toward school improvement and reforms receive attention, so do the concerns for refining professional development as a means for school improvement. Acknowledging the problems of practice surrounding professional development can become an initial step to reform professional development.

» Professional development opportunities are often perceived dichotomously: as either mandated or voluntary participation, either complying to a specific content and pedagogical set of practices versus encouraging flexibility and creative adaptation of curriculum materials, or either anticipating receiving extrinsic or intrinsic rewards for attendance.

» The relationships between how teachers learn within the context of the professional development experience and how the same teachers teach their students in the context of their classroom often have not been explicitly correlated, resulting in a mismatch between expectations and implementation.

» Professional development programs often omit or disregard the input of the very individuals—the teachers—for whom the programs are designed.

» Facilitators of professional development experiences are sometimes selected for attributes such as presentation style without regard for the significance and value of the presentation style on teacher learning.

» Evaluations of professional development experiences sometimes exonerate the participants from assessing their role as a learner during the professional development and their responsibilities to transfer their learning to their own classroom. Instead, evaluations emphasize satisfaction with respect to items such as the venue, time frame, and abundance of materials distributed during the professional development.

» Knowledge and skills to assess and facilitate the translation of the professional development experiences to the classroom are not always stipulated as integral features of the professional development program.

» Evidence of teacher change as a consequence of participating in professional development is difficult to discern and the sustainability of these changes can be elusive.

» There is a difference between a teacher's internalization and integration of the learning from the professional development experience and the visible yet superficial presentation or showcase of the learning when observing in the teacher's classroom.

» The contemporary overemphasis on cognitive student outcomes related to test scores can obliterate the personal and social student outcomes that can also emerge from the teacher's involvement in professional development activities.

Each general problem of practice stimulates an examination of the issues that act as contributors or inhibitors of successful teacher training experiences. Awareness of the general problems of practice allow for the specific definition and application of experiences to educate teachers for gifted education. Acknowledging the problems of practice provides the backdrop to determine the scope and sequence of professional development experiences for teachers of the gifted (see Table 8.3).

Implications for Professional Development: Planning and Assessing Needs

A set of key words often guides the decisions relevant to planning and implementing professional development: why, what, how, and when. Specifically, these key words are used to frame the questions to articulate the professional development experience: (a) Why is the professional development experience important and vital to the mission, goals, and objectives of gifted education? (b) What specific and general features of the professional development experience affect the teachers' practices and the gifted and talented students' learning? (c) How is the professional development experience enhancing the professional expertise of the educational participants? and (d) When is the optimum timing to schedule the professional development experience? The answers to these questions must be supported by evidence representative of single or a collection of needs-assessment data reflective of teachers, students, parents, and/or community members. To be effective, professional development needs to have a central theme or focus. The focus should be perceived as a goal or set of goals that can be attained through a sequence of professional development experiences over a scheduled time frame. Professional development experiences that are episodic or single disjointed incremental learning experiences do not allow for the development of proficiency. Often, this is due to the fact that such learning experiences provide a one-time offer that excites enthusiasm and interest from the participants that is mistaken for proficiency. The focus can attend to

Table 8.3
Problems of Practice

Problems of Practice	Implications for Professional Development in Gifted Education	Examples
Lack of clarity concerning the intent or goals of the professional development.	Differentiate between general versus specific outcomes derived from attendance.	Expectation for the May 6th professional development is to adapt the XYZ science materials in grades 3–8 to meet the needs of gifted students with specific aptitude in science. Lesson plans will be developed and shared among participants.
Exclusion of teachers in the planning stages of the professional development experiences.	The omission of teachers' involvement in planning the professional development experiences enables them to intellectually disassociate from the experience and exonerates them from making a commitment to utilize in classrooms what has been presented in the professional development.	"We need your voice." Plans for the next professional development program regarding the social-emotional needs of the gifted are being organized. Please rank the topics on the list and return the list to the Human Resource Office by Monday, January 10th so that your voice can be counted in the planning of this event.
Lack of or inconsistent follow-up from professional development does not ensure the practical application of what has been learned to the classroom setting.	Follow-up activities must be scheduled over a period of time so that a one-time intervention does not lead to a misunderstanding of the teacher's proficiency and fidelity to what was presented during the professional development experience. There are many methods to provide follow-up for teachers. Each of these methods must be addressed for its feasibility and sustainability over time.	Needs Assessment Form: As a consequence of your participation in today's workshop, please identify the type of follow-up that would best match your needs to transfer what you learned today to your classroom. • In-classroom demonstration • Videotape analysis of my lesson using the pedagogy learned during this in-service • Conference call to discuss my progress applying the pedagogy • Afterschool consultation with the coordinator of gifted programs to discuss the progress made applying the pedagogy
The presentation style of facilitators during the professional development that allow teachers to be passive learners is noted as a reason professional development can be ineffective.	Contemporary emphasis on teaching and learning that encourages active learning and facilitates the learners' construction of their own learning.	Agenda for today's workshop on inquiry learning for gifted students: 1. Work in the assigned mixed-age-level groups to analyze the lesson set using the Inquiry for Gifted Rubric. 2. "Take a Stand." After watching the demonstration of the inquiry lesson, answer or argue this question: Is/isn't this an appropriate pedagogy to stimulate inquiry with gifted learners? 3. Lesson planning: requires working with a partner to draft a lesson in any discipline that applies the inquiry pedagogy appropriate for gifted learners.

The Professional Development Standard 185

multiple programming standards simultaneously if these standards are clustered or bundled to reinforce a single compatible goal.

A variety of data sources provide the many perspectives that can be used to determine the focus for the professional development experiences. All needs-assessment data should yield information addressing the real versus perceived needs for professional development, differentiating between the negotiable versus the nonnegotiable elements of the professional development, and detailing the immediate or short- versus long-term outcomes expected from the professional development experiences (see Table 8.4).

Establishing the Relationship Between Professional Development and Potential Participants

The disassociation or mismatch existing between the actual professional development experiences and the professionals for whom the experiences have been designed is an ever-present complaint registered by educators. The inclusion of the intended participants as members of the planning committee has ameliorated some of the lack of connection between participants and professional development and heightened the support of the future participants for the professional development experiences. Forming professional development committees analogous to small learning communities charged with the responsibility to design professional development has been presented as a means to bridge participant involvement in the planning stages of professional development. Engaging educators in the task of prioritizing the possible topics to be presented during professional development events is another way that potential participants can be involved in the planning stages.

Providing an array or menu of different purposes and formats for professional development also can forge the relationships between potential participants and professional development experiences. Viewing the various options that are feasible widens educators' spectrum of possibilities from which specific plans for professional development can be selected and designed. Many educators express discontent with professional development experiences offered to them that do not meet their needs. It is also important to share the academic, time, resource, and economic limitations that govern decision making and affect the planning of professional development experiences. This allows potential participants to recognize that decisions regarding professional development experiences are contingent on a variety of controllable and uncontrollable fac-

Table 8.4

Data Sources and Professional Development Needs

Data Source	Examples of the Relationship Between Data and Professional Development Needs
Gifted/talented program: mission statement and goals	Identifying curriculum and instructional areas of omission or weakness
Survey or questionnaire data revealing responses to programmatic features, services, and the like received from educators, parents, and/or students	Defining explicit roles and responsibilities of individuals administering the program
Scores from norm- and criterion-referenced standardized and/or district- and teacher-developed tests	Outlining the relationships between basic and differentiated expectations for teaching and learning
Interview data obtained from teacher, student, and parent focus groups	Analyzing the variances between practices and perceptions of curriculum
Analysis of student work examples	Determining pedagogical and environmental needs to reinforce differentiated student outcomes
Observations of teaching and learning within classrooms containing gifted/talented students	Identifying "spill-over" effect from gifted to general education
Evaluations of previously conducted professional development experiences	Developing observation protocol for classroom visits
Review curriculum and instructional references and materials	Determining relationships between fiscal expenditures and program needs

tors and gives them the opportunity to realize that professional development is based on facts rather than whims of the key decision makers.

There are several methods to launch collective decision making to draft professional development experiences. Both of these methods utilize topical cards and the sorting process (see Figure 8.4).

This continuum provides a means by which topical areas related to gifted educational standards are written on 5 x 5 cards and sorted according to their perceived value for different populations of participants. The cards could define the key areas recommended by VanTassel-Baska (2003) to be included in professional development for general education classroom teachers: diagnostic assessment of students' level of knowledge and appropriate instructional levels, selection of instructional materials, grouping and individualized learning methods, knowledge of acceleration, and problem-centered learning.

Another method used to generate collective responses to what and when various topics should be introduced, reinforced, or extended is shown in Figure 8.5. An analysis of the distribution of the topical cards on the chart provides the

Professional Development Spectrum			
Degree of Value	Barely Important	Somewhat Important	Very Important
Administrators			
General Education Teachers			
Teachers of the Gifted			

Figure 8.4. Professional development spectrum.

Population	Level of Presentation		
	Introduce	Reinforce	Extend
General Education Teachers			
Gifted Education Teachers			
Administrators, Coordinators, Counselors			

Figure 8.5. Determining the program.

basis for determining the needs and levels of input for each audience (see Figure 8.6). The chart is also the vehicle to sequence topics included in the professional development program, the types of facilitators and materials needed for the program, and the expectations for teacher participant performance during and after attendance at the professional development.

Selecting Models for Professional Development

There are numerous professional development models proposed by researchers and theorists. Although each model is organized to accomplish its goals for professional development, each model places different emphasis on the components comprising its structure to illustrate its intentions and uniqueness.

Guskey's Model

The Guskey (2002) model highlights the author's belief that professional development is based on affecting teacher change. Significant to this model is the sequence of how teacher change is manifested. Guskey (2002) asserted that

Population	Level of Presentation		
	Introduce	Reinforce	Extend
General Education Teachers		Principles of Differentiation	Problem-Based Learning
Gifted Education Teachers		Diversity Among Gifted Students	Underachievement Issues
Administrators, Coordinators, Counselors	Non-Traditional Identification Procedures		

Figure 8.6. Example of a program.

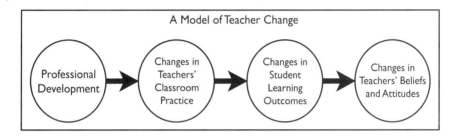

Figure 8.7. A model of teacher change.

teacher change comes after or as a result of successful implementation of practice learned during professional development (see Figure 8.7).

Developmental Model for Participant Involvement

Decisions pertaining to the inclusion of participants in professional development are a constant issue. The decision regarding voluntary versus invitational participation for the professional development opportunities has professional, social, and personal ramifications. There is evidence that institutionally forced or mandated versus personally self-selected attendance in a designated professional development opportunity has differing outcomes for the participants. Experiences with participants have informed a design for deciding which and when teachers could be involved in the professional development process targeted to accomplish a specific goal such as designing and implementing differentiated curriculum or introducing and practicing new pedagogy.

The model is based on the idea of concentric circles of influence. As the initial group of teachers who are involved in a specific goal-oriented professional experience develop proficiency, they communicate and demonstrate their success and intrigue to others, who join them as new participants. An important feature of this type of professional development model is that it has a ripple effect: Each group of participants stimulates awareness of the work it is doing and enlarges the circle of individuals who become aware of and subsequently interested in joining the professional development opportunities. The option to become involved when the teacher perceives the value of training has the potential to increase participation of teachers when their affective filter is lowered and their readiness to learn is respected. This developmental model for professional development parallels the types of concerns educators apply to determine their students' readiness for learning.

Differentiated Model for Professional Development

There is no question that professional development for educators should follow the same educational principles appropriate to educate young learners. The concept of differentiation for educators within the context of the professional development experience is illustrated in Table 8.5. Although it is possible to arrange separate professional development opportunities to meet the varied needs, interests, and abilities of teachers, it is also possible to provide this differentiation within the context of a single professional development opportunity, as Table 8.5 indicates. Primary to the success of a differentiation model for professional development is the need to address the assigned versus self-determined teacher's designation of the self as a novice, conversant, or expert participant.

Differentiated professional development can be organized to accommodate teachers assigned to various program models. Although all teachers of gifted students require exposure and proficiency in similar areas defined by the NAGC programming standards, different degrees of emphasis can be attributed to these standards for teachers in different programmatic structures. Programmatic demands and teachers' needs for training become symbiotically related to determine the scope of professional development. Figure 8.8 exemplifies the possible match between programmatic designs and teachers' needs to develop training experiences.

Differentiating learning experiences to respond to teachers' levels of expertise within the context of professional development can be conducted using this pattern of presentation during the time allocated for the training experience. It should be noted that this pattern is a replica of the type of flexible grouping advocated to teach gifted students within a homogeneous or heterogeneous classroom. It allows for time to work in mixed as well as specific ability and/or interest groups (see Figure 8.9).

Table 8.5

Objectives for the Professional Development: Informing Parents of the Gifted Program and How It Meets the Needs of Students

Novice	Conversant	Expert
Presentation of the alignment of the characteristics of the gifted and the specific elements of the gifted program: grouping, curriculum, and assessment.	Presentation of how general student work examples inform the basic underlying elements of the gifted program and how parents can use children's work examples to discern the outcomes derived from the program participation.	Presentation of how the gifted program facilitates the academic, social, and emotional development of gifted students. Presentation regarding what parents can do to augment the basic underlying elements of the gifted program applying formal and informal methods.

Program Model	Standards-Based Areas of Need	Degree of Emphasis		
		Weak	Some	Strong
Pull-out program	• Grouping • Assessment • Social-emotional needs		X X	 X
Special day class	• Grouping • Assessment • Social-emotional needs		X	 X X
Cluster grouping in the regular or heterogeneous classroom	• Grouping • Assessment • Social-emotional needs			X X X
Afterschool classes	• Grouping • Assessment • Social-emotional needs	X X	 X	

Figure 8.8. Program designs and teachers' needs.

Distance Education Model for Professional Development

The use of technology as a medium to provide professional development has been both credited as beneficial and fraught with skepticism. Advances in technology have reduced some of the skepticism related to the use of online learning as more emphasis is placed on interactive methods of using the technology to provide active participatory learning. Figure 8.10 illustrates a technological delivery system for teaching and learning online and illustrates its potential to design professional development. This three-stage model is based on the current MAT@USC program (2009–2010).

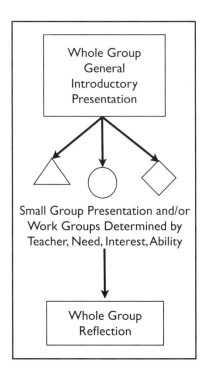

Figure 8.9. Pattern to implement professional development.

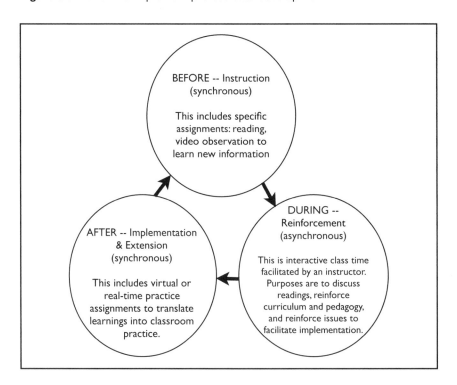

Figure 8.10. Three-stage MAT@USC (2009–2010) model of teacher education.

Online learning experiences have the potential to reduce costs for professional development while still maintaining the opportunities to provide educational experiences to teachers. Often, costs attributed to venue, substitutes, and the like that traditionally have eroded the breadth of professional development available to educators are reduced by online opportunities. Online professional development also affords teachers the opportunities to avail themselves of educational experiences to match personal schedules and needs. Some cautions relative to online learning include the need to ensure that the technology does not obliterate or reduce the learning for which it was designed. In some instances, facilitators have become enamored with the technology and have forgotten, so to speak, its purpose to promote teaching and learning. Another caution is the need to fully orient teacher-users to the norms that guide their successful use of the online program. Such norms include attention to time frames for submission of work and introduction to how to resolve technological problems when they arise.

The Javits Grant Model

The Javits Grant Department of Education (#S206A040072-07): Models of Teaching to Affect Student Achievement awarded to the University of Southern California was the impetus to determine multiple means by which professional development experiences could fulfill the goals of the grant: to develop awareness of the repertoire of models of teaching, their alignment to teaching and learning of content and skills across the disciplines, and their ability to foster learning-to-learn dispositions and behaviors for gifted students (see Figure 8.11).

Although the data indicated that this design did positively affect the education of teachers of the gifted, there were some unintended yet vital questions about teacher learning that emerged from implementing the model: (a) When do teacher support strategies foster teacher dependence rather than encourage teacher independence in the practice and employment of the skills taught during professional development? and (b) What behaviors encourage the translation of being a successful curriculum consumer and user to become a successful curriculum designer or producer?

Dynamic Scaffolding Model

Mathews and Foster (2005) described a model that is tiered and is consultant based (see Figure 8.12). The use of consultants and mentors enhances a more personalized approach to training.

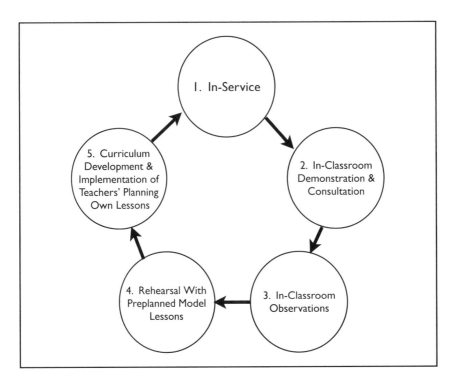

Figure 8.11. Javits model of professional development.

Tier I: Providing professional development oppórtunities emphasizing programming for advanced learners.

Tier II: Providing consulting work with teachers individually or in groups.

Tier III: Establishing networking, curriculum development, and other services.

Figure 8.12. Dynamic scaffolding model.

Training of Trainers Model

The training of trainers model has been a popular model in the literature to describe options for developing professionals. Founded on the idea that well-trained educators can transmit the knowledge and skills they have mastered to others, the trainer of trainers model represents some salient features of learning: (a) people can learn from more adept significant others and those who can model for them, (b) learning can be communicated more effectively and perceived to be more authentic or feasible when it is shared by colleagues who have similar roles and experiences, and (c) there is a cost-effective quality to teachers teaching their peers. Similar to all models, it also has several concerns accompanying it: (a) the training of trainers model has the potential to be analogous to the game of "telephone" wherein the original message becomes diffused as it is sent from the primary receiver to recipients and subsequently, it can erode the integrity of the professional development objective, and (b) the training of trainers model has the potential to shift authority in the educational institution. For example, the teacher-trainer does not have the same evaluative authority as does an administrator. Even though the teacher is the facilitator of the learning, that same individual is often not vested with the role of assessing the outcomes from the learning.

The NAGC Standards and Planning Professional Development

Although all of the Gifted Programming Standards need to be met in various professional development experiences, the selection and organization of these standards to operationalize them in a professional development context can be accomplished in many ways.

» Prioritizing standards (see Figure 8.13) is paramount to program status, scheduling, teacher readiness, and fiscal and administrative outcomes. There are several ways to prioritize the standards: relevancy, prior knowledge, and long-term goals and actions. Prioritizing using multiple indicators enhances the prescriptions for planning and/or developing a scope and sequence for professional development.

» Clustering standards (see Figure 8.14) facilitates achieving simultaneous multiple ends during the professional development. The basis for the clustering of standards is the identification of a single standard that becomes superordinate and subsequently is the centerpiece for defining the subordinate standards that complement it. In this process, all standards are addressed but with differing levels of intensity.

» Sequencing standards refers to the concept of arranging standards to corral the unfolding of the gifted and/or regular education programs. It is acknowledged that some standards reinforce general district or school activities. For example, matching the introduction of gifted education standards to the district's discussion of student progress has some positive possibilities.

Conclusion

Designing and providing professional development to teachers forces educators to acknowledge the similarity between the issues of planning educational

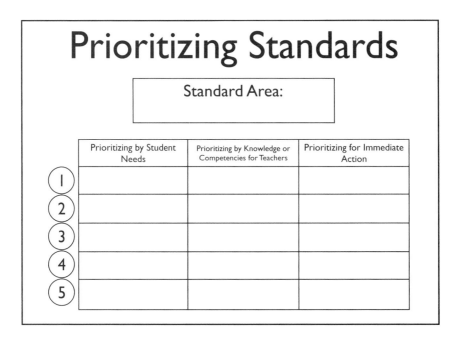

Figure 8.13. Prioritizing standards.

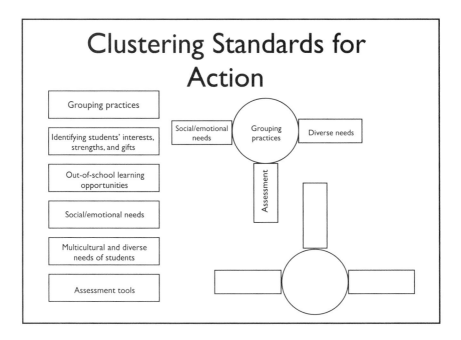

Figure 8.14. Clustering standards for action.

NAGC Pre-K–Grade 12 Gifted Education Programming Standards

experiences for gifted students. Curriculum and instruction, resources and time, and expectations and measures of outcomes derived from teaching and learning are the same concerns that need to be addressed in programs for gifted students and with the teachers responsible to educate them. Just as standards drive decision making for gifted students, the standards of professional development should drive the decisions to educate the teachers of gifted students. In many cases, the fear to afford teachers the opportunity to be educated with the same levels of sophistication that they are expected to make available to their students can underestimate the profession and devalue professionalism.

References

Borko, H. (2004). Professional development and teacher learning: Mapping the terrain. *Educational Researcher, 30*(8), 3–15.

Clark, B. (2008). *Growing up gifted* (7th ed.). Upper Saddle River, NJ: Prentice Hall.

Darling-Hammond, L., Wei, R. C., Andree, A., Richardson, N., & Orphanos, S. (2009). *Professional learning in the learning profession: A status report on teacher development in the United States and abroad.* Retrieved from http://www.learningforward.org/news/NSDCstudy2009.pdf

Donovan, M. S., Bransford, J. D., & Pellegrino, J. W. (Eds.). (2000). *How people learn: Brain, mind, experience, and school.* Washington, DC: National Academy Press.

Gallagher, J. J. (1975). Framing educational personnel for the gifted. In J. J. Gallagher (Ed.), *Teaching the gifted child* (2nd ed.). Boston, MA: Allyn & Bacon.

Guskey, T. A. (1986). Staff development and the process of teacher change. *Educational Researcher, 15*(15), 5–12.

Guskey, T. A. (2002). Professional development and teacher change. *Teachers and Teaching: Theory and Practice, 8,* 381–391.

Hargreaves, A. (1994). *Changing teachers, changing times.* New York, NY: Teachers College Press.

Hawley, W., & Valli, L. (1999). The essence of effective professional development: A new consensus. In G. Sykes & L. Darling-Hammond (Eds.), *Teaching as the learning profession: A handbook of teaching and policy* (pp. 127–150). San Francisco, CA: Jossey-Bass.

Hill, H. (2007). Learning in the teaching workforce. *The Future of Children, 17*(1), 111–127.

Marland, S. P., Jr. (1972). *Education of the gifted and talented: Report to the Congress of the United States by the U.S. Commissioner of Education and background papers submitted to the U.S. Office of Education,* 2 vols. Washington, DC: U.S. Government Printing Office. (Government Documents, Y4.L 11/2: G36)

Mathews, D. J., & Foster, J. F. (2005). A dynamic scaffolding model of teacher development: The gifted education consultant as catalyst for change. *Gifted Child Quarterly, 49,* 222–230.

National Association for Gifted Children. (2010). *NAGC pre-K–grade 12 gifted programming standards: A blueprint for quality gifted education.* Washington, DC: Author.

National College for School Leadership. (2003). *Policies that support professional development in an era of reform.* Retrieved from http://www.oest.oas.org/iten/documentos/Research/randd-engaged-darling.pdf

Rallis, S. F., & Rossman, G. B. (1995). *Dynamic teachers: Leaders of change.* Thousand Oaks, CA: Corwin Press.

Rashid, H. (2000). Professional development and the urban educator: Strategies for promoting school as community. *Contemporary Education, 71*(2), 56–59.

Tannenbaum, A. J. (1983). *Gifted children: Psychological and educational perspectives.* New York, NY: Macmillan.

U.S. Department of Education, Office of Educational Research and Improvement. (1993). *National excellence: A case for developing America's talent.* Washington, DC: U.S. Government Printing Office.

VanTassel-Baska, J. (2003). *Curriculum and instructional planning and design for gifted learners.* Denver, CO: Love.

Chapter 9
Using the NAGC Gifted Programming Standards to Evaluate Progress and Success: Why and How

by Reva Friedman-Nimz

> Give to us clear vision that we may know where to stand and what to stand for—because unless we stand for something, we shall fall for anything.
>
> —Marshall (1951)

The central function of evaluation is to: "[collect systematically] information about the activities, characteristics, and outcomes of programs, personnel, and products for use by specific people to reduce uncertainties, improve effectiveness, and make decisions with regard to what those programs personnel or products are doing and affecting" (Patton, 1981, p. 124). The new NAGC Pre-K–Grade 12 Gifted Programming Standards can provide a method for evaluating a program's progress and its success.

Why use standards as the framework for determining program outcomes, program development, and related action plans? In what ways are standards useful tools for evaluating gifted education programming? Described in a variety of contexts throughout this book, the revised Gifted Programming Standards form the field of gifted education's agreed-on framework for defining and identifying programming quality, which in turn informs the development of defensible policies, practices, and processes. As mentioned in Chapter 1, NAGC's Gifted Programming Standards represent a coordinated effort to provide "coherence, structures, guidelines for professional development, attention to underserved populations, ways to improve programming, and a foundation for advocacy" (p. 3). A key feature of the revised standards is their grounding in evidence-based practice, defined as joining collective professional wisdom with pertinent empirical evidence. Thus, these standards are a de facto statement of where we stand and what we stand for. Their respective indicators serve as intermediate goals—in effect, a task analysis of the actions needed to attain the pertinent standard. Program evaluation in this context results in a coherent, comprehensive picture of cumulative as well as interim programming effects on students, teachers, the school environment, and families.

An Overview of Program Evaluation

In the beginning God created the heaven
and the earth . . .

And God saw every thing that He made.
"Behold," God said, "It is very good."
And the evening and the morning were the
sixth day.

And on the seventh day God rested from
all His work. His archangel came then
unto Him asking: "God how do you know
that what you have created is 'very good'?
What are your criteria? On what data
do you base your judgment? Aren't you a
little close to the situation to make a
fair and unbiased evaluation?"

God thought about these questions all
that day and His rest was greatly disturbed.
On the eighth day God said, "Lucifer,
go to hell."

Thus was evaluation born in a blaze
of glory.
Ever since the status of the profession
has been somewhat in doubt: the road
to salvation or a sure ticket to damnation?

—From Halcom's *The Real Story of Paradise Lost*
(Patton, 1981, p. 1)

Given an opportunity to evaluate a program, drink arsenic, or do anything else, the latter will be the likely choice.
—Coleman (2006, p. 349)

Data? We don't need no stinking data.

—Shapiro (2011)

These three quotes illustrate a regrettably common misunderstanding of the potential value of program evaluation. Rather than viewing evaluation as an attack on the credibility of program developers relative to determining the qualities that signal "very good," evaluation data can provide evidence of program developers' innovative work and promote a transparent program improvement process. Data can be used to support or establish programs, examine growth, identify needed improvements, and gauge effectiveness or impact. They can also be used to determine successful program components, as public relations tools, and to seek support for modifying policy and legal requirements (Callahan, Tomlinson, Hunsaker, Bland, & Moon, 1995). Callahan et al. (1995) sorted reasons for engaging in program evaluation into two categories: program improvement (e.g., seeking information for program improvement) and program protection (e.g., meeting legal requirements). The key point is that regardless of the reasons for engaging in program evaluation, an evaluation can be useful and lead to defensible decision making.

Unfortunately, evaluations are rarely conducted under neutral conditions. Carter (1991) captured the pervasiveness and persistence of this issue: "Program coordinators must routinely convince decision makers that their gifted programs are necessary and make a difference. This is especially true in times of fiscal recession when school boards are required to trim the budget" (p. 245).

Using nationally recognized standards as the basis for program evaluation in gifted education creates an opportunity to enhance programming consistency, because the standards represent the knowledge base in the field rather than experiences in a particular district or state. Ideally, accessible discussions relative to evaluation needs promote open dialogue relative to the metrics (standards and indicators) of program quality (what is meant by "quality?"), and, over the long-term, ensure that standards are represented by data-supported practices relevant to the majority of pertinent educational settings.

When initiating an evaluation plan within a standards-based programming framework, the system needs to be congruent with *what* is being tested and *how it is tested*. For instance, standards-based assessment lends itself to assessing learners' academic performance as compared to similar learners' (norm-referenced assessment). In addition, learners' cognitive growth should be assessed against a standard and/or its indicators (criterion-referenced assessment). The standards themselves should also be open to ongoing scrutiny: Are these guideposts appropriate? For example, VanTassel-Baska (n.d.) asked: "How do we know that students are learning what they need to for high level functioning in the 21st century?" (para. 2). Responding to this question requires a systematic inquiry relative to the 20th-century learning goals as well as the emerging common core standards. VanTassel-Baska further asserted: "Every student has a right to have a challenging curriculum and to receive pedagogical supports to master it effectively" (para. 3). Defining "challenging curriculum" and ascertaining the qualities of pedagogical supports are fitting foci for formative evaluation (i.e., benchmarking progress toward accomplishing a standard).

Evaluating the implementation and outcomes of the Gifted Programming Standards should incorporate two types of program evaluation plans: formative and summative. Analogous to classroom assessments, formative evaluation could be considered as evaluation *for* programming, while summative evaluation could be viewed as evaluation *of* programming. Thus, a regular cycle of evaluation activities is used to determine the ways in which the program is on track to achieving its goals and to provide information that leads to strengthening pertinent policies and procedures, which leads to a clearer picture of overall program effects and outcomes. In the context of the Gifted Programming Standards, assessing the accomplishment of the indicators or practices that elaborate each standard could be considered as process, and examining related learner outcome benchmarks as products.

The goal for this chapter is to demonstrate the process of translating standards, related indicators (evidence-based practice), and learner outcomes (also based on research evidence) into a coherent program development, implementation, and evaluation plan. The chapter focuses on implementing and evaluating the following two outcomes within Standard 2: Assessment, using a series of school-level scenarios to demonstrate how to incorporate program evaluation into an overall plan.

Standard 2: Assessment

Description: Assessments provide information about identification, learning progress and outcomes, and evaluation of programming for students with gifts and talents in all domains.

2.5. Evaluation of Programming. Students identified with gifts and talents demonstrate important learning progress as a result of programming and services.

2.6. Evaluation of Programming. Students identified with gifts and talents have increased access and they show significant learning progress as a result of improving components of gifted education programming. (NAGC, 2010, p. 9)

Scenario Part 1: Evidence-Based Programming

Wheat State Elementary School initiated its gifted education program last year. In the model differentiated education school, the teachers have already implemented some provisions that fit the needs of gifted and talented students: curriculum compacting, tiered instruction, learning contracts, and independent study. Teachers also record learner progress as a regular aspect of instruction and have agreed to use this information as informal documentation of high potential in the referral/team problem-solving process. The gifted education teacher has led staff development sessions during which teachers transformed research-supported lists of characteristics into behavioral guides (negative and positive) that they use as a key component of a body of evidence in making decisions regarding a student's need for gifted education services. The faculty has agreed to pilot test above-grade-level norms for district-wide achievement testing.

The above situation is increasingly common. Developing a comprehensive evaluation plan should be an integral aspect of implementing any programming standards. Collected and analyzed regularly, evaluation data should provide a coherent, evidence-based picture of interim as well as cumulative programming effects on students, teachers, and the school environment.

The revised programming standards embody the assumption that a thoughtful and intentional program design and implementation process is requisite to providing consistent, comprehensive, and coordinated experiences for learners across grade levels and in a variety of contexts. They represent the articulation of enduring and implicit beliefs about the cognitive and affective needs of gifted and talented learners, goals and expectations for programming, and learner outcomes that transcend particular philosophies. The revised programming standards therefore are formed by combining two key components: evidence-based programming practices with clearly defined expectations for student outcomes.

Evidence-Based Practice as a Key Component of Standards

From the practicing professionals' perspective an evidence-based practice is an intervention or strategy that has been sufficiently studied so that professionals can reasonably expect positive results when the practice is implemented as described with a given individual in a given setting or context . . . From this perspective evidence-based practice represents the professional's approach to decision-making that integrates rigorous research evidence; practitioner expertise and accessible contextual resources; and individual and familial preferences and cultural values. (Council for Exceptional Children, 2008, p. 21)

The NAGC Workgroup conceptualized evidence-based practice as encompassing three categories: practice-based, research-based, or literature-based. Employing evidence-based practice as the foundation for building the standards accomplishes two goals: (a) to establish credibility for the standards and their related indicators and (b) to create a roadmap leading to programming and related outcomes whose validity is based on research rather than on local history or politics.

The first category, practice, incorporates field-based experience with practitioner expertise and collective wisdom. However, focusing solely on practice and utility can likewise limit generalizability to a particular context. My personal experience is that when the rationale for particular programming features or key activities fails to include the professional literature (empirical or theoretical), the field of gifted education loses credibility. Therefore, evidence-based practice also needs to incorporate the two types of professional literature indicated above: empirical investigations and theory/reasoning. It is crucial to draw from all three categories when planning program policies and procedures and their related evaluation elements.

Gifted Programming Standards' Focus on Student Outcomes

Although evidence-based practices are important in making decisions about specific provisions that might be implemented, they are not sufficient for determining their effectiveness with individual gifted and talented students. Johnsen (2010) highlighted the fundamental change in focus represented in the revised programming standards: "The number of practices used or how the schools use practices is not as important as whether or not the practice is effective with students (e.g., Do the multiple assessments allow each student to manifest his or her potential?)" (p. 5). The new standards incorporate inputs in the form of evidence-based practice and outcomes in terms of effects on the learner, rather than solely emphasizing inputs/processes as the basis for determining acceptable or exemplary attainment of particular standards, described as a shortcoming of the 1998 standards (Matthews & Shaunessy, 2010).

Callahan and Caldwell (1997) pointed out that most gifted education programs contain common functional components: identification and placement, curriculum and instruction, program design/administration, and staff selection and professional development. Along with evidence-based practices, all of these components are addressed in the standards. Moreover, they are in turn linked to observable outcomes, the majority of which feature learner growth, also derived from related research.

As you explore Standard 2's student outcomes (i.e., 2.5 and 2.6) that relate to evaluation of programming, notice that they are broadly written, providing a general foundation in the area of assessment. Their six related evidence-based practices pertain to program implementation and in effect form the scope and sequence for a program development and improvement plan. Related evaluation data should signal whether there is appropriate progress toward attaining the standard. This process of "benchmarking," or determining the degree of progress, provides an album of program "snapshots" that needs to be employed regularly in an ongoing, in-depth, self-assessment process or to provide the information needed for an advocacy plan.

Scenario Part 2: Conducting a Gap Analysis

Following the procedure established for all innovative district programs, the building administration appoints an evaluation workgroup, consisting of a cross section of classroom teachers, the gifted program teacher who serves the building as well as the pertinent middle-level gifted program teacher, a sampling of families, participating students, and a few nonparticipating peers. A series of informal lunch meetings with school staff reveals several common questions: Do program services positively affect participating students' learning? Is their achievement surpassing predicted academic growth? Families were also invited to contribute their questions about the program. Their questions added a broader perspective: Has the program affected the overall quality of education in the school for all students? The school's equity initiative results in two additional questions: What proportion of the students referred for services are identified? Does the identification rate for traditionally underrepresented groups demonstrate increased access to services? The group agrees that its first task is to conduct a gap analysis related to its evaluation procedures (outlined in NAGC, 2010, p. 5; see Tables 9.1 and 9.2).

A quick scan of the Gap Analysis Charts confirms that the program has made a strong start in its use of data-based decision making but needs more normed data to assess growth of students at all grade levels. There also appears to be limited use of qualitative data, no use of rubrics to evaluate content mastery or higher level thinking in individual research projects, and inadequate analysis of individual learning plans. Moreover, the school's English language learners (ELL) population as a whole is mushrooming. There appears to be noticeable

Table 9.1

Gap Analysis for Student Outcome 2.5

Gap Analysis: Assessment Standard

2.5. Evaluation of Programming. Students identified with gifts and talents demonstrate important learning progress as a result of programming and services.

Evidence-Based Practices	What We Do to Support This Practice	Desired Student Outcomes	What Evidence Do We Have That Current Practices Are Leading to Desired Student Outcomes?	What Additional Evidence Do We Need (Gaps)?
2.5.1. Educators ensure that the assessments used in the identification and evaluation processes are reliable and valid for each instrument's purpose, allow for above-grade-level performance, and allow for diverse perspectives.	Gifted program teachers meet once per quarter with the school psychologist and the interrelated resource room specialist to review formal and informal instruments used for identification. This group has been collecting data so that it can create above-grade-level norms in all content areas.	Ongoing identification. Equity: equal representation of all identifiable school populations receiving gifted program services. Accurate representation of learning progress.	Quarterly data from formal and informal instruments. Identification process is not ongoing—operates on a fixed schedule. Underrepresentation of English language learners and twice-exceptional students. Above-grade-level norms in all content areas. Limited use of individualized learning plans, tiered instruction.	Formative classroom assessments that are used as part of the identification process. Assessments that are sensitive to indicators of potential giftedness among English language learners. Examples of student work evaluated with differentiated rubrics.
2.5.2. Educators ensure that the progress of the assessment of students with gifts and talents uses multiple indicators that measure mastery of content, higher level thinking skills, achievement in specific program areas, and affective growth.	Pretesting, curriculum compacting, work samples, selective questioning. Periodic self-assessment of skills: content, process, and personal.	Decreased numbers of identified students reporting boredom/lack of challenge. More regularized provisions for ascending intellectual demand. Increased self-regulation and self-directedness.	Use of pretests, curriculum compacting contracts, independent study contracts, and work products; observations of questioning; and periodic self-assessments	Rubrics for evaluating higher level thinking skills within contracts as well as products. Individualized learning plans that analyze learner strengths and needs as part of identification process and are updated regularly as aspect of classroom assessments.
2.5.3. Educators assess the quantity, quality, and appropriateness of the programming and services provided for students with gifts and talents by disaggregating assessment data and yearly progress data and making the results public.	Disaggregated data analyzed according to growth rather than status model. Use of above-grade-level norms. Annual report shared with district administration and school board. Program services satisfaction surveys data collected four times per year.	Full implementation of growth model, demonstrating advanced learning rate and quality. Program improvement plans developed and implemented.	Beginning stages of creating norms. Implemented program improvement plans.	Norms for each grade level to compare data. Direct and indirect effects of program changes.

Table 9.2

Gap Analysis for Student Outcome 2.6

Gap Analysis: Assessment Standard

2.6. Evaluation of Programming. Students identified with gifts and talents have increased access and they show significant learning progress as a result of improving components of gifted education programming.

Evidence-Based Practices	What We Do to Support This Practice	Desired Student Outcomes	What Evidence Do We Have That Current Practices Are Learning to Desired Student Outcomes?	What Additional Evidence Do We Need (Gaps)?
2.6.1. Administrators provide the necessary time and resources to implement an annual evaluation plan developed by persons with expertise in program evaluation and gifted education.	Establishment of school-based evaluation workgroup; access to district evaluation and assessment director.	A comprehensive, coherent, current evaluation plan that "grows" as the program develops.	Informal feedback concerning pertinent knowledge, skills, and collaboration of experts with the rest of evaluation workgroup.	See full evaluation report. Evaluation plan needs to be assessed by external evaluation expert.
2.6.2. The evaluation plan is purposeful and evaluates how student-level outcomes are influenced by one or more of the following components of gifted education programming: (a) identification, (b) curriculum, (c) instructional programming and services, (d) ongoing assessment of student learning, (e) counseling and guidance programs, (f) teacher qualifications and professional development, (g) parent/guardian and community involvement, (h) programming resources, and (i) programming design, management, and delivery.	Assessments and procedures identified in 2.5.2 are categorized as "identification," "curriculum, programming, and services," "learning outcomes," "counseling and guidance," and "professional development." Each is assessed for 'consumer satisfaction": how happy students, teachers, and families are with certain categories of services and specific activities within categories.	Learner engagement, producing evidence of advanced learning. Routinely providing ascending intellectual demand through curriculum, resources, and instruction. Seamless interface between general and gifted education.	Identification: Aggregated demographic data for district and school as a whole and disaggregated for students identified as gifted. Programming: Descriptions of program design and management, curriculum, instructional programming and services, ongoing assessment of student learning, guidance and counseling services, and family and community involvement. Teacher qualifications: Analyzing general education as well as gifted program teacher credentials for evidence of formal preparation regarding giftedness: introductory, general/specific methods, and related areas such as differentiation. Programming resources: cataloguing material, human, and electronic resources available to teachers, families, and students. Assessing for currency and comprehensiveness.	Classroom observations focusing on provisions such as differentiated instruction, compacting, flexible grouping, and instruction such as Socratic questioning. Identifying and applying best practices in gifted education to evaluating curriculum and other instructional materials. Grade-level and off-grade-level norms for high-stakes testing.
2.6.3. Educators disseminate the results of the evaluation, orally and in written form, and explain how they will use the results.	Draft copies of report reviewed by work group.	Specific actions recommended.	Educator focus groups meet periodically to share practices that need to be worked on.	Prime interest groups are able to process results and recommend program improvements.

underrepresentation of these students according to gifted programming demographics.

Scenario Part 3: Developing an Action Plan

The evaluation workgroup has prioritized program "gaps," and has selected two for immediate attention. Their strategy was to focus on one practice that would benefit the entire school as well as students with high potential (2.5.2, assessing student learning) and on one practice relative to program evaluation (2.6.1, administrative support for resources beyond the school faculty to develop and implement a comprehensive evaluation plan; see Table 9.3). They agreed that the results of assessing student learning would have the greatest likelihood of providing support for the effects of programming on the cognitive growth of gifted and talented students. Focusing on amending assessments to accommodate a wider range of student achievement could be helpful to the entire school. The evaluation workgroup decides to develop new rubrics to assess learner work samples. A small group of teachers agree to pilot the four-stage process developed by Stevens and Levi (2005) to develop rubrics that extend the learning ceiling: reflecting on the purposes of the assignment, listing the most important attributes for this assignment, grouping and labeling similar terms, and constructing a rubric grid wherein each level represents increasingly complex and abstract thinking. Despite initial concerns that constructing and implementing ongoing program evaluation would be far from benign, members of the workgroup now perceive the process as creating a venue for conversations and collaborations that improve the learning climate of the entire school program.

Callahan (2009) raised two key decisions that need to be addressed prior to undertaking program evaluation activities. The first concerns who should handle the data—program staff (comprehensive familiarity with programming, but there is potential for bias) or an external expert (quality of evaluation plan, more sophisticated analyses, but can be expensive). There is no single correct choice; however, it is best to think through a rationale for particular actions.

The second involves ensuring that key stakeholders understand the focus of the evaluation. For example, in the above scenario, the gifted program teacher could conceptualize learning in the context of problem-based learning (PBL); the classroom teacher might have in mind documenting the frequency of successful curriculum compacting. In contrast, the principal is likely to focus on global achievement test scores.

Table 9.3

Action Plan for Student Outcomes 2.5 and 2.6

Action Plan Assessment Standard

2.5 Evaluation of Programming. Students identified with gifts and talents demonstrate important learning progress as a result of programming and services.

Evidence-Based Practices	Desired Student Outcomes	Identified Gaps	Information to Be Collected	Responsible Person(s) and Timeline
2.5.2. Educators ensure that the assessment of the progress of students with gifts and talents uses multiple indicators that measure mastery of content, higher level thinking skills, achievement in specific program areas, and affective growth.	More regularized provisions for ascending intellectual demand. Increased self-regulation and self-directedness. Decreased numbers of identified students reporting boredom/lack of challenge.	Better rubrics for evaluating contracts and products. Individualized learning plans that analyze learner strengths and needs as part of identification process and are updated regularly as aspect of classroom assessments.	Updated publications about building rubrics; rubrics that have been field-tested by other schools in assessing higher level thinking. Review pertinent instruments; analysis of strengths and needs in current individualized learning plans.	Designated workgroup members to collect information and construct new rubrics. Designated workgroup members to review instruments.

2.6. Evaluation of Programming. Students identified with gifts and talents have increased access and they show significant learning progress as a result of improving components of gifted education programming.

Evidence-Based Practices	Desired Student Outcomes	Identified Gaps	Information to Be Collected	Responsible Person(s) and Timeline
2.6.1. Administrators provide the necessary time and resources to implement an annual evaluation plan developed by persons with expertise in program evaluation and gifted education.	A comprehensive, coherent, current evaluation plan that "grows" as the program develops.	Current evaluation plan is incomplete. School workgroup has not worked with evaluation expert.	Evaluation plans for other innovative district programs. District evaluation expert reviews of draft plans.	Building principal, workgroup leaders, evaluation consultant.

Selecting the types of information and data courses that will best inform a systematic program improvement plan can also be challenging. Should there be a narrow spotlight only on identified gifted and talented students? Or, because the program features an in-class differentiation component, should the entire class participate? Objective, quantitative assessments range from formal, norm-referenced tests to rating scales and surveys (see Appendix B for a varied catalogue of possible assessments). In contrast, qualitative assessments could emphasize portfolios that encompass a variety of work by a student or learning products whose impact extends well beyond the school. In order to decide whether an assessment is appropriate, one needs to examine it carefully. In what contexts has the assessment been used and how useful were the results? What are the assessment's psychometric qualities (validity and reliability)? Were gifted/high-achieving students included in the norming sample? Does the assessment's content appear to represent the domain (content/concepts) of instruction?

If a variety of assessments are planned (quantitative and qualitative), it is important to ascertain that a staff member has the requisite skill to analyze and interpret the results. Administration time, cost, and availability need to be considered as well. Johnsen (2004) offered a succinct exemplar in which she summarized types of information, related source, data collection method, and scoring pertaining to evaluating student growth as a key feature of programming (see Table 9.4).

For example, achievement test data can be gathered from students as well as the district as a whole. A related evaluation procedure would be to compare test performance across years, which would be considered as a quantitative assessment. In contrast, teacher ratings and summaries of student performance are provided by teachers. A related quantitative analysis would be to examine the relationship between test results with other types of student performance information, and a qualitative analysis would be to look for patterns in the attributes and quality of student work.

Design and measurement issues particular to evaluating gifted education program effects need to be considered, such as ceiling effects, regression to the mean, limited availability of comparison groups, and the metric for determining learning growth. Regression to the mean refers to the diminished probability of a second unusual occurrence. For example, a student whose test score is extremely high in May of Year 1 is more likely to score lower in May of Year 2. Ceiling effects refer to the pervasive issue of a score range that falls short for an advanced learner. In this situation, it is not possible to assess cognitive growth accurately unless off-level norms are developed. Last, the conceptual frame for assessing learner growth can exert a profound effect on judgments of learner growth: status or growth. Status models are commonly employed to calculate the number of learners who attain a minimum competency level. "Status models tend to focus a school's attention and resources on those students who are *not* achieving proficiency rather than those who are *above* proficiency" (Council for Exceptional Children, The Association for the Gifted [CEC-TAG], n.d., p. 1). In contrast, "the term growth model should be clearly defined as measurement of academic success on the basis of how much student achievement improves and should be based on individual student gains" (CEC-TAG, n.d., p. 3). Using a growth model allows for using the learner as his or her own comparison: The expected rate of learning can be contrasted with the actual rate.

Table 9.4

Type of Information, Source, Method, and Measurement of One Key Feature

Key Feature: Student Academic Benefit			
Type of Information	**Source**	**Method**	**Assessment**
Achievement tests (ITBS, AP)	Student and district	Compare performance on tests from one year to the next.	Quantitative
SAT tests	Student and district	Mean comparisons across years of students who participate and who do not participate in the program.	Quantitative
Portfolios	Student and teacher	Description of products using the state performance criteria.	Qualitative
Ratings and summaries of performance	Teacher	Relationship between performance and achievement tests; description of performance in classroom.	Quantitative and qualitative
Observations of students	Outside evaluator	Relationship between performance, teacher ratings and achievement tests; description of interactions in the classroom.	Quantitative and qualitative

Note. From "Evaluating the Effectiveness of Identification Procedures," by S. K. Johnsen in *Identifying Gifted Students: A Practical Guide* (2nd ed., p. 154), by S. K. Johnsen (Ed.), 2011, Waco, TX: Prufrock Press. Copyright 2011 by Prufrock Press. Reprinted with permission.

Scenario Part 4: Positive Effects of Program Evaluation

According to the results of a preliminary attitude survey administered at the close of the program's first full implementation year, identified students, their families, and classroom and gifted program teachers were highly satisfied with the program design, and believed that program services were worthwhile. However, recent cuts to the district's budget have sparked a review of all non-mandated programs, and the gifted education program is especially visible. The building administrators want to know if the program is a worthwhile investment. The campus in this scenario now has data that can be used to examine the value of its program: differentiated rubrics, individualized growth plans, and a plan for systematic program evaluation.

As an outgrowth of the accountability movement, evaluation provides useful, systematic, generalizable information that highlights the relative effectiveness of various programming components, congruence between stated and enacted goals and services, impact on participating learners, and incidental benefit to their nonparticipating peers. Although standards and related evaluation activities are not a cure-all for all programming issues, thoughtful use of both strengthens the distinct identity of the field and provides a setting for continuing important conversations about providing comprehensive programming that promotes rather than suppresses extraordinary performance.

If you don't know where you're going, you'll probably wind up someplace else.

—Yogi Berra

References

Callahan, C. M. (2009). Making the grade or achieving the goal?: Evaluating learner and program outcomes in gifted education. In F. A. Karnes & S. M. Bean (Eds.), *Methods and materials for teaching the gifted* (3rd ed., pp. 221–260). Waco, TX: Prufrock Press.

Callahan, C. M., & Caldwell, M. S. (1997). *A practitioner's guide to evaluating programs for the gifted*. Washington, DC: National Association for Gifted Children.

Callahan, C. M., Tomlinson, C. A. Hunsaker, S. L., Bland, L., & Moon, T. (1995). *Instruments and evaluation designs used in gifted programs*. Storrs: University of Connecticut, The National Research Center on the Gifted and Talented.

Carter, K. R. (1991). Evaluation of gifted programs. In N. Buchanan & J. Feldhusen (Eds.), *Conducting research and evaluation in gifted education: A handbook of methods and applications* (pp. 245–274). New York, NY: Teachers College Press.

Coleman, L. J. (2006). A report card on the state of research on the talented and gifted. *Gifted Child Quarterly, 50,* 346–350.

Council for Exceptional Children. (2008). *Classifying the state of evidence for special education professional practices: CEC practice study manual*. Retrieved from http://www.cec.sped.org/Content/NavigationMenu/ProfessionalDevelopment/ProfessionalStandards/Practice_Studies_Manual_1_25.pdf

Council for Exceptional Children, The Association for the Gifted. (n.d.). *Growth in achievement of advanced students*. Retrieved from http://www.gifted.uconn.edu/siegle/TAG/Growth%20Models.pdf

Johnsen, S. K. (Ed.). (2004). *Identifying gifted students: A practical guide*. Waco, TX: Prufrock Press.

Johnsen, S. K. (2010). Principles underlying the 2010 programming standards in gifted education. *Gifted Child Today, 34*(2), 5, 65.

Johnsen, S. K. (2011). Evaluating the effectiveness of identification procedures. In S. K. Johnsen (Ed.), *Identifying gifted students: A practical guide* (2nd ed., pp. 149–157). Waco, TX: Prufrock Press.

Marshall, C. (1951). *A man called Peter: The story of Peter Marshall*. Grand Rapids, MI: Chosen Books.

Matthews, M. S., & Shaunessy, E. (2010). Putting standards into practice: Evaluating the utility of the NAGC pre-K–grade 12 gifted program standards. *Gifted Child Quarterly, 54,* 159–167.

National Association for Gifted Children. (2010). *NAGC pre-K–grade 12 gifted programming standards: A blueprint for quality gifted education programs.* Washington, DC: Author.

Patton, M. Q. (1981). *Creative evaluation.* Beverly Hills, CA: Sage.

Shapiro, S. (2011, May 1). *We don't need no stinking data.* Retrieved from http://www.alan.com/2011/05/01/we-dont-need-no-stinking-data

Stevens, D. D., & Levi, A. (2005). *Introduction to rubrics: An assessment tool to save grading time, convey effective feedback, and promote student learning.* Herndon, VA: Stylus Publishing.

VanTassel-Baska, J. (n.d.). *Standards of learning and gifted education: Goodness of fit.* Retrieved from http://www.vagifted.org.

Chapter 10

State Models for Implementing the Standards

by Chrystyna V. Mursky

Standards provide a basis for developing policies, rules, procedures, plans, programming and services, assessment systems, and professional development at both the state and local levels. State departments of education use national standards for two additional purposes: (a) to evaluate and improve state standards, and (b) to approve gifted plans and programs and monitor for compliance with state regulations. In the 2008–2009 *State of the Nation in Gifted Education* report, "28 states mandate some form of programs or services for gifted children," but it is a "piecemeal, inconsistent, and at times bewildering collection of policies and programs that vary sharply from state to state . . . Ultimately gifted and talented students are ill-served by this fragmented and uncoordinated method of delivery" (NAGC, 2009, p. 3). The NAGC Pre-K–Grade 12 Gifted Programming Standards (2010b) provide promise for bringing consistency among states. This chapter will explore how three states are presently implementing the standards and suggest additional ideas about how they might be used.

Alabama

In conjunction with its Administrative Code, Alabama plans to use the 2010 Gifted Programming Standards to revise how they monitor gifted programs in all of the school systems in the state. Currently, they have two forms for their review process. The first form breaks the Administrative Code and Title VI Resolution Agreement into 10 statements, which rate the school system as Below Standard, Meets Standards, or Exceeds Standards. The second form lists a variety of quality of service indicators that use the same rating system. Following the lead of the Gifted Programming Standards, the state department has convened a task force to rewrite the descriptors on these documents so they reflect student outcomes rather than program evaluation. The task force will determine what these student outcomes will look like in both general education and gifted education classrooms and how they will be rated according to the new Gifted Programming Standards.

Maryland

Jeanne Paynter, the Specialist for Gifted Education in the Maryland State Department of Education, developed an introduction to the 2010 Gifted Programming Standards that she uses with program coordinators from different school systems in the state. She notes, however, that it could be used with a variety of audiences.

Dr. Paynter begins with a PowerPoint that provides an overview to the standards. It includes information on how to use the standards, how the 2010 standards differ from the 1998 standards, the characteristics of evidence-based practices, how to assess student outcomes, and a very brief description of each of the six standards. After the PowerPoint presentation, participants divide into six groups, each one focusing on a standard.

Each group uses the Gifted Programming Standards booklet (NAGC, 2010b) to examine its standard in two parts: (a) key concepts and (b) evidence-based practices. Dr. Paynter refers to this as "Unpacking the 2010 NAGC Pre-K–Grade 12 Gifted Programming Standards." The activity emphasizes three of the four ways in which the 2010 standards differ from the 1998 standards: the importance of diversity, the focus on student outcomes, and the emphasis on evidence-based practices from current research. Let's look at each of the two parts of this activity in more detail.

Key Concepts

Directions for this part of the activity state that participants should review the definition of each of the identified terms in the Gifted Programming Standards' Glossary of Terms (NAGC, 2010b, pp. 14–15). Then they identify new understandings that they acquire from discussing the definition. For example, for Standard 1: Learning and Development, four terms are explored (see Table 10.1).

Terms for Standard 2 are assessment, diversity, off-level/above-grade-level, qualitative instruments, quantitative instruments, and technical adequacy. Terms for Standard 3 are aptitude, culturally relevant, differentiated curriculum, differentiated instruction, and diversity. Terms for Standard 4 are cultural competence, diversity, and social competence. Terms for Standard 5 are collaboration, cognitive and affective growth, coordinated services, diversity, programs/programming, and services/servicing. Terms for Standard 6 are diversity, ser-

Table 10.1
Glossary of Terms

Glossary of Terms	New Understandings
Cognitive and affective growth	
Diversity	
Social competence	
Socio-emotional development	

vices/servicing, socio-emotional development, twice-exceptional, and under-achieving. Note that each group discusses the meaning of the term diversity, thus accentuating the critical nature of this thread in the standards.

Evidence-Based Practices

The second part of the Unpacking Activity focuses on two important organizational components of the standards: student outcomes and evidence-based practices. Directions for the first half read: "While the new Programming Standards emphasize student outcomes, we are more familiar with looking at our program practices. Review the list of evidence-based program practices for (your standard) in order to identify three (3) that your group agrees are currently established in your school systems. Fill in those practices in the table."

Once discussion about these practices has taken place, group members are asked to consider the following: "How might we move from practices to student outcomes? Review the student outcomes for those three practices. In what ways might we assess those outcomes?" The chart for this part of the activity is found in Table 10.2.

Dr. Paynter reports that groups she worked with had rich discussion around the standards using this framework. She notes that the next logical step is to design a data collection system to assess the student outcomes, perhaps by first focusing on data sources already available in schools, but not presently used for this particular purpose.

Texas

In 1987, the Texas Legislature mandated that all school districts in the state identify and serve K–12 gifted and talented students. As a result, the Texas Education Agency (TEA) developed a state plan, revised in 2009, that forms the basis for G/T services and accountability. The revision, however, does not reflect the Gifted Programming Standards.

Table 10.2
Assessment of Outcomes

How to Assess/Evaluate Student Outcomes	Evidence-Based Practices (Established)

Johnsen (2011) first compared the standards in the 2009 Texas state plan to the Gifted Programming Standards and then suggested a process for school districts to use both sets of standards to develop, implement, and improve programming for students with gifts and talents. Her analysis can serve as a model for other states.

Johnsen (2011) acknowledged that the Texas state plan focuses on specific practices rather than on student outcomes, as the Gifted Programming Standards do. In her mind, this variation is significant, as it may lead to very different results. Johnsen stated,

> If educators focus on practices rather than outcomes, they may use the standards simply as a yes/no checklist (e.g., Are policies in place? Do I have multiple assessments? . . .). Whereas if the standards are focused on student outcomes, the practices become a means to an end (e.g., How do the policies affect students services? How are multiple assessments including more diverse students in the gifted program?). (p. 17)

The Texas state plan does, however, use evidence-based practices that are listed in the Gifted Programming Standards. The Texas standards emphasize five components of gifted education programs: student assessment, service design, curriculum and instruction, professional development, and family/community involvement. As such, Johnsen (2011) noted that the Texas state plan most closely reflects aspects of NAGC Standard 2 (Assessment) and Standard 5 (Programming). To a lesser degree, the plan reflects aspects of NAGC Standard 3 (Curriculum Planning and Instruction) and Standard 6 (Professional Development). Johnsen also identified Gifted Programming Standards that are only peripherally addressed or are not found at all in the Texas state plan. These include Standard 1 (Learning and Development) and Standard 4 (Learning Environments). Finally, she identified other gaps that exist, most notably several components related to diversity, reference to preassessments, and online learning and other technological resources.

The self-assessment that Johnsen (2011) completed, comparing state standards to the Gifted Programming Standards, is an important process that other states might want to consider. The author suggested that this could be the first step for school districts as well. She recommended that they examine to what degree they are meeting the Texas standards and the Gifted Programming Standards that are not reflected in the state document. Johnsen then outlined the next three steps in developing, implementing, and improving programming for students with gifts and talents: (a) identifying what student outcomes might look like, (b) selecting assessments to determine if the students outcomes have been met, and (c) developing an action plan to establish short- and long-term goals for improvement.

Other Suggestions

Alabama, Maryland, and Texas provide examples of how states are using the Gifted Programming Standards. I would like to offer two other suggestions that states and schools may find helpful.

NAGC Guiding Questions

NAGC (2010a) has developed a set of guiding questions to help implement the Gifted Programming Standards. They can also serve as a form of self-assessment, generating conversation around the topics. NAGC (2010a) stated,

Overall, the questions focus attention on the steps to be taken and the resources to be accessed that will help education leaders and advocates develop high-level curriculum, organize a dynamic classroom setting, and provide appropriate guidance and community opportunities that will meet the needs of a diverse group of students with a wide range of gifts and talents. (para. 2)

Following are examples of these guiding questions, one from each standard.

» **Standard 1. Learning and development.** Considering the range of student interest, ability, and talent, what steps are necessary to ensure that educators are able to recognize the learning and developmental differences of gifted and talented students, promote student ongoing self-understanding, and promote student cognitive and affective growth in school, at home, and in community settings? (NAGC, 2010a, para. 3)

» **Standard 2. Assessment.** In planning for initial student identification, do selected assessment instruments provide qualitative and quantitative information from a variety of non-biased, equitable, and technically adequate sources that ensure an accurate representation of the local student population? Are there ongoing, comprehensive identification procedures in place and have families been kept fully informed? (NAGC, 2010a, para. 4)

» **Standard 3. Curriculum planning and instruction.** Does the curriculum used integrate career exploration experiences and allow for deep exploration of cultures, languages, and other diversity-related issues? (NAGC, 2010a, para. 9)

» **Standard 4. Learning environments.** Has a learning environment that is conducive to intellectual safety, trust, and self-exploration been created by recognizing the importance of positive communication, social skill and leadership development, and cultural competence as students explore their individual, intellectual, and creative differences? (NAGC, 2010a, para. 10)

» **Standard 5. Programming.** Has a system been put in place, including articulated policies and procedures, that allows for educators to develop multi-year plans, plan and coordinate programming and services with the school's professional service providers, and communicate with family and community members to meet student needs and program goals? (NAGC, 2010a, para. 11)

» **Standard 6. Professional development.** Are all teachers, counselors and instructional support staff given sufficient time and funds to regularly participate in a variety of research-supported professional development options in order to increase their expertise in the pedagogy and practice of gifted and talented education and to familiarize themselves with the resources available to meet the academic and socio-emotional needs of their students? (NAGC, 2010a, para. 12)

Common Core State Standards

The Common Core State Standards (CCSS) in English Language Arts and Mathematics were released in 2010 and have been adopted by 48 states (see Common Core State Standards Initiative [CCSSI] at http://www.core standards.org). They are benchmarked—each standard is mapped so educators can guide students in acquiring increasingly complex knowledge and skills from kindergarten through 12th grade. Because they provide a clear pathway, states can use them as NAGC Evidence-Based Practice 3.1.1 suggests, "to align and expand curriculum and instructional plans" (NAGC, 2010b, p. 10). The CCSS also emphasize higher level skills, which reflects NAGC Evidence-Based Practice 3.1.4: "Educators design differentiated curricula that incorporate advanced, conceptually challenging, in-depth, distinctive, and complex content for students with gifts and talents" (NAGC, 2010b, p. 10). The CCSS, then, can provide a foundational scope and sequence from which Student Outcome 3.1 can be met: "Students with gifts and talents demonstrate growth commensurate with aptitude during the school year" (NAGC, 2010b, p. 10).

In addition, as decisions are made about how to implement the CCSS, states have the opportunity to connect or embed other Gifted Programming Standards into this process or to use the evidence-based practices to inform how the Common Core State Standards are put into practice. Following are examples of how this might be done in both English Language Arts and Mathematics. For both CCSSI content areas, I will summarize key design concepts, identify related NAGC student outcomes and evidence-based practices, and then discuss the implications. These suggestions are not exhaustive, merely illustrative of how states might proceed.

English Language Arts. The CCSS include four strands: Reading, Writing, Speaking and Listening, and Language. A key design element is that these strands are closely connected, resulting in an integrated model of literacy. Following is a discussion of these strands.

Reading. The CCSS define a "grade-by-grade 'staircase' of increasing text complexity" (CCSSI, 2010a, p. 8) for both literature and informational text. Students must make "an increasing number of connections among ideas and between texts, consider a wider range of textual evidence, and become more sensitive to inconsistencies, ambiguities, and poor reasoning in text" (CCSSI, 2010a, p. 8).

» Related NAGC Student Outcome 5.1. Students with gifts and talents participate in a variety of evidence-based programming options that enhance performance in cognitive and affective areas (NAGC, 2010b, p. 12).

» Related NAGC Evidence-Based Practice 5.1.2. Educators regularly use enrichment options to extend and deepen learning opportunities within and outside of the school setting (NAGC, 2010b, p. 12).

» Discussion. Depth refers to the exploration of content within a discipline and includes looking for trends and patterns (i.e., seeing connections). Because the CCSS emphasize making connections, there are built-in opportunities in these standards to extend and deepen learning.

There is a shared responsibility for developing literacy in the CCSS. This is evidenced in the section on literacy in history/social studies, science, and technical subjects for grades 6–12. These standards emphasize being able to read complex informational text *independently* in order to be successful in the workplace and in postsecondary programs.

» Related NAGC Student Outcome 4.1. Students with gifts and talents demonstrate growth in personal competence and dispositions for exceptional academic and creative productivity. These include self-awareness, self-advocacy, self-efficacy, confidence, motivation, resilience, independence, curiosity, and risk taking (NAGC, 2010b, p. 11).

» Related NAGC Evidence-Based Practice 4.1.2. Educators provide opportunities for self-exploration, development and pursuit of interests, and development of identities supportive of achievement (NAGC, 2010b, p. 11).

» Discussion. Using informational text to develop independence is one way that students with gifts and talents can develop characteristics that will support achievement.

Writing. The CCSS provide opportunities to write for a variety of purposes including argumentative, informative/exploratory, and narrative. The CCSS document noted, "Because of the centrality of writing to most forms of inquiry, research standards are prominently included" (CCSSI, 2010a, p. 8).

» Related NAGC Student Outcome 4.5. Students with gifts and talents develop competence in interpersonal and technical communication skills . . . They display fluency with technologies that support effective communication (NAGC, 2010b, p. 11).

» Related NAGC Evidence-Based Practice 4.5.2. Educators provide resources to enhance oral, written, and artistic forms of communication, recognizing students' cultural context (NAGC, 2010b, p. 11).

» Discussion. This strand provides opportunities for states to recommend resources and effective strategies that will benefit all students, but will encourage students with gifts and talents to flourish.

Speaking and listening. The CCSS require students to "develop a range of broadly useful oral communication and interpersonal skills" (CCSSI, 2010a, p. 8).

» Related NAGC Student Outcome 1.3. Students with gifts and talents demonstrate understanding of and respect for similarities and differences between themselves and their peer group and others in the general population (NAGC, 2010b, p. 8).

» Related NAGC Evidence-Based Practice 1.3.1. Educators provide a variety of research-based grouping practices for students with gifts and talents that allow them to interact with individuals of various gifts, talents, abilities, and strengths (NAGC, 2010b, p. 8).

» Discussion. Affective development is as important as cognitive development, and the Gifted Programming Standards reflect this belief. Self-understanding and social awareness are key areas that contribute to this growth. The CCSS use speaking and listening as a vehicle for cultivating interpersonal skills.

Language. This strand includes "rules" of standard written and spoken English and vocabulary skills such as understanding words and phrases and their nuances (CCSSI, 2010a).

» Related NAGC Student Outcome 4.5. Students with gifts and talents develop competence in interpersonal and technical communication skills. They demonstrate advanced oral and written skills, balanced biliteracy or multiliteracy, and creative expression (NAGC, 2010b, p. 11).

» Related NAGC Evidence-Based Practice 4.5.1. Educators provide opportunities for advanced development and maintenance of first and second language(s) (NAGC, 2010b, p. 11).

» Discussion. The Interagency Language Roundtable (2011) described skills that are characteristic of different levels of interpretation. The highest level, Master Professional Performance, includes the ability to "convey the meaning of the speaker faithfully and accurately, including all details and nuances" (Interagency Language Roundtable, 2011, para. 16). It's evident from this description that understanding and being able to use shades of meaning is an advanced communication skill. Emphasizing aspects of language such as this will benefit students with gifts and talents.

The Common Core State Standards also provide a portrait of literate students, describing seven key characteristics. Below, I discuss five of these traits and provide examples of connections to the Gifted Programming Standards.

- » They demonstrate independence.
    - ◇ Related NAGC Student Outcome 3.2. Students with gifts and talents become more competent in multiple talent areas and across dimensions of learning (NAGC, 2010b, p. 10).
    - ◇ Related NAGC Evidence-Based Practice 3.2.2. Educators use metacognitive models to meet the needs of students with gifts and talents (NAGC, 2010b, p. 10).
    - ◇ Related NAGC Student Outcome 3.4. Students with gifts and talents become independent investigators (NAGC, 2010b, p. 10).
    - ◇ Related NAGC Evidence-Based Practice 3.4.2. Educators use creative-thinking strategies to meet the needs of students with gifts and talents (NAGC, 2010b, p. 10).
    - ◇ Discussion. Two NAGC student outcomes and evidence-based practices are relevant here. Bonds, Bonds, and Peach (1992) asserted that developing meta-cognitive skills contribute to independence. Lee (2005) found a strong connection between creative thinking ability and independence. Teaching students to use metacognitive strategies and creative thinking models, then, nurtures independence.
- » They comprehend and critique.
    - ◇ Related NAGC Student Outcome 3.4. Students with gifts and talents become independent investigators (NAGC, 2010b, p. 10).
    - ◇ Related NAGC Evidence-Based Practice 3.4.1. Educators use critical-thinking strategies to meet the needs of students with gifts and talents (NAGC, 2010b, p. 10).
    - ◇ Discussion. Critical thinking skills involve higher order thinking. Bloom's (1956) taxonomy identifies evaluation (i.e., critique) as one of the three higher order thinking levels. If states keep this CCSS characteristic of literate students in mind when developing implementation plans, then students with gifts and talents will be served.
- » They value evidence. Research and media skills are integrated into the CCSS. The English Language Arts document stated,

students need the ability to gather, comprehend, evaluate, synthesize, and report on information and ideas, to conduct original research in order to answer questions or solve problems, and to analyze and create a high volume and extensive range of print and nonprint texts in media forms old and new. (CCSSI, 2010a, p. 4)

◇ Related NAGC Student Outcome 3.4. Students with gifts and talents become independent investigators (NAGC, 2010b, p. 10).

◇ Related NAGC Evidence-Based Practice 3.4.4. Educators use inquiry models to meet the needs of students with gifts and talents (NAGC, 2010b, p. 10).

◇ Discussion. Inquiry is strongly related to research. In this model, students explore and evaluate existing research and evidence and identify and research new areas of interest. This results in independent investigators.

» They use technology and digital media strategically and capably.

◇ Related NAGC Student Outcome 4.5. Students with gifts and talents develop competence in interpersonal and technical communication skills. . . . They display fluency with technologies that support effective communication (NAGC, 2010b, p. 11).

◇ Related NAGC Evidence-Based Practice 4.5.3. Educators ensure access to advanced communication tools, including assistive technologies, and use of these tools for expressing higher-level thinking and creative productivity (NAGC, 2010b, p. 11).

◇ Discussion. It's evident that there is a strong similarity between this CCSS student characteristic and the Gifted Programming Standards.

» They come to understand other perspectives and cultures.

◇ Related NAGC Student Outcome 3.5. Students with gifts and talents develop knowledge and skills for living and being productive in a multicultural, diverse, and global society (NAGC, 2010b, p. 10).

◇ Related NAGC Evidence-Based Practice 3.5.3. Educators use curriculum for deep explorations of cultures, languages, and social issues related to diversity (NAGC, 2010b, p. 10).

◇ Discussion. If this CCSS trait is emphasized in curricular and instructional decisions, then growth of students with gifts and talents will be supported.

Mathematics. The Common Core State Standards for Mathematics are organized differently than the CCSS for English Language Arts (CCSSI, 2010b). They begin with Eight Standards for Mathematical Practice that describe ways in which students should engage with the subject matter. Following these are the Standards for Mathematical Content that set expectations for what students will understand about specific topics. K–8 standards provide mathematical learning trajectories that incorporate new concepts and skills within and across domains. The high school standards are organized around topics such as algebra, functions, modeling, geometry, and probability and statistics. In all grades, the CCSS emphasize not only procedural skills, but conceptual understanding as well. They place a priority on students' ability to explain math problems, not simply compute them. This is good news for students with gifts and talents who thrive on opportunities to learn deeply.

Standards of mathematical practice. The CCSS described "varieties of expertise that mathematics educators at all levels should seek to develop in their students. These practices rest on important 'processes and proficiencies' with longstanding importance in mathematics education" (p. 6). These are referred to as the Eight Standards for Mathematical Practice. I discuss four of them below.

» Make sense of problems and persevere in solving them. Mathematically proficient students start by explaining to themselves the meaning of a problem and looking for entry points to its solution . . . They monitor and evaluate their progress and change course if necessary (CCSSI, 2010b, p. 6).

◇ Related NAGC Student Outcome 3.2. Students with gifts and talents become more competent in multiple talent areas and across dimensions of learning (NAGC, 2010, p. 10).

◇ Related NAGC Evidence-Based Practice 3.2.2. Educators use metacognitive models to meet the needs of students with gifts and talents (NAGC, 2010, p. 10).

◇ Related NAGC Student Outcome 4.1. Students with gifts and talents demonstrate growth in personal competence and dispositions for exceptional academic and creative productivity. These include self-awareness, self-advocacy, self-efficacy, confidence, motivation, resilience, independence, curiosity, and risk taking (NAGC, 2010b, p. 11).

◇ Related NAGC Evidence-Based Practice 4.1.5. Educators provide examples of positive coping skills and opportunities to apply them (NAGC, 2010b, p. 11).

◇ Discussion. It's evident that there is a strong similarity between this CCSS mathematical practice and the Gifted Programming Standards, with an emphasis on metacognition, flexibility, and resiliency.

» Construct viable arguments and critique the reasoning of others. Mathematically proficient students make conjectures and build a logical progression of statements to explore the truth of their conjectures . . . They justify their conclusions, communicate them to others, and respond to the arguments of others (CCSSI, 2010b, pp. 6–7).

◇ Related NAGC Student Outcome 3.4. Students with gifts and talents become independent investigators (NAGC, 2010b, p. 10).

◇ Related NAGC Evidence-Based Practice 3.4.1. Educators use critical-thinking strategies to meet the needs of students with gifts and talents (NAGC, 2010b, p. 10).

◇ Discussion. The CCSS discuss the importance of constructing viable arguments and critiquing the reasoning of others. Questioning assumptions, examining the structure and validity of reasoning, and applying these conclusions to new lines of reasoning are all components of critical thinking and independent investigation. The field of gifted education can provide substantial guidance in developing these skills in a mathematical context.

» Model with mathematics. Mathematically proficient students can apply the mathematics they know to solve problems arising in everyday life, society, and the workplace (CCSSI, 2010b, p. 7).

◇ Related NAGC Student Outcome 3.4. Students with gifts and talents become independent investigators (NAGC, 2010b, p. 10).

◇ Related NAGC Evidence-Based Practice 3.4.3. Educators use problem-solving model strategies to meet the needs of students with gifts and talents (NAGC, 2010b, p. 10).

◇ Discussion. There are a variety of effective problem-solving models in gifted education that can inform instruction in this mathematical practice. Among these models are the six-step process developed by Torrance (1982) and used in the Future Problem Solving Program and Treffinger and Isaksen's (2005) Creative Problem Solving (CPS) framework.

» Use appropriate tools strategically. Mathematically proficient students can consider the available tools when solving a mathematical problem. These tools might include pencil and paper, concrete models, a ruler, a protractor, a calculator, a spreadsheet, a computer algebra system, a statistical package, or dynamic geometry software . . . [They] make sound decisions about when each of these tools might be helpful, recognizing both the insight to be gained and their limitations (CCSSI, 2010b, p. 7).

◇ Related NAGC Student Outcome 3.1. Students with gifts and talents demonstrate growth commensurate with aptitude during the school year (NAGC, 2010b, p. 10).

◇ Related NAGC Evidence-Based Practice 3.1.7. Educators use information and technologies, including assistive technologies (NAGC, 2010b, p. 10).

◇ Discussion. This CCSS mathematical practice acknowledges the variety of tools that are available to students and the importance of using the correct one for the situation. The Gifted Programming Standards also give a nod to this idea. Educators are well advised to remember that effective tools do not necessarily have to be glitzy. They range from the common pencil to higher tech assistive technologies.

Conclusion

State educational agencies can provide significant leadership in establishing policies, rules, plans, and assessments for general education and for gifted education. The NAGC Pre-K–Grade 12 Gifted Programming Standards hold promise for informing this work and can be particularly powerful when braided with other local, state, or national efforts. Making connections between initiatives that are already in place (such as balanced assessment systems that school districts have developed) or are in the process of being implemented (such as the Common Core State Standards) strengthens the impact of our work. The Gifted Programming Standards have tremendous potential for guiding conversations and shaping instructional decisions.

References

Bloom, B. S. (1956). *Taxonomy of educational objectives, handbook 1: The cognitive domain*. New York, NY: David McKay.

Bonds, C. W., Bonds, L. G., & Peach, W. (1992). Metacognition: Developing independence in learning. *The Clearing House, 66*(1), 56–59.

Common Core State Standards Initiative. (2010a). *Common core state standards for English language arts and literacy in history/social studies, science, and technical subjects.* Retrieved from http://www.corestandards.org/assets/CCSSI_ELA%20 Standards.pdf

Common Core State Standards Initiative. (2010b). *Common core standards for mathematics.* Retrieved from http://www.corestandards.org/assets/CCSSI_Math%20 Standards.pdf

Interagency Language Roundtable. (2011). *ILR skill level descriptions for interpretation performance.* Retrieved from http://www.govtilr.org/skills/interpretationSLD sapproved.htm#l

Johnsen, S. K. (2011). A comparison of the Texas state plan for the education of gifted/talented students and the 2010 NAGC Pre-K–Grade 12 Gifted Programming standards. *Tempo, 31*(1), 10–20.

Lee, K. H. (2005). The relationship between creative thinking ability and creative personality of preschoolers. *International Education Journal, 6,* 194–199.

National Association for Gifted Children. (2009). *State of the nation in gifted education.* Retrieved from http://www.nagc.org/uploadedFiles/Information_and_ Resources/State_of_the_States_2008-2009/2008-09%20State%20of%20 the%20Nation%20overview.pdf

National Association for Gifted Children. (2010a). *Applying the standards: Guiding questions.* Retrieved from http://www.nagc.org/index.aspx?id=6526

National Association for Gifted Children. (2010b). *NAGC pre-k–grade 12 gifted programming standards: A blueprint for quality gifted education programs.* Washington, DC: National Association for Gifted Children.

Texas Education Agency. (2009). *Texas state plan for the education of gifted/talented students.* Austin, TX: Author.

Torrance, E. P. (1982). Future problem solving and quality circles in schools. *New Jersey Education Association Review, 56*(1), 20–23.

Treffinger, D. J., & Isaksen, S. G. (2005). Creative problem solving: The history, development, and implications for gifted education and talent development. *Gifted Child Quarterly, 49,* 342–353.

Chapter 11

Action Plans: Bringing the Gifted Programming Standards to Life

by Alicia Cotabish and Sally Krisel

Accountability of school districts has increasingly placed gifted educators in the position of having to prove their worth and demonstrate their impact on student achievement. Without programming standards to guide them, educators may struggle to document the effects of gifted programming on student performance. In addition, standards often serve as benchmarks or indicators of progress and can be used to document gaps in program services. Because of their utility, programming standards can be used not only to evaluate program effectiveness but also to plan and develop district action plans.

The 2010 NAGC Pre-K–Grade 12 Gifted Programming Standards focus on student outcomes; reflect a stronger emphasis on diversity; emphasize a stronger relationship between gifted education, general education, and special education; and integrate cognitive science research. In addition, the revised Gifted Programming Standards emphasize evidence-based practices that are based on research (National Association for Gifted Children [NAGC], 2010).

This chapter is guided by two questions:

» How might educators use the NAGC Pre-K–Grade 12 Gifted Programming Standards?
» Where do educators begin?

How Might Educators Use These Standards?

The Venn diagram represented in Figure 11.1 suggests six categories in which state department personnel, gifted program coordinators, and classroom teachers can use the Gifted Programming Standards.

State department personnel may use the Gifted Programming Standards to develop, improve, and evaluate state standards; approve gifted plans and programs; and monitor programs for compliance with state regulations. Program coordinators may use the standards to assess, evaluate, and improve local plans

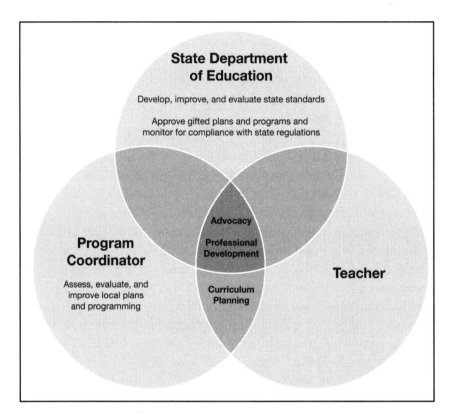

Figure 11.1. Six categories of use.

and programming. Both program coordinators and teachers may find the programming standards to be a valuable tool for curriculum planning. All three groups may use the programming standards to inform and guide professional development activities. Moreover, the programming standards may also provide language, rationale, and direction for effective advocacy for high-quality services for students with gifts and talents.

As noted in the *2010 NAGC Pre-K–Grade 12 Gifted Programming Standards: A Blueprint for Quality Gifted Programs*, other uses may include:

» early stages of planning for programming,
» internal analysis of programming,
» defensibility of plans/programming,
» documenting the need for the programming,
» justifying programming approach,
» identifying strengths and weaknesses of programming,
» determining new directions or components, and
» providing support to maintain current programs and services.

Figure 11.2. Road map. ©2011, Lindsey Schichtl Goodwin

Where Do Educators Begin?
Charting a Course of Action

The term "evidence-based practices" implies *action*. When referring to education, a course of action requires navigating through content or programming standards with skillful planning. In this chapter, we will examine three tools: The Snapshot Survey of Gifted Programming Effectiveness Factors (Lord & Cotabish, 2010), the Gap Analysis Chart (NAGC, 2010), and the Action Plan Chart (NAGC, 2010). Utilizing a roadmap-type of approach, the three tools will help educators evaluate current programming services, set goals, and plan strategically for meeting those goals. Working in concert, the three tools can assist educators in program planning and avoiding roadblocks or a dead end while carrying out an action plan (see Figure 11.2).

Snapshot Survey of Gifted Programming Effectiveness Factors

The Snapshot Survey of Gifted Programming Effectiveness Factors (Snapshot Survey; Lord & Cotabish, 2010) is a tool educators can use to (a) assess the extent to which their programs employ best practices as identified by national standards, (b) rate the extent to which changes in current practices on specific standards would likely improve student outcomes, and (c) determine the amount of effort it would take to significantly modify their practices and/or develop new initiatives targeting specific evidence-based practices. Additionally, the Snapshot Survey will help educators identify program strengths and weaknesses, focus on potential trouble spots, determine new directions and new components, or maintain current status of programs and services. Used as a planning tool, the Snapshot Survey can be used as the initial step toward documenting or monitoring progress toward compliance with state regulations and implementation of evidence-based practices.

A partial graphic depiction of the Snapshot Survey is displayed in Table 11.1. The survey is organized by standard and includes all of the Gifted Programming Standards' evidence-based practices. Three questions are used to help users:

> » reflect on the degree to which they are already engaged in the evidence-based practices enumerated in the Gifted Programming Standards,
> » predict the potential impact the particular practice would have on student achievement or other desired student outcomes, and
> » consider the effort required to significantly change the practice.

An additional column has been added to remind users of the Snapshot Survey to consider policy implications of any practices they may target in an action plan. Is a particular practice, for example, allowable under state law and rule? Would it require adoption of a new board of education policy or an amendment to local administrative procedures? These may prove to be important considerations as gifted program personnel complete the Snapshot Survey, use the results to set goals, and strategically create a roadmap to meet those goals in a timely manner.

In the left-hand column of the Snapshot Survey, users will see the evidence-based practices for Standard 1: Learning and Development. To get started, users should read each evidence-based practice and rate the extent to which it is included in their services for gifted learners. Their responses will range from *not at all* to *to a great extent*.

Table 11.1
Snapshot Survey of Gifted Programming Effectiveness Factors

Standard 1	Question 1 — To what extent do we engage in this behavior or address this issue?				Question 2 — How much will a change in our practices on this item increase access or the academic achievement of our students?				Question 3 — How much effort will it take to significantly change our practices regarding this issue?				Are there policy implications? (✓) if yes
	Not at all			To a great extent	Not at all			To a great extent	Not at all			To a great extent	
Standard 1: Learning and Development	1	2	3	4	1	2	3	4	1	2	3	4	
Evidence-Based Practices in My School													
1.1.1 Educators engage students with gifts and talents in identifying interests, strengths, and gifts.													
1.1.2 Educators assist students with gifts and talents in developing identities supportive of achievement.													
1.2.1 Educators develop activities that match each student's developmental level and culture-based learning needs.													
1.3.1 Educators provide a variety of research-based grouping practices for students with gifts and talents that allow them to interact with individuals of various gifts, talents, abilities and strengths.													
1.3.2. Educators model respect for individuals with diverse abilities, strengths, and goals.													
1.4.1 Educators provide role models (e.g., through mentors, bibliotherapy) for students with gifts and talents that match their abilities and interests.													

Note. Adapted from Marzano (2003).

Next, using the same scale, users should evaluate the potential power of focusing program improvement efforts on that practice by considering the way a change would impact students. Remember that the Gifted Programming Standards are framed as student outcomes instead of best practices, which were the focus of the 1998 standards. The Snapshot Survey helps school districts move beyond the focus on practices alone to the relationship between certain practices and desired student outcomes.

Although positive changes in student outcomes (e.g., cognitive, academic, and affective growth) are the primary concern of gifted program coordinators and teachers, it is wise for decision makers also to consider the effort that would be required to change the practices associated with targeted outcomes. For each evidence-based practice, users should continue their analysis by rating the time and resources (both human and material) that would be required to change the practice. They should also make note of policy implications of potential changes in their current practices.

If only one person is the sole provider of gifted programming services in her district, she will complete the Snapshot Survey by herself; however, if there is more than one person available, it would be better to use a consensus approach to rating.

After rating each evidence-based practice, users should go back and review their responses to Questions 1–3 to analyze their programming needs. When choosing programming areas on which to focus, users should give careful consideration to the evidence-based practices that are not currently addressed or are only minimally addressed. It would be too daunting to address every single one, so users will want to choose a limited number of evidence-based practices to tackle during a single school year. To help users prioritize their selection, consider three questions:

» Will addressing the evidence-based practice positively and significantly affect student outcomes?

» Is it doable at this time or do other components need to be in place first?

» Is it a good allocation of my time? In other words, is it worth the effort at this time or would addressing another evidence-based practice first have greater impact?

After considering these three questions, users should choose several evidence-based practices to address.

Gap Analysis Chart

After using the Snapshot Survey to identify which standards and evidence-based practices will be the focus, users will be ready to explore gaps between current practices and those that have been shown to improve outcomes for gifted learners. A gap analysis chart is a simple tool they can use to identify methods for closing a gap (see Table 11.2). The results of the gap analysis will help determine what steps must be taken to "move from a current state of affairs to a future desired state" (Reference for Business, 2011, para. 1). To do this, educators will use a Gap Analysis Chart (NAGC, 2010).

To use the chart, users should list the standard in Column 1 and the evidence-based practice they chose to address in Column 2. Then users should list what they are currently doing to support this practice in the third column. In Column 4, users should describe the desired student outcome associated with the evidence-based practice. Column 5 allows users to document efforts to date in that area of programming and the evidence they have that is leading to desired student outcomes. Although the reality may indicate that the users do not have any evidence, certainly they should give themselves credit for work that may serve as the foundation for continuous improvement. In the final column, users are asked to consider what additional evidence or information is needed to determine if there is a gap between current procedures and practices and those that are based on research. These last two columns will help users identify specific issues or gaps in programming practice(s).

Action Plan Chart

The third and final piece of the roadmap is the Action Plan Chart (see Table 11.3; NAGC, 2010). An action plan highlights the steps that must be taken, or activities that must be performed well, for a strategy to succeed. The Action Plan Chart components include: the evidence-based practice to be addressed, the desired student outcome tied to the evidence-based practice, the identified gap, the information to be collected, the person(s) responsible for carrying out the action, and a timeline for carrying out the action.

To use the Action Plan Chart, users should list the standard and evidence-based practice they want to address in the first and second column. In the next column, they should describe the desired student outcome tied to the evidence-based practice. In Column 4, users will record the gap they identified on the Gap Analysis Chart, and in Column 5 they will list all of the information to be collected or the actions to be completed to implement the evidence-based practice. The last two columns allow users to designate the person(s) responsible and the time period in which they plan to carry out the action.

Table 11.2
Gap Analysis Chart

Gap Analysis Chart

Standard	Evidence-Based Practice	What We Do to Support This Practice	Desired Student Outcomes	What Evidence Do We Have That Current Practices Are Leading to Desired Student Outcomes?	What Additional Evidence/Information Do We Need? (Gaps)

Note. From *NAGC Pre-K–Grade 12 Gifted Programming Standards: A Blueprint for Quality Gifted Education Programs* (p. 5), by National Association for Gifted Children, 2010, Washington, DC: Author. Copyright 2010 by National Association for Gifted Children. Reprinted with permission.

Table 11.3
Action Plan Chart

Action Plan Chart					
Standard	Evidence-Based Practice	Desired Student Outcomes	Identified Gaps	Information to Be Collected/Action to Be Carried Out	Person(s) Responsible	Timeline

Note. From *NAGC Pre-K–Grade 12 Gifted Programming Standards: A Blueprint for Quality Gifted Education Programs* (p. 6), by National Association for Gifted Children, 2010, Washington, DC: Author. Copyright 2010 by National Association for Gifted Children. Reprinted with permission.

Putting the Standards Into Practice

We will now present two scenarios that will illustrate the use of the three planning documents. The first scenario is an example of how a gifted program coordinator might address Standard 2: Assessment.

Program Coordinator Scenario

The Juniper School District is located in a low-income suburban community. Seventy-four percent of the district's students qualify for free or reduced lunches; however, only 10% of the students identified for gifted programming services qualify for free or reduced lunches. Mrs. Jones, the district's gifted program coordinator, wants to find ways for students to reveal their exceptionalities or potential through assessment evidence so that an increased number of low-income students will be identified for programming services and appropriate instructional accommodations and modifications can be made. Currently, the district utilizes standardized test scores as well as a student characteristics/behavior checklist completed by the classroom teacher to inform program placement. Locally-developed norms or assessment tools in nonverbal formats are not considered. Although the program coordinator accepts nominations from multiple sources, most of the student nominations are received from teachers. An identification committee is in place and is made up of the elementary principal, the school counselor, one elementary teacher, one middle school teacher, and one high school teacher. Program guidelines were developed 12 years ago and include procedures for identifying students, committee guidelines, and appeal procedures for both entry and exit.

Mrs. Jones completed the Snapshot Survey. A partial listing of her Snapshot Survey ratings can be found in Table 11.4. Mrs. Jones combed through the evidence-based practices and marked the extent to which she engaged in behaviors associated with each practice, assessed the extent to which a change in the behavior would increase access or the academic achievement of students, and determined the amount of effort it would take to significantly change the practice regarding the issue. She felt that she minimally addressed Evidence-Based Practice 2.1.1 regarding the development of environments and instructional activities that encourage students to express diverse characteristics and behaviors associated with giftedness. She acknowledged that a change in the practice would benefit students, and she indicated that it would not require a great amount of effort to change the practice.

Table 11.4

Snapshot Survey of Gifted Programming Effectiveness Factors

Standard 2	Question 1: To what extent do we engage in this behavior or address this issue?				Question 2: How much will a change in our practices on this item increase access or the academic achievement of our students?				Question 3: How much effort will it take to significantly change our practices regarding this issue?				Are there policy implications? (√) if yes
	Not at all 1	2	3	To a great extent 4	Not at all 1	2	3	To a great extent 4	Not at all 1	2	3	To a great extent 4	
Standard 2: Assessment													
Evidence-Based Practices in My School													
2.1.1. Educators develop environments and instructional activities that encourage students to express diverse characteristics and behaviors that are associated with giftedness.		√					√			√			
2.1.2. Educators provide parents/guardians with information regarding diverse characteristics and behaviors that are associated with giftedness.	√						√			√			
2.2.1. Educators establish comprehensive, cohesive, and ongoing procedures for identifying and serving students with gifts and talents. These provisions include informed consent, committee review, student retention, student reassessment, student exiting, and appeals procedures for both entry and exit from gifted program services.			√					√	√				√
2.2.2. Educators select and use multiple assessments that measure diverse abilities, talents, and strengths that are based on current theories, models, and research.								√			√		√
2.2.3 Assessments provide qualitative and quantitative information from a variety of sources, including off-level testing, are nonbiased and equitable, and are technically adequate for the purpose.		√						√			√		√

Table 11.4, continued

Standard 2	Question 1 – To what extent do we engage in this behavior or address this issue?				Question 2 – How much will a change in our practices on this item increase access or the academic achievement of our students?				Question 3 – How much effort will it take to significantly change our practices regarding this issue?				Are there policy implications? (√) if yes
	Not at all 1	2	3	To a great extent 4	Not at all 1	2	3	To a great extent 4	Not at all 1	2	3	To a great extent 4	
Standard 2: Assessment													
Evidence-Based Practices in My School													
2.2.4. Educators have knowledge of student exceptionalities and collect assessment data while adjusting curriculum and instruction to learn about each student's developmental level and aptitude for learning.			√		√				√				
2.2.5. Educators interpret multiple assessments in different domains and understand the uses and limitations of the assessments in identifying the needs of students with gifts and talents.	√							√			√		
2.3.1. Educators select and use non-biased and equitable approaches for identifying students with gifts and talents, which may include using locally developed norms or assessment tools in the child's native language or in nonverbal formats.	√							√			√		√

As noted, Mrs. Jones felt relatively the same way about Evidence-Based Practice 2.1.2, which focuses on educators providing parents with information regarding diverse characteristics and behaviors associated with giftedness. When reviewing 2.2.1, however, Mrs. Jones realized that although the identification committee went through the motions of identifying students for services, the Juniper School District's program procedures were outdated and did not reflect the latest research or practice outlined in Evidence-Based Practice 2.2.1. She decided that this particular evidence-based practice was one she wanted to focus on and shaded it accordingly.

She also discovered that the use of multiple and varied assessments including nonverbal testing and information from a variety of sources was not considered. In particular, Evidence-Based Practice 2.2.2 stood out to her as needing her most immediate attention, and seemed reasonably doable this semester. As documented on the Snapshot Survey for Evidence-Based Practice 2.2.2, Mrs. Jones collected only standardized test scores and a student behavior checklist. She recognized that she needed to administer multiple assessments, and apparently felt that a change in this practice could increase access for students, but she also indicated it would require some effort.

Mrs. Jones highlighted Evidence-Based Practice 2.2.5 because she felt that the extra effort to address this standard would give her the greatest effect for the least amount of effort. She acknowledged her committee's failure to utilize multiple assessments addressing different domains and recognized her committee's lack of understanding of how to interpret assessments, including assessment uses and limitations in identifying the needs of students with gifts and talents.

When reviewing her ratings, Mrs. Jones focused on Evidence-Based Practice 2.3.1. She admitted that she and her committee never considered using locally-developed norms or adding nonverbal testing to the mix of identification assessments.

Now, Mrs. Jones plotted her selected evidence-based practices on a Gap Analysis Chart (see Table 11.5). For Evidence-Based Practice 2.2.1, which is "Educators establish comprehensive, cohesive, and ongoing procedures for identifying and serving students with gifts and talents" (NAGC 2010, p. 9), Mrs. Jones wrote in the third column, "We have procedures in place, although dated and ineffective." In the next column, she wrote the student outcome tied to the evidence-based practice. In the next column, Mrs. Jones stated that she had very little evidence that the current practices in place were leading to desired student outcomes. She also stated that few low-income students were identified for gifted programming services. In the last column, she noted that additional evidence was needed, and that she intended to compare timely research-based identification practices against the district's current identification practices.

Table 11.5

Gap Analysis Chart Example

Gap Analysis Chart					
Standard	Evidence-Based Practice	What We Do to Support This Practice	Desired Student Outcomes	What Evidence Do We Have That Current Practices Are Leading to Desired Student Outcomes?	What Additional Evidence/ Information Do We Need? (Gaps)
2	2.2.1	We have procedures in place, although dated and ineffective.	Each student reveals his or her exceptionalities or potential through assessment evidence so that appropriate accommodations and modifications can be made.	Very little. Few low-income students are identified and served through gifted programming services.	**Additional evidence is needed.** Compare timely research-based identification practices against district's current identification practices.
2	2.2.2	We address this minimally; a variety of assessments are not considered.	Each student reveals his or her exceptionalities or potential through assessment evidence so that appropriate accommodations and modifications can be made.	Very little. Few low-income students are identified and served through gifted programming services.	Very little additional evidence is needed as we only use standardized tests and a teacher checklist for identifying students. **This is a documented gap.**
2	2.2.5	We do not address this at all.	Each student reveals his or her exceptionalities or potential through assessment evidence so that appropriate accommodations and modifications can be made.	No evidence related to 2.2.5.	None needed. We do not currently address. **This is a documented gap.**
2	2.3.1	We do not address this at all.	Students with identified needs represent diverse (in this case low-income) backgrounds and reflect the total student population of the district.	No evidence related to 2.3.1.	None needed. We do not currently address. **This is a documented gap.**

For Evidence-Based Practice 2.2.2, which is "Educators select and use multiple assessments that measure diverse abilities, talents, and strengths that are based on current theories, models, and research" (NAGC 2010, p. 9), Mrs. Jones noted in the last column that she has very little evidence. She also recognized that few low-income students were identified for programming services. In the last column, she stated that she needed very little additional evidence, as they only used standardized tests and a behavior checklist to identify students. She recognized that she had a documented gap. For Evidence-Based Practices 2.2.5 and 2.3.1, Mrs. Jones stated that they did not address these, and there was no evidence to support that they addressed either evidence-based practice; therefore, she documented both as gaps in programming services as is noted in bold.

Now we are going to take a look at Mrs. Jones's Action Plan Chart (see Table 11.6). For Evidence-Based Practice 2.2.1, Mrs. Jones listed the identified gap as being outdated identification procedures. She assigned herself the task of seeking out research-based, nonbiased, and equitable identification procedures, and based on the findings, revised the program's identification procedures. She allotted herself one grading period to carry out the action.

For Evidence-Based Practice 2.2.2, Mrs. Jones stated that her program did not utilize multiple assessments as part of the identification procedure. In the fifth column, she assigned herself the task of seeking out a variety of assessments that measure diverse abilities, talents, and strengths and are based on current theories, models, and research. As noted in the last column, she allotted herself one semester to carry out the task.

For Evidence-Based Practice 2.2.5, Mrs. Jones documented that the identification committee failed to use/interpret multiple assessments in different domains; additionally, the committee does not understand the uses and limitations of the assessments in identifying the needs of students with gifts and talents. She assigned herself and the school's assessment coordinator the task of seeking out information on a variety of assessments testing different domains and studying them so the committee would understand the limitations of each. She allotted herself the spring semester to carry out the task.

For Evidence-Based Practice 2.3.1, Mrs. Jones acknowledged that they do not use nonbiased and equitable approaches for identifying students, nor do they use locally-developed norms. Mrs. Jones decided to seek out more information about how to use locally-developed norms to inform identification. She delegated herself and the assessment coordinator as the persons responsible for carrying out the action during the fourth grading period of the year.

At this point, we have completed an example Action Plan Chart. We will now look at a classroom teacher scenario. This particular scenario highlights Standard 5: Programming.

Table 11.6
Action Plan Chart Example

Action Plan Chart						
Standard	Evidence-Based Practice	Desired Student Outcomes	Identified Gaps	Information to Be Collected / Action to Be Carried Out	Person(s) Responsible	Timeline
2	2.2.1	Each student reveals his or her exceptionalities through assessment evidence so that appropriate instructional accommodations and modifications can be made.	Additional evidence revealed outdated identification procedures.	Seek out research-based, nonbiased, and equitable identification procedures.	Program coordinator, identification committee members	One grading period (first 9 weeks)
2	2.2.2	Each student reveals his or her exceptionalities through assessment evidence so that appropriate instructional accommodations and modifications can be made.	Lack of variety of sources used to identify students for gifted programming services.	Seek out a variety of qualitative and quantitative sources, including off-level testing, that are nonbiased and equitable, and are technically adequate for the purpose.	Program coordinator	One semester (fall; first and second 9-week grading periods)
2	2.2.5	Each student reveals his or her exceptionalities through assessment evidence so that appropriate instructional accommodations and modifications can be made.	The identification committee fails to use/interpret *multiple* assessments in *different* domains. Additionally, the committee does not understand the uses and limitations of the assessments in identifying the needs of students with gifts and talents.	Seek out information on a variety of assessments testing different domains. Understand the limitations of each.	Program coordinator, assessment coordinator	One semester (spring; third and fourth 9-week grading periods)
2	2.3.1	Students with identified needs represent diverse (in this case low-income) backgrounds and reflect the total student population of the district.	We do not use nonbiased and equitable approaches for identifying students, nor do we use locally-developed norms.	Seek out how to use locally-developed norms to inform identification.	Program coordinator, assessment coordinator	One grading period (fourth 9 weeks)

Classroom Teacher Scenario

Ms. Wilhelm, a third-grade teacher in the Pleasant Valley School District, finds that her gifted students consistently finish their work early and are often bored. In the past, she has assigned gifted students the enrichment activities found in her teacher's edition; however, students' reactions to the enrichment activities have been less than enthusiastic, and there appears to be no evidence that her students have benefited from the activities. Although Ms. Wilhelm engages with families during the required parent-teacher conferences, no efforts have been made to include families and community members in classroom planning. Ms. Wilhelm feels the need to do more to accommodate these students with special needs. Not knowing what to do or where to turn, Ms. Wilhelm decided to search online. She was thrilled to come across the NAGC website highlighting the 2010 NAGC Pre-K–Grade 12 Gifted Programming Standards along with resources to assist her with understanding and implementing the programming standards in her classroom.

Ms. Wilhelm completed the Snapshot Survey (see Table 11.7). When reviewing Evidence-Based Practice 5.1.1, "Educators regularly use multiple alternative approaches to accelerate learning" (NAGC, 2010, p. 12), Ms. Wilhelm marked *not at all* when assessing the extent to which she engaged in this behavior or addressed this practice. Furthermore, she marked *to a great extent* when assessing how much a change in her practices on this item would increase the academic achievement of her students. When sizing up Question 3, "How much effort will it take to significantly change our practices regarding this item?," Ms. Wilhelm marked "3," indicating that it would require some effort on her part to change this practice; however, because she highlighted it as one of the items to address in her classroom, she acknowledged it would be a worthwhile effort.

She gave similar marks for Evidence-Based Practices 5.1.4, which is "Educators regularly use individualized learning options such as mentorships, internships, online courses, and independent study" (NAGC, 2010, p. 12), and 5.3.1, which focuses on collaboration. There is one remark to be made here. Although she acknowledged there was a complete failure to address Evidence-Based Practice 5.2.1, she must have felt it was not "doable" or would require too much effort on her part to change this practice; therefore, she did not highlight it as one of the practices she would address at this time.

After rating the Standard 5 Evidence-Based Practices using the Snapshot Survey, Ms. Wilhelm chose to address Evidence-Based Practices 5.1.1, 5.1.4, and 5.3.1.

Table 11.7
Snapshot Survey of Gifted Programming Effectiveness Factors

Standard 5	Question 1: To what extent do we engage in this behavior or address this issue?				Question 2: How much will a change in our practices on this item increase access or the academic achievement of our students?				Question 3: How much effort will it take to significantly change our practices regarding this issue?				Are there policy implications? (✓) if yes
	Not at all 1	2	3	To a great extent 4	Not at all 1	2	3	To a great extent 4	Not at all 1	2	3	To a great extent 4	
Standard 5: Programming													
Evidence-Based Practices in My School													
5.1.1. Educators regularly use multiple alternative approaches to accelerate learning.	✓							✓			✓		✓
5.1.2. Educators regularly use enrichment options to extend and deepen learning opportunities within and outside of the school setting.		✓						✓		✓			
5.1.3. Educators regularly use multiple forms of grouping, including clusters, resource rooms, special classes, or special schools.		✓				✓				✓			✓
5.1.4. Educators regularly use individualized learning options such as mentorships, internships, online courses, and independent study.	✓							✓		✓			✓
5.2.1. Educators in gifted, general, and special education programs, as well as those in specialized areas, collaboratively plan, develop, and implement services for learners with gifts and talents.	✓						✓					✓	
5.3.1. Educators regularly engage families and community members for planning, programming, evaluating, and advocating.	✓						✓			✓			

NAGC Pre-K–Grade 12 Gifted Education Programming Standards

Next, Ms. Wilhelm completed the Gap Analysis Chart (see Table 11.8). For Evidence-Based Practice 5.1.1, Ms. Wilhelm acknowledged that she did assign enrichment activities found in her teacher's edition, but she also noted that there was no evidence that these activities impacted her students. In the last column, she recognized that she needed additional evidence because she had no clue as to what she should be doing for high-ability students.

For Evidence-Based Practice 5.1.4, she stated that nothing had been done to support the practice, which is "Educators regularly use individualized learning options such as mentorships, internships, online courses, and independent study" (NAGC, 2010, p. 12). The same is documented for Evidence-Based Practice 5.3.1, which is "Educators regularly engage families and community members for planning, programming, evaluating, and advocating" (NAGC, 2010, p. 12). In the last column, she stated that little to no additional evidence is needed, as individualized learning options are not utilized and collaboration with the community and families is limited. She acknowledged both as documented gaps.

Now, we will take a look at the Action Plan Chart (see Table 11.9). Ms. Wilhelm identified the gap for Evidence-Based Practice 5.1.1 as being "a lack of alternative approaches that can be used to accelerate learning" (NAGC, 2010, p. 12). To address the issue, she appointed herself the task of gathering information about multiple alternative approaches to accelerate learning. She stated she is going to check out the "Acceleration Works" link located at the NAGC website under Teacher's Corner. She allotted herself one month to carry out the task, as noted in the last column.

For Evidence-Based Practice 5.1.4, Ms. Wilhelm identified the gap as being the lack of individualized learning options for students. She assigned herself the task of seeking out mentorship opportunities, online courses, and independent study options for her students. For Evidence-Based Practice 5.3.1, Ms. Wilhelm identified that gap as being the lack of engagement with families and community members for planning, programming, evaluating, and advocating. She delegated herself, as well as the school counselor and parent facilitator, the task of seeking input and collaborative opportunities with parents and community members. She wrote "ongoing" under the Timeline column, indicating that she will continually seek out opportunities to engage families and community members.

Table 11.8
Gap Analysis Chart Example

Gap Analysis Chart

Standard	Evidence-Based Practice	What We Do to Support This Practice	Desired Student Outcomes	What Evidence Do We Have That Current Practices Are Leading to Desired Student Outcomes?	What Additional Evidence/ Information Do We Need? (Gaps)
5	5.1.1	Assign enrichment activities found in my teacher's edition. Not sure what other alternative approaches can be used to accelerate learning.	Students with gifts and talents participate in a variety of evidence-based programming options that enhance performance in cognitive and affective areas.	No evidence related to 5.1.1.	**Additional evidence is needed.** Search for research-based approaches to accelerate learning and compare against current classroom practice.
5	5.1.4	Nothing has been done to support this practice.	Students with gifts and talents participate in a variety of evidence-based programming options that enhance performance in cognitive and affective areas.	No evidence related to 5.1.4.	Very little additional evidence is needed because individualized learning options have not been utilized. **This is a document gap.**
5	5.3.1	Very little other than communicating with parents once a semester during parent-teacher conferences.	Students with gifts and talents participate in a variety of evidence-based programming options that enhance performance in cognitive and affective areas.	No evidence related to 5.3.1.	Very little additional evidence is needed because individualized learning options have not been utilized. **This is a document gap.**

Table 11.9

Action Plan Chart Example

Action Plan Chart

Standard	Evidence-Based Practice	Desired Student Outcomes	Identified Gaps	Information to Be Collected/ Action to Be Carried Out	Person(s) Responsible	Timeline
5	5.1.1	Students with gifts and talents participate in a variety of evidence-based programming options that enhance performance in cognitive and affective areas.	A lack of alternative approaches that can be used to accelerate learning.	Gather information about multiple alternative approaches to accelerate learning. Check out the "Acceleration Works" link located at the NAGC's website under Teacher's Corner.	Me, the classroom teacher; I will also ask the curriculum coordinator for assistance.	One month (September)
5	5.1.4	Students with gifts and talents participate in a variety of evidence-based programming options that enhance performance in cognitive and affective areas.	Individualized learning options have not been utilized.	Seek out student mentorship opportunities, online courses, and independent study options for my students.	Me, the classroom teacher.	One month (October) for initial information (but continue to be ongoing)
5	5.3.1	Educators regularly engage families and community members for planning, programming, evaluating, and advocating.	Very little engagement with families and community members for planning, programming, evaluating, and advocating.	Seek parents' and community members' input to inform classroom planning and programming, evaluating and advocating.	Me, the classroom teacher; I will also ask the school counselor and parent facilitator for assistance.	Ongoing

Figure 11.3. Driving in circles. ©2011, Lindsey Schichtl Goodwin

Bringing It All Together

Well, did you follow the charted course, or are you driving in circles (see Figure 11.3)?

Hopefully, you stayed the course. To implement the programming standards effectively requires thoughtful planning and careful consideration. There are several NAGC resources available that can assist you in your quest to bring the standards to life. These include a full glossary of terms available on the NAGC website, as well as links to references for many of the strategies recommended in the Gifted Programming Standards. The early stages of program planning and development are ideal times to use the three planning documents. Evidence-based practices provide the most compelling support for effective programming. Regardless of whether you are a novice or an old pro, utilizing district action plans is a smart way to organize data collection and resources and put informed judgments into practice.

References

Lord, E. W., & Cotabish, A. (2010, November). *Using the national gifted teacher preparation standards and NAGC program standards to inform practice: Snapshot survey of gifted programming effectiveness factors.* Paper presented at the annual meeting of the National Association for Gifted Children, Atlanta, GA.

Marzano, R. J. (2003). Snapshot survey of school effectiveness factors. In R. J. Marzano (Ed.), *What works in schools: Translating research into action* (pp. 179–187). Alexandria, VA: ASCD.

National Association for Gifted Children. (2010). *NAGC pre-K–grade 12 gifted programming standards: A blueprint for quality gifted education programs.* Washington, DC: Author.

Reference for Business. (2011). *Strategy formulation*. Retrieved from http://www.referenceforbusiness.com/management/Sc-Str/Strategy-Formulation.html

Chapter 12

Off the Page and Into Practice: Advocating for Implementation of the Gifted Programming Standards

by E. Wayne Lord and Jane Clarenbach

Can you have too many standards? Evidently, the answer to this question is a resounding "No!" Since the release of *A Nation at Risk* (National Commission on Excellence in Education,1983), there has been a rising tide of academic standards established in individual state curriculum frameworks, then through national professional associations, followed by more state curriculum standards, and now in the Common Core State Standards (Council of Chief State School Officers [CCSSO] & National Governors Association [NGA], 2010). Across the country, educators are breathing a sigh of relief: at last, standards driven by the mission to "provide a consistent clear understanding of what students are expected to learn" (Common Core Standards Initiative, n.d., para 1.).

And let's not forget the panoply of teacher preparation standards, accrediting organization standards, and specialty area teacher standards such as the Interstate Teacher Assessment and Support Consortium Model Core Teaching Standards (InTASC; CCSSO, 2011) and the National Council for Accreditation of Teacher Education Unit Standards (NCATE, 2007) and 21 specialized professional associations that partner with NCATE. The recent merger of NCATE and the Teacher Education Accreditation Council (TEAC) into a single accrediting body most likely will yield new accreditation challenges for institutions of higher education.

Program standards or opportunity-to-learn standards also describe or prescribe conditions that must exist in order for students to reach the expected academic standards. These standards, which address input, learning environment, management, and resources, began to appear in response to state curriculum standards (National Coalition of Educational Equity Advocates, 1994). Professional organizations such as the National Association for Gifted Children (NAGC) gradually introduced quality program standards (Landrum & Shaklee, 1998) that outlined requirements or criteria to guide processes for implementation.

Attached to each iteration of standards have been the challenges of documenting student learning progress and achievement, equipping teachers with professional development, identifying resources to support instruction, and convincing the public that our schools and students are performing at high levels.

In this tsunami of standards, educators are tossed about by federal regulations and funding enticements. Districts and schools are overwhelmed by federal, state, and local expectations when defining what students should know and be able to do. Add to these the tensions of autonomy in the classroom and accountability for student achievement, competition of funding amidst difficult economic times, and policymakers with good intentions yet less than comprehensive understanding. No wonder thinking about standards brings mixed emotions for most educators.

As the grip of accountability continues to tighten on educators, standards built solely around program expectations rather that evidence of impact on learners are no longer viable. Whether we are racing to the top, not leaving anyone behind, or scrambling to demonstrate yearly progress, the accountability refrain is clear. Enter the NAGC Pre-K–Grade 12 Gifted Programming Standards—revised, updated, and emphasizing student outcomes. Another set of standards by another well-intentioned professional organization. Will these programming standards be catalysts for action? Just as the 1992 Clinton campaign kept a sharp focus with "It's the economy, stupid," gifted educators, leaders, and advocates must brand these programming standards with "It's the student outcomes, _____!"

The 1998 Gifted Program Standards mainly addressed program expectations (input and processes) rather than student outcomes. Although they were reportedly widely used, there is little quantitative or qualitative data to demonstrate how gifted programs were affected by the earlier set of Gifted Program Standards (Matthews & Shaunessy, 2010). How do standards move off the page and into practice? Leadership is required. Leadership is needed to move beyond adopting and into implementing.

Here, we discuss two of the most critical elements necessary for standards to become a reality: collaboration with education colleagues and ensuring an open, receptive environment in which standards, along with accompanying change in practice, occur as intended by standards developers. We then move on to how those who accepted the leadership role for the gifted education program standards can advocate for their use. Whether with school leaders, colleagues, volunteers, or elected officials, we suggest inserting into various conversations one or more of the standards, the strategies, or the research on which the standards are founded. We suggest three strategies for advocate leaders to keep in mind when presenting the standards for others to consider and provide a sample scenario for each.

Depending on the environment—molded by the effectiveness of gifted education leaders—advocacy can be slow and sometimes frustrating, particularly when the advocate encounters deeply held misunderstandings about high-ability students. However, advocacy is essential for positive change. As Ford (2011) recently reminded us, the time expended in developing and distributing standards is wasted if there is no implementation.

Key Factors for Standards Success

Leadership

Who are these leaders? Potential leaders are classroom teachers, school principals, district staff, parents and grandparents of students, school boards, state education agencies, community organizations and businesses, and elected governmental representatives. Where are these leaders? Everywhere—but implementation will occur at the classroom level, in school buildings with general educators, gifted educators, media specialists, counselors, support staff, and administrators. Policymakers may pass mandates, and state education agencies may issue guidelines; however, school leaders, both teachers and administrators, will bring life to gifted programming standards and most directly affect student learning outcomes.

There are no easy ways for implementing the Gifted Programming Standards that are addressed in this book, and to offer a single approach or roadmap for achieving implementation would be naïve. Implementation will require bringing together a wide array of people for chiseling away at problems, barriers, and commitments. In many educational settings, implementation will require substantive changes; in others, refinement or modest adaptation of current practices will suffice.

As school leaders plan to advocate for and guide the implementation of Gifted Programming Standards, recalling some essential ideas related to collaboration and culture might prove useful. These areas are continuously addressed in leadership literature (e.g., Collins, 2001; Deal & Peterson, 1999; Leithwood & Riehl, 2003; Sergiovanni, 1992), and an intensive or extensive discussion of these is impractical for this short chapter. However, reflecting on the challenges of collaboration and culture is critical for guiding how one leads and advocates.

Collaboration

Whether implementing the 2010 Gifted Programming Standards in a classroom or in a school, district, or state, collaboration is critical. Although most leaders, advocates, and stakeholders might agree with this in theory, the practice of collaboration is hard work. Competing agendas, differing beliefs, unique personalities, and unwillingness to expend energy often create barriers to collaborating. Teachers, gifted education coordinators, administrators, state directors, and advocates face these same challenges.

The Wallace Foundation (2006) monograph reported, "Close collaboration and coordination between states and districts has not been the historic norm. It is complex, time-consuming, and challenging to maintain. And it takes top government and education leaders with authority to make change happen" (p. 6). Although this study did not focus on gifted education policy, it reaffirms the collaboration challenge gifted advocates face when working in the policy arena and reinforces the focus for leading through collaboration at the building level.

A collaborative environment thrives when healthy, positive relationships exist; central to such relationships is trust. Trust is critical when seeking rapid improvement and when requiring exceptional effort and competence (Evans, 1996). A recent Rand Corporation study (Augustine et al., 2009) emphasized the importance of trust when collaborating and working to build cohesion. The strategies that relate to collaboration that were found to be effective include creating networks (formal and informal), facilitating communication, working to build capacity, and linking to other educational reform efforts (Augustine et al., 2009).

Trust clearly can be seen as a factor affecting how successful these additional collaboration strategies will be. Networks (horizontal and vertical) will not be productive without trust. Communication will not be open without trust. Capacity building, which includes taking risks, acknowledging needs, creating learning communities, and providing resources, will not occur without trust. Lastly, connecting to other reform initiatives will not be an option when prior evidence of trusting relationships cannot be found.

As an advocate and leader, what is your trust factor? What can you do to foster collaboration for implementing the Gifted Programming Standards?

Culture

The culture within a school will either facilitate implementation of gifted programming standards or present a resilient barrier to any change. Barth (2007) defined school culture as "the complex pattern of norms, attitudes, beliefs, behaviors, values, ceremonies, traditions, and myths that are deeply ingrained in the very core of the organization" (p. 160). These separate elements interact to form school culture, which may be fixed or fluid, rigid, or open to adaptation.

When considering culture and its impact on conversations and actions related to the Gifted Programming Standards, leaders and advocates may encounter resistance based on myths or lack of knowledge related to the needs of gifted learners. Beyond understanding the school culture, leaders promoting gifted education must acknowledge school and community values and attitudes about giftedness. A respectful appreciation of the personal as well as the institutional beliefs and practices will serve leaders and advocates well.

Reeves (2009) advised leaders to be clear about which aspects of the culture will not change—what we will continue to do. Trying to implement Gifted Programming Standards in a top-down approach will not bring about the desired cultural change. A skillful leader or advocate strategizes carefully and uses various tools for introducing and supporting change within an educational system. Context is important.

A leader must understand the nature of a school's culture and how the culture responds to implementing different ideas and approaches—especially when changes in teaching practices are proposed. According to Senge and colleagues (1999), "The fundamental flaw in most innovators' strategies is that they focus on their innovations, on what they are trying to do—rather than on understanding how the larger culture, structures, and norms will react to their efforts" (p. 26). Sparks (2008) echoed this truth during a presentation at the National Staff Development Council conference saying, "Culture trumps innovation."

As a leader, how well do you understand the culture of your school, district, community, and state for implementing the Gifted Programming Standards? What can you do to guide any cultural changes that may be needed so that advocacy for the standards can be successful?

Advocating for Gifted Learners

Most of us advocate daily, as we discuss ideas with friends and colleagues; join, volunteer, or contribute to special-interest organizations; or propose new initiatives, strategies, or budgets as part of our jobs.

Advocating for education policy or practice changes is similar in that it involves making value judgments, but is different in that success typically involves persuading decision makers to take specific action that will have a broad and lasting impact. Robinson and Moon (2003) identified several factors about advocates that support positive advocacy outcomes. In their research, successful advocates are knowledgeable about both best practices in gifted education and decision-making processes, they check for clarity and accuracy in communication, and they are persistent and collaborative rather than adversarial in approach. These last two factors—persistence and collaboration—are also discussed by Gallagher and Coleman (1992) in the context of successful leadership for advocacy. At the risk of sounding overly simplistic, all successful advocacy on the Gifted Programming Standards requires at least one individual taking the responsibility—the leadership role—to promote the standards to others.

Role of Standards in Advocacy

Standards in education influence school, district, and state priorities, including curriculum development, teacher training, staff hiring, development of student assessments, development of specialized services, and evaluation of programs and services (Johnsen, 2011), among other critical components of teaching and learning.

As a subset of education standards, standards in gifted education programming provide the foundation on which to ensure gifted and talented students, as well as high-potential students who could achieve at high levels with appropriate supports, are identified and served (Johnsen, 2011). High-quality, evidence-based standards can also provide clarity, guidance to educators, and consistency across buildings within the same district and between districts across the state (Ford, 2011), which is critical to garnering support for the resources necessary to sustain the programs and services. As has been stated so well elsewhere, standards provide a structure that allows for a commitment to common values and rules and as such, function as consensus-building agents within institutions (VanTassel-Baska & Johnsen, 2007).

Powerful stuff. If school leadership on the Gifted Programming Standards can spur support for appropriate services for advanced students, the standards become a new tool in an advocate's toolbox. So then, how might we successfully advocate for the implementation of the Gifted Programming Standards to help develop support for our high-ability students and improve instruction for all students?

Inserting the Gifted Programming Standards Into the Conversation

Depending on the individual school and district circumstances, standards proponents could advocate for the Gifted Programming Standards as a set or for individual standards and corresponding services or gifted education strategy within each practice area. Advocates searching for opportunities to advance the standards may find that advocating for the complete set of standards is practicable in settings where some support for gifted and talented education services already exists. In this context, the standards inform improvements to or expansion of those services in the six areas covered by the standards. Conversely, in an environment where there is a lack of or uneven support for gifted and talented education services, advocates may be able to insert one or more of the Gifted Programming Standards into key decisions being made in a building, district, or state by linking gifted education strategies and the standards to one or more of the numerous education issues school leaders are confronting. For example, state and district discussions about the Common Core State Standards (CCSSO & NGA, 2010) or the new InTASC teacher preparation standards (CCSSO, 2011) provide opportunities, or "hooks," to ask how the implementation of those initiatives will take into account the needs of advanced and high-potential students. From there, it's a short step to discussing the new Gifted Programming Standards on curriculum planning and instruction and professional development.

Make no mistake, though, getting to agreement on changes to policy and practice can be elusive for advocates and decision makers. We propose three key ways to present the standards to colleagues and school leaders based on a framework that has proved successful for advocates promoting gifted education services.

Present the standards as part of the solution. Successful advocates present themselves as willing to be part of the solution, rather than only pointing out the problems a policy or practice, or lack thereof, presents for gifted students (Reeves, 2008). Providing the standards as a resource for school leaders or work teams involved in numerous complex issues such as total school improvement not only brings the needs of gifted students into the discussion, but can also contribute specific, high-quality recommendations. The viability of the standards as an authoritative resource for policy or practice is bolstered by the fact that the standards are backed with research support for the strategies leading to each student outcome. Policymakers and school leaders are more likely to be receptive to recommendations that have a research base on the impact on students and are already written in the language of education.

Key questions to help you prepare your advocacy discussion points are:

» What issues are of greatest concern to my school's (district's, state's) leaders?

» How can I position one or more of the Gifted Programming Standards, and their corresponding student outcomes, as addressing these concerns?

Sample Scenario

A K–8 school district just received word that its budget will be significantly cut for the upcoming school year. This means a reduction in the math magnet program, art, music, and afterschool enrichment opportunities. The school district is like many in the area, with a very diverse student population coming from mixed economic backgrounds. Several veteran teachers are leading a school improvement work team that is examining professional development needs, potential community resources and partnerships, and instructional delivery changes as a way to conserve resources while retaining some of the emphases that made school a positive place for the students. Ms. Taylor, the math magnet teacher, brought the NAGC Pre-K–Grade 12 Gifted Programming Standards to the attention of the workgroup as a way to focus on student outcomes in its planning. She emphasized several outcomes directly related to the team's goals.

In looking at ways to enhance student performance in cognitive and affective areas (5.1), Ms. Taylor pointed out that there are several schoolwide strategies from gifted education that are built on a deep research base that they could consider, including enrichment and cluster grouping options (5.1.3). She also suggested that they could take advantage of community resources to enhance advanced student learning (5.3) through individualized learning options such as mentorships, internships, and independent study opportunities (5.1.4; 1.3.1). Collaboration with families and the larger community would also allow infusion of arts and music and other areas of student interest into classroom instruction and out-of-school opportunities (1.4.2).

In considering the diversity of the district's student population, Ms. Taylor suggested increased professional development to focus on helping teachers recognize and respond to the diverse characteristics and behaviors associated with giftedness (6.1.2), to provide activities that match culture-based learning needs (1.2.1), and to design interventions for high-ability students who may be underperforming (1.6.2). She also recommended in-service training for school counselors, administrators, teachers, and instructional staff that models appreciation for and sensitivity to students' diverse backgrounds and languages (4.4.1) and also supports the social-emotional needs of students (6.2.1).

Keep the focus on the students. Just as it is important to make the connection between capable students of today and participating citizens of tomorrow (Reeves, 2008) in advocating for changes in education policy and practice, it is also crucial to connect student outcomes to specific strategies you are recommending when you suggest adoption or implementation of one or more of the standards.

In some districts and states, the topic of the day is the "brain drain" from the state; in others, it's about improving test scores, differentiation, or developing 21st-century skills, all of which can be connected to gifted education pedagogy and to specific programming standards. In other schools, districts, and states, advocates could use the Gifted Programming Standards in discussions about developing student assessments or effective program evaluation. Many parents bring concerns about student boredom and disengagement to the attention of teachers and school leaders. In each case, it is critical to explain how students, both those identified as gifted and the larger student population, will benefit from your recommendations to implement one or more of the standards.

As you prepare to discuss the standards with colleagues, school and district leaders, and elected officials, ask yourself the following questions:

>> Which of the student outcomes are connected to the priorities of the school (district, state)?

>> How can I position the strategies I advocate for, connecting them to student outcomes, as helping all students, including high-ability students, in the school (district, state) to achieve at higher levels?

Sample Scenario

The Lakeview Elementary School principal is concerned about the school's flat test scores over the past 3 years. She is new to the building and has heard a general concern from parents that their children are often bored in class. The principal has appointed a workgroup to suggest ways in which the school could address both concerns by increasing academic rigor for some students who may need it. One of the teachers (who is pursuing a degree in gifted education), brought the Gifted Programming Standards to the meeting. When the group began talking about what changes the school might make, the teacher drew the workgroup's attention to Standard 1: Learning and Development and its research support that focuses on how high-ability students, including those who are underachieving, can benefit from meaningful and challenging learning activities (1.6). She suggested that they might plan for schoolwide professional development on assessment strategies that would contribute to advanced student learning outcomes (2.4), such as using off-level standardized assessments (2.4.3). The teacher knew from her own coursework that in planning for curriculum and instruction, it's essential to preassess student knowledge (3.1.6) so that time isn't wasted on material that students already know, which may have been the cause of the reported boredom. She also emphasized the link between student interest and learning (3.3.3) and to be sure that the school made every effort to collaborate with families in accessing resources to develop their child's interests and talents (1.4.1; 1.5.1). Armed with the standards and the supporting research base, the teacher was able to show her colleagues how many of the strategies used with gifted and talented students can be used to improve the performance of all students.

Keep the audience focus as wide as possible. Recognizing that all educators are responsible for the education of high-ability students (Johnsen, 2011), the Gifted Programming Standards broadly define the term "educators" to include administrators, teachers, counselors, and other instructional support staff. This inclusive definition of educators means that there are other building and district-level professionals with whom the standards should be shared and discussed, as the student outcomes may depend on their support and expertise. The process of educating colleagues to the needs of high-ability students through the standards lens provides opportunities for consultation and collaboration that ultimately increase the number of advocates for this special population of learners. Likewise, families and parents, who play critical roles in supporting their high-ability children, should be informed about the standards and invited to share their concerns and questions. Parents are often formidable allies in advocacy.

As you consider potential audiences for your message, ask yourself the following questions:

» Who in the school (district, state) makes decisions or recommendations about serving gifted and talented students?

» Who in the school (district, state) has primary responsibility for each of the practice areas covered by the standards? Are there workgroups or committees also working on any of these areas?

» What are the opportunities to present the standards to the audiences identified above?

Sample Scenario

All it took was one meeting, about 4 weeks into the school year, to know that the new principal, who had a background in special education with an emphasis on gifted education, would be running things a bit differently. Mr. Davis told his staff that he wanted to be sure that the school was matching services to student needs across the entire student population. He had observed a silo-like approach to serving students, where teachers talked about "my" kids and "your" kids and "our" program versus "your" program. He wanted to encourage a shared responsibility for all of the students. He distributed the Gifted Programming Standards to the teachers and asked them to come to a future meeting prepared to recommend strategies for how the entire school community could collaborate in support of the students.

To kick off the discussion at the subsequent meeting, one teacher pointed out that all students would benefit from coordinated curriculum and instruction, and that it would take collaboration across gifted, general, and special education programs, as well as the counselors and psychologists, to plan, develop, and implement those services effectively (5.2.1). Other teachers recommended several collaboration strategies:

- Educators could support students' cognitive and affective needs by working with families to access resources to develop their child's talents (1.5.1), share information with families about the diverse characteristics and behaviors associated with giftedness (2.1.2), and provide information that explains the nature and purpose of gifted programming options. And, in order to make appropriate instructional accommodations and modifications (2.2), educators must elicit from families evidence regarding the child's interests and potential outside of the classroom setting (2.2.6).

- To help students understand themselves and others (1.3), the school could implement more grouping practices across subjects and grades to allow students to interact with a wide range of learners (1.3.1) and provide structured opportunities to collaborate with diverse peers on a common goal (4.4.3).
- To encourage social responsibility and leadership development, and to support talent development and future career goals, school personnel could share with each other the leadership (4.3.2) or internship and mentorship opportunities (5.1.4; 5.7.2) available that they might encourage students to take on as well as ensure that colleagues are aware of school and community resources that support differentiation (3.3.2).

Mr. Davis was pleased with the suggestions and could see that some cross-department and program training and professional development would help the entire community better understand the wide range of student learning needs as well as the possible responses. He also wanted to broaden the expertise on several ongoing teams, including the Response to Intervention (RtI) group and the career and vocational opportunities team, to ensure that students being considered for special services and opportunities would benefit from as broad a range of perspectives as possible.

As more gifted education leaders and advocates initiate conversations about desired student outcomes at the district and building levels, and as more gifted education professionals share proven strategies with colleagues in general and special education, the result is more likely to be increased excellence in general education classrooms and more equity in gifted education services (Tomlinson, Coleman, Allan, Udall, & Landrum, 1996).

Exemplary Leaders and Advocates

Off the page and into practice—an opportunity for leaders and advocates to develop, inform, implement, and support education policies based on research and best practices that will be effective and long-lasting. Gallagher and Coleman (1992) found that highly motivated individuals willing to persist in both policy development and policy approval efforts are critical to a successful outcome. However, Fullan (2001) cautioned, "Being sure of yourself when you shouldn't be can be a liability. Decisive leaders can attract many followers, but it is usually more a case of dependency than enlightenment" (p. 49).

In many schools and districts, before policy can be adopted, much work must be done to dispel myths and misconceptions. Moreover, the consequences of implementing these gifted programming standards for education and training cannot be ignored. Raising awareness of the nature of high ability and how it is developed and nurtured must be grown into a pedagogy of advanced learning that supports gifted learners and improves student outcomes. Building awareness and transforming practices are important tasks for gifted education leaders and advocates.

There are specific behaviors that can guide leaders and advocates when confronting the challenges of collaboration and culture. The research on leadership conducted by Kouzes and Posner (2007) provided a framework for leading and advocating. Leaders and advocates "model the way, inspire a shared vision, challenge the process, enable others to act, encourage the heart" (Kouzes & Posner, 2007, p. 14). Collaboration will flourish and organizational culture will be responsive to change as leaders and advocates for gifted and talented students match words with actions, engage stakeholders in pursuing a common good, press on as obstacles are encountered, empower those engaged in making a positive difference, and acknowledge progress made in difficult settings.

References

Augustine, C. H., Gonzalez, G., Ikemoto, G. S., Russell, J., Zellman, G. L., Constant, L., . . . Dembosky, J. W. (2009). *Building cohesive leadership systems to improve school leadership*. Santa Monica, CA: RAND Corporation.

Barth, R. (2007). Culture in question. In *The Jossey-Bass reader on educational leadership* (pp. 159–168). San Francisco, CA: Jossey-Bass.

Collins, J. (2001). *Good to great: Why some companies make the leap . . . and others don't*. New York, NY: HarperCollins.

Common Core Standards Initiative. (n.d.). *Mission statement*. Retrieved from http://www.corestandards.org

Council of Chief State School Officers. (2011). *InTASC model core teaching standards: A resource for state dialogue*. Washington, DC: Author. Retrieved from http://www.ccsso.org/Documents/2011/InTASC_Model_Core_Teaching_Standards_2011.pdf

Council of Chief State School Officers, & National Governors Association. (2010). *Common core state standards initiative*. Retrieved from http://www.corestandards.org

Deal, T. E., & Peterson, K. D. (1999). *Shaping the school culture: The heart of leadership*. San Francisco, CA: Jossey-Bass.

Evans, R. (1996). *The human side of school change*. San Francisco, CA: Jossey-Bass.

Ford, D. (2011). Don't waste trees: Standards must be culturally responsive and their implementation monitored. *Tempo, 31*(1), 35–38.

Fullan, M. (2001), *Leading in a culture of change.* San Francisco, CA: Jossey-Bass.

Gallagher, J. J., & Coleman, M. R. (1992). *State policies on the identification of gifted students from special populations: Three states in profile.* Chapel Hill: University of North Carolina, Gifted Education Policy Study Program.

Johnsen, S. K. (2011). A comparison of the Texas state plan for the education of gifted/ talented students and the 2010 NAGC pre-K–grade 12 gifted programming standards. *Tempo, 31*(1), 10–19.

Kouzes, J., & Posner, B. (2007). *The leadership challenge* (4th ed.). San Francisco, CA: Jossey-Bass.

Landrum, M. S., & Shaklee, B. D. (Eds.). (1998). *Pre-K–grade 12 gifted program standards.* Washington, DC: National Association for Gifted Children.

Leithwood, K. A., & Riehl, C. (2003). *What we know about successful school leadership.* Philadelphia, PA: Temple University, Laboratory for Student Success.

Matthews, M., & Shaunessy, E. (2010). Putting standards into practice: Evaluating the utility of the NAGC pre-K–grade 12 gifted program standards. *Gifted Child Quarterly, 54,* 159–167.

National Coalition of Educational Equity Advocates. (1994). *Educate America: A call for equity in school reform.* Chevy Chase, MD: The Mid-Atlantic Equity Consortium.

National Commission on Excellence in Education. (1983). *A nation at risk: The imperatives for educational reform.* Washington, DC: United States Government Printing Office.

National Council for Accreditation of Teacher Education. (2007). *Professional standards for the accreditation of teacher preparation institutions.* Washington, DC: Author.

Reeves, D. (2008, December). Dancing toward district advocacy. *Parenting for High Potential,* 11-13.

Reeves, D. (2009). *Leading change in your school: How to conquer myths, build commitments, and get results.* Alexandria, VA: ASCD.

Robinson, A., & Moon, S. M. (2003). A national study of local and state advocacy in gifted education. *Gifted Child Quarterly, 47,* 8–25.

Senge, P., Kleiner, A., Roberts, C., Roth, G., Ross, R., & Smith, B. (1999). *The dance of change.* New York, NY: Doubleday.

Sergiovanni, T. J. (1992). *Moral leadership: Getting to the heart of school improvement.* San Francisco, CA: Jossey-Bass.

Sparks, D. (2008, December). *Leadership for re-culturing schools.* Paper presented at the annual meeting of National Staff Development Council, Washington, DC.

Tomlinson, C. A., Coleman, M. R., Allan, S., Udall, A., & Landrum, M. (1996). Interface between gifted education and general education: Toward communication, cooperation, and collaboration. *Gifted Child Quarterly, 40,* 165–171.

VanTassel-Baska, J., & Johnsen, S. K. (2007). Teacher education standards for the field of gifted education. *Gifted Child Quarterly, 51,* 182–204.

The Wallace Foundation. (2006). *Leadership for learning: Making connections among state, district, and school policies and practices.* New York, NY: Author.

2010 Pre-K–Grade 12 Gifted Programming Standards

Gifted Education Programming Standard 1: Learning and Development

Introduction

To be effective in working with learners with gifts and talents, teachers and other educators in PreK-12 settings must understand the characteristics and needs of the population for whom they are planning curriculum, instruction, assessment, programs, and services. These characteristics provide the rationale for differentiation in programs, grouping, and services for this population and are translated into appropriate differentiation choices made at curricular and program levels in schools and school districts. While cognitive growth is important in such programs, affective development is also necessary. Thus many of the characteristics addressed in this standard emphasize affective development linked to self-understanding and social awareness.

Standard 1: Learning and Development

Description: *Educators, recognizing the learning and developmental differences of students with gifts and talents, promote ongoing self-understanding, awareness of their needs, and cognitive and affective growth of these students in school, home, and community settings to ensure specific student outcomes.*

Student Outcomes	Evidence-Based Practices
1.1. Self-Understanding. Students with gifts and talents demonstrate self-knowledge with respect to their interests, strengths, identities, and needs in socio-emotional development and in intellectual, academic, creative, leadership, and artistic domains.	1.1.1. Educators engage students with gifts and talents in identifying interests, strengths, and gifts. 1.1.2. Educators assist students with gifts and talents in developing identities supportive of achievement.

Student Outcomes	Evidence-Based Practices
1.2. Self-Understanding. Students with gifts and talents possess a developmentally appropriate understanding of how they learn and grow; they recognize the influences of their beliefs, traditions, and values on their learning and behavior.	1.2.1. Educators develop activities that match each student's developmental level and culture-based learning needs.
1.3. Self-Understanding. Students with gifts and talents demonstrate understanding of and respect for similarities and differences between themselves and their peer group and others in the general population.	1.3.1. Educators provide a variety of research-based grouping practices for students with gifts and talents that allow them to interact with individuals of various gifts, talents, abilities, and strengths. 1.3.2. Educators model respect for individuals with diverse abilities, strengths, and goals.
1.4. Awareness of Needs. Students with gifts and talents access resources from the community to support cognitive and affective needs, including social interactions with others having similar interests and abilities or experiences, including same-age peers and mentors or experts.	1.4.1. Educators provide role models (e.g., through mentors, bibliotherapy) for students with gifts and talents that match their abilities and interests. 1.4.2. Educators identify out-of-school learning opportunities that match students' abilities and interests.
1.5. Awareness of Needs. Students' families and communities understand similarities and differences with respect to the development and characteristics of advanced and typical learners and support students with gifts and talents' needs.	1.5.1. Educators collaborate with families in accessing resources to develop their child's talents.
1.6. Cognitive and Affective Growth. Students with gifts and talents benefit from meaningful and challenging learning activities addressing their unique characteristics and needs.	1.6.1. Educators design interventions for students to develop cognitive and affective growth that is based on research of effective practices. 1.6.2. Educators develop specialized intervention services for students with gifts and talents who are underachieving and are now learning and developing their talents.
1.7. Cognitive and Affective Growth. Students with gifts and talents recognize their preferred approaches to learning and expand their repertoire.	1.7.1. Teachers enable students to identify their preferred approaches to learning, accommodate these preferences, and expand them.
1.8. Cognitive and Affective Growth. Students with gifts and talents identify future career goals that match their talents and abilities and resources needed to meet those goals (e.g., higher education opportunities, mentors, financial support).	1.8.1. Educators provide students with college and career guidance that is consistent with their strengths. 1.8.2. Teachers and counselors implement a curriculum scope and sequence that contains person/social awareness and adjustment, academic planning, and vocational and career awareness.

Gifted Education Programming Standard 2: Assessment

Introduction

Knowledge about all forms of assessment is essential for educators of students with gifts and talents. It is integral to identification, assessing each student's learning progress, and evaluation of programming. Educators need to establish a challenging environment and collect multiple types of assessment information so that all students are able to demonstrate their gifts and talents. Educators' understanding of non-biased, technically adequate, and equitable approaches enables them to identify students who represent diverse backgrounds. They also differentiate their curriculum and instruction by using pre- and post-, performance-based, product-based, and out-of-level assessments. As a result of each educator's use of ongoing assessments, students with gifts and talents demonstrate advanced and complex learning. Using these student progress data, educators then evaluate services and make adjustments to one or more of the school's programming components so that student performance is improved.

Standard 2: Assessment	
Description: *Assessments provide information about identification, learning progress and outcomes, and evaluation of programming for students with gifts and talents in all domains.*	

Student Outcomes	Evidence-Based Practices
2.1. Identification. All students in grades PK–12 have equal access to a comprehensive assessment system that allows them to demonstrate diverse characteristics and behaviors that are associated with giftedness.	2.1.1. Educators develop environments and instructional activities that encourage students to express diverse characteristics and behaviors that are associated with giftedness. 2.1.2. Educators provide parents/guardians with information regarding diverse characteristics and behaviors that are associated with giftedness.
2.2. Identification. Each student reveals his or her exceptionalities or potential through assessment evidence so that appropriate instructional accommodations and modifications can be provided.	2.2.1. Educators establish comprehensive, cohesive, and ongoing procedures for identifying and serving students with gifts and talents. These provisions include informed consent, committee review, student retention, student reassessment, student exiting, and appeals procedures for both entry and exit from gifted program services.

Student Outcomes	Evidence-Based Practices
	2.2.2. Educators select and use multiple assessments that measure diverse abilities, talents, and strengths that are based on current theories, models, and research. 2.2.3 Assessments provide qualitative and quantitative information from a variety of sources, including off-level testing, are nonbiased and equitable, and are technically adequate for the purpose. 2.2.4. Educators have knowledge of student exceptionalities and collect assessment data while adjusting curriculum and instruction to learn about each student's developmental level and aptitude for learning. 2.2.5. Educators interpret multiple assessments in different domains and understand the uses and limitations of the assessments in identifying the needs of students with gifts and talents. 2.2.6. Educators inform all parents/guardians about the identification process. Teachers obtain parental/guardian permission for assessments, use culturally sensitive checklists, and elicit evidence regarding the child's interests and potential outside of the classroom setting.
2.3. Identification. Students with identified needs represent diverse backgrounds and reflect the total student population of the district.	2.3.1. Educators select and use non-biased and equitable approaches for identifying students with gifts and talents, which may include using locally developed norms or assessment tools in the child's native language or in nonverbal formats. 2.3.2. Educators understand and implement district and state policies designed to foster equity in gifted programming and services. 2.3.3. Educators provide parents/guardians with information in their native language regarding diverse behaviors and characteristics that are associated with giftedness and with information that explains the nature and purpose of gifted programming options.
2.4. Learning Progress and Outcomes. Students with gifts and talents demonstrate advanced and complex learning as a result of using multiple, appropriate, and ongoing assessments.	2.4.1. Educators use differentiated pre- and post- performance-based assessments to measure the progress of students with gifts and talents. 2.4.2. Educators use differentiated product-based assessments to measure the progress of students with gifts and talents.

Student Outcomes	Evidence-Based Practices
	2.4.3. Educators use off-level standardized assessments to measure the progress of students with gifts and talents. 2.4.4. Educators use and interpret qualitative and quantitative assessment information to develop a profile of the strengths and weaknesses of each student with gifts and talents to plan appropriate intervention. 2.4.5. Educators communicate and interpret assessment information to students with gifts and talents and their parents/guardians.
2.5. Evaluation of Programming. Students identified with gifts and talents demonstrate important learning progress as a result of programming and services.	2.5.1. Educators ensure that the assessments used in the identification and evaluation processes are reliable and valid for each instrument's purpose, allow for above-grade-level performance, and allow for diverse perspectives. 2.5.2. Educators ensure that the assessment of the progress of students with gifts and talents uses multiple indicators that measure mastery of content, higher level thinking skills, achievement in specific program areas, and affective growth. 2.5.3. Educators assess the quantity, quality, and appropriateness of the programming and services provided for students with gifts and talents by disaggregating assessment data and yearly progress data and making the results public.
2.6. Evaluation of Programming. Students identified with gifts and talents have increased access and they show significant learning progress as a result of improving components of gifted education programming.	2.6.1. Administrators provide the necessary time and resources to implement an annual evaluation plan developed by persons with expertise in program evaluation and gifted education. 2.6.2. The evaluation plan is purposeful and evaluates how student-level outcomes are influenced by one or more of the following components of gifted education programming: (a) identification, (b) curriculum, (c) instructional programming and services, (d) ongoing assessment of student learning, (e) counseling and guidance programs, (f) teacher qualifications and professional development, (g) parent/guardian and community involvement, (h) programming resources, and (i) programming design, management, and delivery. 2.6.3. Educators disseminate the results of the evaluation, orally and in written form, and explain how they will use the results.

Gifted Education Programming Standard 3: Curriculum Planning and Instruction

Introduction

Assessment is an integral component of the curriculum planning process. The information obtained from multiple types of assessments informs decisions about curriculum content, instructional strategies, and resources that will support the growth of students with gifts and talents. Educators develop and use a comprehensive and sequenced core curriculum that is aligned with local, state, and national standards, then differentiate and expand it. In order to meet the unique needs of students with gifts and talents, this curriculum must emphasize advanced, conceptually challenging, in-depth, distinctive, and complex content within cognitive, affective, aesthetic, social, and leadership domains. Educators must possess a repertoire of evidence-based instructional strategies in delivering the curriculum (a) to develop talent, enhance learning, and provide students with the knowledge and skills to become independent, self-aware learners, and (b) to give students the tools to contribute to a multicultural, diverse society. The curriculum, instructional strategies, and materials and resources must engage a variety of learners using culturally responsive practices.

Standard 3: Curriculum Planning and Instruction

Description: *Educators apply the theory and research-based models of curriculum and instruction related to students with gifts and talents and respond to their needs by planning, selecting, adapting, and creating culturally relevant curriculum and by using a repertoire of evidence-based instructional strategies to ensure specific student outcomes.*

Student Outcomes	Evidence-Based Practices
3.1. Curriculum Planning. Students with gifts and talents demonstrate growth commensurate with aptitude during the school year.	3.1.1. Educators use local, state, and national standards to align and expand curriculum and instructional plans. 3.1.2. Educators design and use a comprehensive and continuous scope and sequence to develop differentiated plans for PK–12 students with gifts and talents. 3.1.3. Educators adapt, modify, or replace the core or standard curriculum to meet the needs of students with gifts and talents and those with special needs such as twice-exceptional, highly gifted, and English language learners.

Student Outcomes	Evidence-Based Practices
	3.1.4. Educators design differentiated curricula that incorporate advanced, conceptually challenging, in-depth, distinctive, and complex content for students with gifts and talents. 3.1.5. Educators use a balanced assessment system, including pre-assessment and formative assessment, to identify students' needs, develop differentiated education plans, and adjust plans based on continual progress monitoring. 3.1.6. Educators use pre-assessments and pace instruction based on the learning rates of students with gifts and talents and accelerate and compact learning as appropriate. 3.1.7. Educators use information and technologies, including assistive technologies, to individualize for students with gifts and talents, including those who are twice-exceptional.
3.2. Talent Development. Students with gifts and talents become more competent in multiple talent areas and across dimensions of learning.	3.2.1. Educators design curricula in cognitive, affective, aesthetic, social, and leadership domains that are challenging and effective for students with gifts and talents. 3.2.2. Educators use metacognitive models to meet the needs of students with gifts and talents.
3.3. Talent Development. Students with gifts and talents develop their abilities in their domain of talent and/or area of interest.	3.3.1. Educators select, adapt, and use a repertoire of instructional strategies and materials that differentiate for students with gifts and talents and that respond to diversity. 3.3.2. Educators use school and community resources that support differentiation. 3.3.3. Educators provide opportunities for students with gifts and talents to explore, develop, or research their areas of interest and/or talent.
3.4. Instructional Strategies. Students with gifts and talents become independent investigators.	3.4.1. Educators use critical-thinking strategies to meet the needs of students with gifts and talents. 3.4.2. Educators use creative-thinking strategies to meet the needs of students with gifts and talents. 3.4.3. Educators use problem-solving model strategies to meet the needs of students with gifts and talents. 3.4.4. Educators use inquiry models to meet the needs of students with gifts and talents.

Student Outcomes	Evidence-Based Practices
3.5. Culturally Relevant Curriculum. Students with gifts and talents develop knowledge and skills for living and being productive in a multicultural, diverse, and global society.	3.5.1. Educators develop and use challenging, culturally responsive curriculum to engage all students with gifts and talents. 3.5.2. Educators integrate career exploration experiences into learning opportunities for students with gifts and talents, e.g. biography study or speakers. 3.5.3. Educators use curriculum for deep explorations of cultures, languages, and social issues related to diversity.
3.6. Resources. Students with gifts and talents benefit from gifted education programming that provides a variety of high quality resources and materials.	3.6.1. Teachers and administrators demonstrate familiarity with sources for high quality resources and materials that are appropriate for learners with gifts and talents.

Gifted Education Programming Standard 4: Learning Environments

Introduction

Effective educators of students with gifts and talents create safe learning environments that foster emotional well-being, positive social interaction, leadership for social change, and cultural understanding for success in a diverse society. Knowledge of the impact of giftedness and diversity on social-emotional development enables educators of students with gifts and talents to design environments that encourage independence, motivation, and self-efficacy of individuals from all backgrounds. They understand the role of language and communication in talent development and the ways in which culture affects communication and behavior. They use relevant strategies and technologies to enhance oral, written, and artistic communication of learners whose needs vary based on exceptionality, language proficiency, and cultural and linguistic differences. They recognize the value of multilingualism in today's global community.

Standard 4: Learning Environments

Description: *Learning environments foster personal and social responsibility, multicultural competence, and interpersonal and technical communication skills for leadership in the 21st century to ensure specific student outcomes.*

Student Outcomes	Evidence-Based Practices
4.1. Personal Competence. Students with gifts and talents demonstrate growth in personal competence and dispositions for exceptional academic and creative productivity. These include self-awareness, self-advocacy, self-efficacy, confidence, motivation, resilience, independence, curiosity, and risk taking.	4.1.1. Educators maintain high expectations for all students with gifts and talents as evidenced in meaningful and challenging activities. 4.1.2. Educators provide opportunities for self-exploration, development and pursuit of interests, and development of identities supportive of achievement, e.g., through mentors and role models. 4.1.3. Educators create environments that support trust among diverse learners. 4.1.4. Educators provide feedback that focuses on effort, on evidence of potential to meet high standards, and on mistakes as learning opportunities. 4.1.5. Educators provide examples of positive coping skills and opportunities to apply them.
4.2. Social Competence. Students with gifts and talents develop social competence manifested in positive peer relationships and social interactions.	4.2.1. Educators understand the needs of students with gifts and talents for both solitude and social interaction. 4.2.2. Educators provide opportunities for interaction with intellectual and artistic/creative peers as well as with chronological-age peers. 4.2.3. Educators assess and provide instruction on social skills needed for school, community, and the world of work.
4.3. Leadership. Students with gifts and talents demonstrate personal and social responsibility and leadership skills.	4.3.1. Educators establish a safe and welcoming climate for addressing social issues and developing personal responsibility. 4.3.2. Educators provide environments for developing many forms of leadership and leadership skills. 4.3.3. Educators promote opportunities for leadership in community settings to effect positive change.
4.4. Cultural Competence. Students with gifts and talents value their own and others' language, heritage, and circumstance. They possess skills in communicating, teaming, and collaborating with diverse individuals and across diverse groups.[1] They use positive strategies to address social issues, including discrimination and stereotyping.	4.4.1. Educators model appreciation for and sensitivity to students' diverse backgrounds and languages. 4.4.2. Educators censure discriminatory language and behavior and model appropriate strategies. 4.4.3. Educators provide structured opportunities to collaborate with diverse peers on a common goal.

Student Outcomes	Evidence-Based Practices
4.5. Communication Competence. Students with gifts and talents develop competence in interpersonal and technical communication skills. They demonstrate advanced oral and written skills, balanced biliteracy or multiliteracy, and creative expression. They display fluency with technologies that support effective communication	4.5.1. Educators provide opportunities for advanced development and maintenance of first and second language(s). 4.5.2. Educators provide resources to enhance oral, written, and artistic forms of communication, recognizing students' cultural context. 4.5.3. Educators ensure access to advanced communication tools, including assistive technologies, and use of these tools for expressing higher-level thinking and creative productivity.

1   Differences among groups of people and individuals based on ethnicity, race, socioeconomic status, gender, exceptionalities, language, religion, sexual orientation, and geographical area.

Gifted Education Programming Standard 5: Programming

Introduction

The term programming refers to a continuum of services that address students with gifts and talents' needs in all settings. Educators develop policies and procedures to guide and sustain all components of comprehensive and aligned programming and services for PreK-12 students with gifts and talents. Educators use a variety of programming options such as acceleration and enrichment in varied grouping arrangements (cluster grouping, resource rooms, special classes, special schools) and within individualized learning options (independent study, mentorships, online courses, internships) to enhance students' performance in cognitive and affective areas and to assist them in identifying future career goals. They augment and integrate current technologies within these learning opportunities to increase access to high level programming such as distance learning courses and to increase connections to resources outside of the school walls. In implementing services, educators in gifted, general, special education programs, and related professional services collaborate with one another and parents/guardians and community members to ensure that students' diverse learning needs are met. Administrators demonstrate their support of these programming options by allocating sufficient resources so that all students within gifts and talents receive appropriate educational services.

Standard 5: Programming

Description: *Educators are aware of empirical evidence regarding (a) the cognitive, creative, and affective development of learners with gifts and talents, and (b) programming that meets their concomitant needs. Educators use this expertise systematically and collaboratively to develop, implement, and effectively manage comprehensive services for students with a variety of gifts and talents to ensure specific student outcomes.*

Student Outcomes	Evidence-Based Practices
5.1. Variety of Programming. Students with gifts and talents participate in a variety of evidence-based programming options that enhance performance in cognitive and affective areas.	5.1.1. Educators regularly use multiple alternative approaches to accelerate learning. 5.1.2. Educators regularly use enrichment options to extend and deepen learning opportunities within and outside of the school setting. 5.1.3. Educators regularly use multiple forms of grouping, including clusters, resource rooms, special classes, or special schools. 5.1.4. Educators regularly use individualized learning options such as mentorships, internships, online courses, and independent study. 5.1.5. Educators regularly use current technologies, including online learning options and assistive technologies to enhance access to high-level programming. 5.1.6. Administrators demonstrate support for gifted programs through equitable allocation of resources and demonstrated willingness to ensure that learners with gifts and talents receive appropriate educational services.
5.2. Coordinated Services. Students with gifts and talents demonstrate progress as a result of the shared commitment and coordinated services of gifted education, general education, special education, and related professional services, such as school counselors, school psychologists, and social workers.	5.2.1. Educators in gifted, general, and special education programs, as well as those in specialized areas, collaboratively plan, develop, and implement services for learners with gifts and talents.
5.3. Collaboration. Students with gifts and talents' learning is enhanced by regular collaboration among families, community, and the school.	5.3.1. Educators regularly engage families and community members for planning, programming, evaluating, and advocating.
5.4. Resources. Students with gifts and talents participate in gifted education programming that is adequately funded to meet student needs and program goals.	5.4.1. Administrators track expenditures at the school level to verify appropriate and sufficient funding for gifted programming and services.

Student Outcomes	Evidence-Based Practices
5.5. Comprehensiveness. Students with gifts and talents develop their potential through comprehensive, aligned programming and services.	5.5.1. Educators develop thoughtful, multi-year program plans in relevant student talent areas, PK–12.
5.6. Policies and Procedures. Students with gifts and talents participate in regular and gifted education programs that are guided by clear policies and procedures that provide for their advanced learning needs (e.g., early entrance, acceleration, credit in lieu of enrollment).	5.6.1. Educators create policies and procedures to guide and sustain all components of the program, including assessment, identification, acceleration practices, and grouping practices, that is built on an evidence-based foundation in gifted education.
5.7. Career Pathways. Students with gifts and talents identify future career goals and the talent development pathways to reach those goals.	5.7.1. Educators provide professional guidance and counseling for individual student strengths, interests, and values. 5.7.2. Educators facilitate mentorships, internships, and vocational programming experiences that match student interests and aptitudes.

Gifted Education Programming Standard 6: Professional Development

Introduction

Professional development is essential for all educators involved in the development and implementation of gifted programs and services. Professional development is the intentional development of professional expertise as outlined by the NAGC-CEC teacher preparation standards and is an ongoing part of gifted educators' professional and ethical practice. Professional development may take many forms ranging from district-sponsored workshops and courses, university courses, professional conferences, independent studies, and presentations by external consultants and should be based on systematic needs assessments and professional reflection. Students participating in gifted education programs and services are taught by teachers with developed expertise in gifted education. Gifted education program services are developed and supported by administrators, coordinators, curriculum specialists, general education, special education, and gifted education teachers who have developed expertise in gifted education. Since students with gifts and talents spend much of their time within general education classrooms, general education teachers need to receive professional development in gifted education that enables them to recognize the characteristics of giftedness in diverse populations, understand the school or district referral and identification process, and possess an array of high quality, research-based differentiation strategies that challenge students. Services for students with gifts and talents are enhanced by guidance and counseling professionals with expertise in gifted education.

Standard 6: Professional Development

Description: *All educators (administrators, teachers, counselors, and other instructional support staff) build their knowledge and skills using the NAGC-CEC Teacher Standards for Gifted and Talented Education and the National Staff Development Standards. They formally assess professional development needs related to the standards, develop and monitor plans, systematically engage in training to meet the identified needs, and demonstrate mastery of standard. They access resources to provide for release time, funding for continuing education, and substitute support. These practices are judged through the assessment of relevant student outcomes.*

Student Outcomes	Evidence-Based Practices
6.1. Talent Development. Students develop their talents and gifts as a result of interacting with educators who meet the national teacher preparation standards in gifted education.	6.1.1. Educators systematically participate in ongoing, research-supported professional development that addresses the foundations of gifted education, characteristics of students with gifts and talents, assessment, curriculum planning and instruction, learning environments, and programming.
	6.1.2. The school district provides professional development for teachers that models how to develop environments and instructional activities that encourage students to express diverse characteristics and behaviors that are associated with giftedness.
	6.1.3. Educators participate in ongoing professional development addressing key issues such as anti-intellectualism and trends in gifted education such as equity and access.
	6.1.4. Administrators provide human and material resources needed for professional development in gifted education (e.g. release time, funding for continuing education, substitute support, webinars, or mentors).
	6.1.5. Educators use their awareness of organizations and publications relevant to gifted education to promote learning for students with gifts and talents.

Student Outcomes	Evidence-Based Practices
6.2. Socio-emotional Development. Students with gifts and talents develop socially and emotionally as a result of educators who have participated in professional development aligned with national standards in gifted education and National Staff Development Standards.	6.2.1. Educators participate in ongoing professional development to support the social and emotional needs of students with gifts and talents.
6.3. Lifelong Learners. Students develop their gifts and talents as a result of educators who are life-long learners, participating in ongoing professional development and continuing education opportunities.	6.3.1. Educators assess their instructional practices and continue their education in school district staff development, professional organizations, and higher education settings based on these assessments. 6.3.2. Educators participate in professional development that is sustained over time, that includes regular follow-up, and that seeks evidence of impact on teacher practice and on student learning. 6.3.3. Educators use multiple modes of professional development delivery including online courses, online and electronic communities, face-to-face workshops, professional learning communities, and book talks. 6.3.4. Educators identify and address areas for personal growth for teaching students with gifts and talents in their professional development plans.
6.4. Ethics. Students develop their gifts and talents as a result of educators who are ethical in their practices.	6.4.1. Educators respond to cultural and personal frames of reference when teaching students with gifts and talents. 6.4.2. Educators comply with rules, policies, and standards of ethical practice.

Note. From *NAGC Pre-K–Grade 12 Gifted Programming Standards: A Blueprint for Quality Gifted Education Programs* (pp. 8–13), by National Association for Gifted Children, 2010, Washington, DC: Author. Copyright 2010 by National Association for Gifted Children. Reprinted with permission.

The Association for the Gifted (TAG), a Division of the Council for Exceptional Children, and its Board of Directors have reviewed these standards and express support of the NAGC Pre-K-Grade 12 Programming Standards. April 2010.

About TAG

The Association for the Gifted (TAG) was organized as a division of The Council for Exceptional Children in 1958. TAG plays a major part in helping both professionals and parents work more effectively with one of our most precious resources: the gifted child. Visit http://www.cectag.org for more information.

Appendix B
Assessments for Measuring Student Outcomes

by Tracey N. Sulak and
Susan K. Johnsen

The assessments in this Appendix were gathered from journals in gifted education, state departments of education, gifted education associations, universities, university-based centers in gifted education, and other centers, regional laboratories, foundations, and institutes that assess outcomes found in the gifted education programming standards. Our process included these steps:

1. We searched the dissertations and theses database for "gifted education," "gifted assessment," "gifted students," and "gifted" and found instruments used in studies with gifted U.S. samples. These instruments were then examined more closely by checking to see if they were published in the Buros Institute of Mental Measurement's (n.d.) *Mental Measurement Yearbook* or used in other studies.

2. We reviewed journals in gifted education (e.g., *Gifted Child Quarterly, Journal for the Education of the Gifted, Journal of Secondary Gifted Education*, and *Roeper Review*) from 1986 to present. We looked for instruments that appeared in the journal that were accessible and/or used in research studies with U.S. gifted students. Again, these were cross-referenced with those in the Buros Institute of Mental Measurement's (n.d.) *Mental Measurement Yearbook* and examined to see if they were used in other studies.

3. We examined all of the information listed on the websites of state departments of education and state associations in gifted education. With the exception of identification instruments, we listed unpublished or free instruments.

4. We examined university centers in gifted education to identify instruments that might be available for free.

5. Finally, we examined other centers, laboratories, and foundations that might provide additional instruments.

In all of our searches, we attempted to find assessments that might be used informally in assessing student outcomes and were available without charge or with only the author's permission. We therefore did not include any assessments that were available primarily from publishers at a particular cost. We also did not include any assessments that were older than 25 years.

Although some of these instruments do have technical information, which we included in Table B.1 and in our descriptions, others do not. Therefore, users are obligated to conduct their own validity and reliability studies if they plan to use the assessments in high-stakes testing such as in identification, program evaluation, or research. In those cases, we recommend that users seek test information from Buros Institute of Mental Measurement's (n.d.) *Mental Measurements Yearbook* and test publishers. When evaluating the technical qualities of tests, Robins and Jolly (2011) provided these questions:

» What is the purpose for the assessment?
» Is the assessment valid for this purpose?
» Is the test reliable?
» When was the test last normed?
» Does the sample used to norm the test reflect current national census data and the school district's population?
» What type of scores does the instrument provide?
» How is the test administered?
» Are there qualified personnel to administer the instrument?
» What is the cost of the instrument? (pp. 75–76)

Along with these criteria, Robins and Jolly (2011) provided a list of 28 instruments that are frequently used in the identification of gifted students and their technical qualities. It is important that educators review assessments in terms of these questions before using instruments to assess student outcomes in their classrooms.

Although many of the referenced assessments do not have technical information, they still may provide helpful guidance in developing informal classroom assessments. As educators administer assessments that lack technical information, data can be collected to determine their technical adequacy over time. In all cases, you need to contact the author to make sure that using the instrument is acceptable.

Assessments with technical information are presented in Table B.1. Following this table are descriptions of all of the assessments. Specific assessments are organized alphabetically by category. Within each category, instruments with technical information, those with an asterisk beside their name, are described and listed first. These instruments are followed by descriptions of tests without technical information and resources that might assist you in finding other assessments. Descriptions include the purpose of the test, its format, age or grade level of students who were administered the test, technical data (if available), and retrieval information. We acknowledge from the outset that this list of assessments is not by any means complete and that more work needs to be done in developing a bank of assessments that all educators might use in assessing student outcomes. We would appreciate your sending any assessments that may have been inadvertently omitted to Dr. Susan K. Johnsen, Baylor University, Department of Educational Psychology, One Bear Place #97301, Waco, TX, or e-mail them to Susan_Johnsen@baylor.edu. Any assessments that you find helpful in your program will be shared online with others.

References

Buros Institute of Mental Measurements. (n.d.). *Buros mental measurements yearbook.* Lincoln, NE: Buros Center for Testing. Retrieved from http://buros.unl.edu/buros

Robins, J. H., & Jolly, J. L. (2011). Technical information regarding assessment. In S. K. Johnsen (Ed.), *Identifying gifted students: A practical guide* (pp. 75–118). Waco, TX: Prufrock Press.

Assessments

Creativity

Resource: Assessing Creativity (Center for Creative Learning). The Center for Creative Learning provides an index of 72 tests used to assess creative thinking. For some tests, they provide the author, copyright date, age/grade level, cost, source, technical qualities, use, and reviews. The index may be retrieved from http://www.creativelearning.com/creative-problem-solving/3/42-assessing-creativity-index.html.

Resource: Creativity Guide (Wisconsin Association for Talented and Gifted). This guide contains teacher, parent, student, and peer nomination forms for identifying creative potential. The forms are appropriate for all grade levels. The guide may be retrieved from http://www.watg.org/creativity.html.

Resource: Creativity Tests (Indiana University). This Indiana University website provides example items from divergent thinking, convergent thinking, and artistic assessments, as well as self-assessments. Tests examples include Guilford Alternative Uses Task, Wallas and Kogan, Torrance Tests of Creative Thinking, Insight Problems, Remote Association Task, Barron-Welsh Art Scale, Khatena-Torrance Creative Perception Inventory, Creativity Assess-

Table B.1

Assessments With Technical Information

Name	Purpose	Date	Sample	Internal Consistency	Test-Retest	Interrater	Validity	Source of Information
Clark's Drawing Abilities Test (CDAT)	To screen gifted students who are talented in the visual arts.	1999	Elementary to high school			.86–.94	Criterion-related; discriminant	Clark, G., & Wilson, T. (1991). Screening and identifying gifted/talented students in the visual arts with Clark's Drawing Abilities Test. *Roeper Review, 13,* 92–97. Clark, G., & Zimmerman, E. (1992). *Issues and practices related to identification of gifted and talented students in the visual arts* (Research Monograph No. 9202). Storrs: University of Connecticut, The National Research Center on the Gifted and Talented. Clark, G., & Zimmerman, E. (2001). Identifying artistically talented students in four rural communities in the United States. *Gifted Child Quarterly, 46,* 104–114.
Classroom Instructional Practices Scale	To assess how teachers organize their classrooms in adapting for learner differences in content, rate, preference, and environment.	1992	Teachers			.92	Content	Johnsen, S. K., Haensly, P. A., Ryser, G. R., & Ford, R. F. (2002). Changing general education classroom practices to adapt for gifted students. *Gifted Child Quarterly, 46,* 45–63.
Classroom Observation Scales, Revised	To evaluate gifted education teachers' classroom practices.	2003	Teachers	.91–.93			Content	http://cfge.wm.edu/COSR%20Form.pdf VanTassel-Baska, J., Feng, A. X., Brown, E., Bracken, B., Stambaugh, T., French, H., . . . Bai, W. (2008). A study of differentiated instructional change over 3 years. *Gifted Child Quarterly, 52,* 297–312. VanTassel-Baska, J., Feng, A. X., MacFarlane, B., Heng, M. A., Tee, C. T., Wong, M. L., . . . Kohng, B. C. (2008). A cross-cultural study of teachers' instructional practices in Singapore and the United States. *Journal for the Education of the Gifted, 31,* 214–239.
Cross-Cultural Counseling Inventory-R	To assess cross-cultural competence.	1991	Adolescents and young adults	.95			Construct; factor analysis	LaFromboise, T. D., Coleman, H. L., & Hernandez, A. (1991). Development and factor analysis of the Cross-Cultural Counseling Inventory-Revised. *Professional Psychology: Research and Practice, 22,* 380–388.

Table B.1, continued

Name	Purpose	Date	Sample	Internal Consistency	Test-Retest	Interrater	Validity	Source of Information
Dance, Music, and Theater Talent Items and Behavioral Descriptors	To assess artistic talents and identify those who are ready for advanced instruction in the arts.	2003	Grades 2–6	.67–.82	.67–.82		Content; construct; factor analysis; convergent; discriminant	Oreck, B. A., Owen, S. V., & Baum, S. M. (2003). Validity, reliability, and equity issues in an observational talent assessment process in the performing arts. *Journal for the Education of the Gifted, 27,* 62–94.
Diet Cola Test	To assess science process skills; some sources indicate the test may be appropriate for identification of gifted students.	1990	All grade levels		.76	.89–.91	Discriminant	http://cfge.wm.edu/Documents/diet%20cola%20test.pdf http://www.gifted.uconn.edu/nrcgt/reports/rm95130/rm95130.pdf
ElemenOE	To measure overexcitability.	2004	Elementary	.88 total scale; .66–.90 subscales			Construct; factor analysis; discriminant	Bouchard, L. L. (2004). An instrument for the measure of Dabrowskian overexcitabilities to identify gifted elementary students. *Gifted Child Quarterly, 48,* 339–350.
Goals and Work Habits Survey	To assess perfectionism.	1994	Middle and high school	.87			Content	Schuler, P. A. (1999). *Voices of perfectionism: Perfectionistic gifted adolescents in a rural middle school.* Storrs: University of Connecticut, The National Research Center on the Gifted and Talented. http://www.gifted.uconn.edu/nrcgt/reports/rm99140/rm99140.pdf
Harter's Self-Perception Profile for Adolescents	To measure eight domains of self-concept and a general domain of self-worth.	1988	Middle and high school	.62–.94			Construct; factor analysis	Harter, S., Whitesnell, N. R., & Junkin, L. J. (1998). Similarities and differences in domain-specific and global self-evaluation of learning disabled, behaviorally disabled, and normally achieving adolescents. *American Educational Research Journal, 35,* 653–680.
Learning Behaviors Scale	To measure effective learning behaviors.	1999	Secondary students	.61–.86			Criterion-related; convergent and discriminant	Worrell, F. C., & Schaefer, B. A. (2004). Reliability and validity of Learning Behaviors Scale (LBS) scores with academically talented students: A comparative perspective. *Gifted Child Quarterly, 48,* 287–308.

Table B.1, continued

Name	Purpose	Date	Sample	Internal Consistency	Test-Retest	Interrater	Validity	Source of Information
Life Skills Development Scale-Adolescent Form (LSDS-B)	To measure an adolescent's perceived life skills.	1996	Ages 13–18	.94 total scale; .72–.87 subscales			Content	Darden, C. A., Ginter, E. J., & Gazda, G. M. (1996). Life Skills Development Scale–Adolescent Form: The theoretical and therapeutic relevance of life-skills. *Journal of Mental Health Counseling, 18,* 142–163.
Metacognitive Awareness Inventory	To identify metacognition in academic settings.	2001		.88			Construct; factor analysis	Sperling, R. A., Howard, B. C., Miller, L. A., & Murphy, C. (2002). Measures of children's knowledge and regulation of cognition. *Contemporary Educational Psychology, 27,* 57–79.
Multidimensional Inventory of Black Identity (MIBI)	To measure racial identity along three dimensions: centrality, ideology, and regard.			Data available for some subscales: .60–.79			Construct; factor analysis; criterion-related	Kearney, L. J. (2010). *Differences in self-concept, racial identity, self-efficacy, resilience, and achievement among African-American gifted and non-gifted students: Implications for retention and persistence of African Americans in gifted programs* (Doctoral dissertation). Available from ProQuest Dissertations and Theses database. (UMI 3404513) Sellers, R. M., Rowley, S. A., Chavous, T. M., Shelton, J. N., & Smith, M. A. (1997). Multidimensional Inventory of Black Identity: A preliminary investigation of reliability and construct validity. *Journal of Personality and Social Psychology, 73,* 805–815. Sellers, R. M., Smith, M. A., Shelton, J. N., Rowley, S. J., & Chavous, T. M. (1998). Multidimensional model of racial identity: A reconceptualization of African-American racial identity. *Personality and Social Psychology Review, 2,* 18–36.
The Multigroup Ethnic Identity Measure	To measure ethnic identity.	1992	High school	.81			Construct; factor analysis	Phinney, J. S. (1992). The Multigroup Ethnic Identity Measure: A new scale for use with diverse groups. *Journal of Adolescent Research, 7,* 156–176. Worrell, F. C. (2007). Ethnic identity, academic achievement, and global self-concept in four groups of academically talented adolescents. *Gifted Child Quarterly, 51,* 23–58.

Table B.1, continued

Name	Purpose	Date	Sample	Internal Consistency	Test-Retest	Interrater	Validity	Source of Information
My Way . . . An Expression Style Inventory	To assess students' interests in developing different types of products.	1998	All grades	.72–.95		.	Construct; factor analysis; content	Kettle, K. E., Renzulli, J. S., & Rizza, M. G. (1998). Products of mind: Exploring student preferences for product development using My Way . . . An Expression Style Instrument. *Gifted Child Quarterly, 42,* 48–61.
Peer Competition Rating Scale; Teacher Competition Rating Scale; Self-Competition Rating Scale	To measure perceptions of competitive goal orientations.	2005; 2006	Middle and high school	.55–.82			Construct; factor analysis; criterion-related	Schapiro, M., Schneider, B. H., Shore, B. M., Margison, J. A., & Udvari, S. J. (2009). Competitive goal orientations, quality, and stability in gifted and other adolescents' friendships: A test of Sullivan's theory about the harm caused by rivalry. *Gifted Child Quarterly, 53,* 71–88. Schneider, B. H., Soteras de Toro, M. P., Woodburn, S., Fulop, M., Cervino, C., Bernstein, S., & Sandor, M. (2006). Cross-cultural differences in competition among children and adolescents. In X. Chen, D. C. French, & B. H. Schneider (Eds.), *Peer relationships in cultural context* (pp. 310–338). New York, NY: Cambridge University Press.
Psychological Well-Being Scale	To measure six domains of psychological well-being.	1989	Adolescents	.86–.93	.81–.88		construct; factor analysis; criterion-related; discriminant and convergent	Jin, S., & Moon, S. M. (2006). A study of well-being and school satisfaction among academically talented students attending a science high school in Korea. *Gifted Child Quarterly, 50,* 169–184. Ryff, C. D. (1989). Beyond Ponce de Leon and life satisfaction: New directions in quest successful aging. *International Journal of Behavioral Development, 12,* 35–55.
Rubric for Scoring Persuasive Writing	To assess persuasive writing.	1996	Upper elementary through high school			92%	Content	VanTassel-Baska, J., Johnson, D. T., Hughes, C. E., & Boyce, L. N. (1996). A study of language arts curriculum effectiveness with gifted learners. *Journal for the Education of the Gifted, 19,* 461–480.
Student Product Assessment Form (SPAF)	To assess both individual aspects and overall excellence of products.	1997	All			86%–100%	Content	http://www.gifted.uconn.edu/sem/pdf/spaf.pdf

Table B.1, continued

Name	Purpose	Date	Sample	Internal Consistency	Test-Retest	Interrater	Validity	Source of Information
Student Social Attribution Scale	To assess the causal attributions (ability, effort, chance, and task difficulty) for success and failure by using social situations.	1995	Grades 4–6	.76–.93	.74–.84		Content	Bain, S. K., & Bell, S. M. (2004). Social self-concept, social attributions, and peer relationships in fourth, fifth, and sixth graders who are gifted compared to high achievers. *Gifted Child Quarterly, 48,* 167–178.
Teacher Observation Scales for Assessing Programs	To provide feedback on effective classroom practices in gifted education.	2010	Teachers	.95			Criterion-related	Peters, S. J., & Gates, J. C. (2010). The teacher observation form: Revisions and updates. *Gifted Child Quarterly, 54,* 179–188.
Teacher Rating of Student Performance	To measure the degree to which students meet overall program objectives.	1997	Teachers	.97			Content	Johnsen, S. K., & Ryser, G. R. (1997). The validity of portfolios in predicting performance in a gifted program. *Journal for the Education of the Gifted, 20,* 253–257.
Test of Critical Thinking	To assess formulation of a written argument.	2003	Grades 3–6	.83–.89			Content	http://cfge.wm.edu/publications.htm

ment Packet, and others. The assessments may be administered by anyone and are appropriate for a variety of ages. Examples from these assessments may be retrieved from http://www.indiana.edu/~bobweb/Handout/d4.ips.htm.

Critical Thinking

*Test of Critical Thinking (Center for Gifted Education, The College of William & Mary, 2003). The instrument uses scenarios and requires the student to select among the provided choices. The selection of choices requires use of critical thinking skills and assesses across seven life domains: social, affect, competence, environmental, physical, family, and academic. The instrument is appropriate for grades 3–6. A manual for interpretation and administration is available on the website. Reliability ranges from a = .83 to .89 and a validity study indicated scores from the TCT correlate with other ability measures. The assessment may be retrieved from http://cfge.wm.edu/publications.htm.

Course Evaluation Form of Critical Thinking (Foundation for Critical Thinking). The student-completed evaluation form of course content and delivery assesses the level of critical thinking supported by course instruction. It is appropriate for use with high school and older populations. The instrument may be retrieved from http://criticalthinking.org/resources/assessment/index.cfm.

Critical Thinking Reading and Writing Test (Paul & Elder, Foundation for Critical Thinking). The purpose of this test is to assess secondary students' abilities to think in particular disciplined and skilled ways. Results from the test are meant to determine the extent to which students have and have not learned foundational critical thinking, reading, and writing skills. This publication provides ways of creating your own prompts and grading rubrics and test forms. An example book may be retrieved from http://criticalthinking.org/resources/assessment/index.cfm.

Protocol for Interviewing Students Regarding Critical Thinking (Foundation for Critical Thinking). The structured interview assesses adoption of critical thinking skills and was initially constructed for college students. It can be adapted for high school students. The protocol may be retrieved from http://criticalthinking.org/resources/assessment/index.cfm.

Rubrics for Assessing Student Reasoning Abilities (Foundation for Critical Thinking). The critical thinking grid rubric assesses critical thinking skills and was initially designed for high school students. It may be adapted for use with younger students. Components include purpose; key question, problem, or issue; point of view; information; concepts; assumptions; interpretations, inferences; and implications, consequences. The rubrics may be retrieved from http://criticalthinking.org/resources/assessment/index.cfm.

Seven Levels of Interaction in Seminar: Metric and Reflection (Scarborough, n.d.). This instrument provides a measure of student engagement in seminar discussions. It is a self-report and is used as a discussion tool for adolescents and older populations. The metric includes descriptors for the least to most interactive behaviors. The instrument may be retrieved from http://www.evergreen.edu/washcenter/resources/acl/d2.html.

Resource: Critical Thinking (Kansas State Department of Education). The Kansas State Department of Education provides a website with rubrics and other evaluation resources for assessing critical thinking. These assessments may be retrieved from http://www.ksde.org/Default.aspx?tabid=2955.

Curriculum Assessments

*Clark's Drawing Abilities Test (CDAT; Clark & Wilson, 1991).** This instrument may be used as a screening device for identifying elementary through high school gifted students who are talented in the visual arts. The instrument correlates with the Torrance Tests of Creativity and state achievement tests. The articles referenced below found the CDAT differentiated between students with and without artistic instruction. Additional information may be found in these references:

Clark, G., & Wilson, T. (1991). Screening and identifying gifted/talented students in the visual arts with Clark's Drawing Abilities Test. *Roeper Review, 13,* 92–97.

Clark, G., & Zimmerman, E. (1992). *Issues and practices related to identification of gifted and talented students in the visual arts* (Research Monograph No. 9202). Storrs: University of Connecticut, The National Research Center on the Gifted and Talented.

Clark, G., & Zimmerman, E. (2001). Identifying artistically talented students in four rural communities in the United States. *Gifted Child Quarterly, 46,* 104–114.

Dance, Music, and Theater Talent Items and Behavioral Descriptors (Oreck, Owen, & Baum, 2003). This instrument is designed to assess artistic talents of elementary students, grades 2–6, and identify those who are ready for advanced instruction in the arts area. Two trained arts instructors may administer it to classes over a five-class series. Each student is rated on a written checklist of 8 music, 10 dance, or 4 theater items. Scoring is done on a simple notice/not notice scale for each. Each assessor then gives an overall, holistic score for each student at the end of every class. Students are invited to a fifth session based either on predetermined cutoff scores or by the number of students who can be accommodated in the fifth session. Reported interrater reliability coefficients were .67 for music, .82 for dance, and .74 for theater. Stability reliability estimates were calculated over three separate intervals and ranged from .35 to .68. Ratings were able to predict future ratings, with 82% of identified students making good to excellent progress on written semiannual evaluations by arts instructors. More technical information and the instrument may be found in this reference:

Oreck, B. A., Owen, S. V., & Baum, S. M. (2003). Validity, reliability, and equity issues in an observational talent assessment process in the performing arts. *Journal for the Education of the Gifted, 27,* 62–94.

*Diet Cola Test (Fowler, 1990). The Diet Cola Test, or Fowler Science Process Skills Assessment, may be used to assess science process skills at all grade levels. The checklist contains descriptors related to safety, problem statement, hypotheses, steps, materials, repeat testing, definitions, observations, types of measurements, data collection, interpretation of data, conclusions, and control variables. The checklist may be used as a formative and summative assessment. Interrater reliability has been reported in the range of .89–.91 and test-retest reliability is .76. The Diet Cola Test may be retrieved from http://cfge.wm.edu/Documents/diet%20cola%20test.pdf.

*Rubric for Scoring Persuasive Writing (VanTassel-Baska, Johnson, Hughes, & Boyce, 1996). This performance-based persuasive writing assessment requires students to develop an argument in written form. It was developed as a pre- and postmeasure for use in a curriculum unit and scored using a rubric. Interrater reliability agreement was reported at 92%. The rubric and more technical information may be found in the following reference:

VanTassel-Baska, J., Johnson, D. T., Hughes, C. E., & Boyce, L. N. (1996). A study of language arts curriculum effectiveness with gifted learners. *Journal for the Education of the Gifted, 19,* 461–480.

Resource: Curriculum-Based Measurements (CBM). Several websites have curriculum-based generators that may be used to create off-level materials for gifted students. The assessments may be customized to meet the specific needs for progress monitoring and may be modified for use with all grade levels. The following websites contain tools for creating curriculum-based measures:

http://www.aimsweb.com (CBM, research)
http://www.studentprogress.org (CBM)
http://www.interventioncentral.org (reading passage generators)

Resource: Florida Assessments for Instruction in Reading (Florida Center for Reading Research). This website contains reading assessments for students in kindergarten through high school. The assessments are considered broad screening devices and may be used to screen for students performing above the current grade level. The assessments are linked the Florida State Educational Standards. Additional information may be retrieved from http://www.fcrr.org.

Resource: Toolkit of Assessments (Northwest Educational Regional Laboratory). This website contains training activities and rubrics for a variety of assessments in core content areas for all grade levels. The toolkit may be retrieved from http://educationnorthwest.org/resource/700.

Interest Assessments

Interest-A-Lyzer: Family of Instruments (Renzulli, 1997). This self-report instrument helps students identify interests that can be used to plan gifted and talented enrichment experiences. It uses situations, both actual and hypothetical, to stimulate reflection. The instrument should be untimed and the results should not be associated with any type of reward. It is designed for use with middle- and high-school-age students. Further information may be found at Creative Learning Press, Inc., P.O. Box 320, Mansfield Center, CT 06250; http://www.creativelearningpress.com.

Primary Interest-A-Lyzer (Renzulli & Rizza, 1997). This self-report interest inventory is designed for students in grades K–3. Picture cues are provided for each question. Teachers may use this instrument informally to identify their students' nonacademic interests. It may be retrieved from http://www.pedagonet.com/quickies/interest.pdf.

Secondary Interest-A-Lyzer (Hébert, Sorensen, & Renzulli, 1997). This informal interest inventory is used to identify secondary students' interests so that educators might plan ways of nurturing their talents and challenging their learning potential. A copy of the instrument may be retrieved from http://www.gifted.uconn.edu/siegle/CurriculumCompacting/SEC-IMAG/ialsecon.pdf.

If I Ran the School (Reis & Siegle, 2002). This instrument is designed for students in grades K–3 to identify their interests within the traditional content areas. Scores from the instrument may be useful for curriculum compacting because it provides information on areas of high interest for the student. It is appropriate for both elementary and secondary students and may be retrieved from http://www.gifted.uconn.edu/siegle/CurriculumCompacting/SEC-IMAG/ranschol.pdf.

Things My Child Likes to Do (The National Research Center on the Gifted and Talented, University of Connecticut). This instrument is a parent report of child interests, strengths, and weaknesses and may be used to plan enrichment. It contains 14 statements about gifted behaviors and the reporting parents assign a rating from *seldom or never* to *almost always* to each statement. The instrument is appropriate for all ages. The instrument may be retrieved from http://www.gifted.uconn.edu/sem/pdf/thingsdo.pdf.

Learning and Motivation Assessments

*ElemenOE (Bouchard, 2004). This instrument measures overexcitabilty in elementary students with a 61-item Likert scale. The author suggests it may be used as a possible identification measure for students less than 13 years of age. Research shows the internal consistency of the total scale as a = .88, with subscale internal consistency ranging from a = .66 to .90. Validity studies show a five-factor structure supporting Dabrowski's theory of positive disintegration. The instrument is located in this reference:

Bouchard, L. L. (2004). An instrument for the measure of Dabrowskian overexcitabilities to identify gifted elementary students. *Gifted Child Quarterly, 48,* 339–350.

*Learning Behaviors Scale (McDermott, Green, Francis, & Stott, 1999). The instrument uses 29 teacher-rated items related to effective learning of secondary students. Internal consistency for the instrument ranges from a = .61 to .86, and validity studies have indicated a four-factor structure explaining 48% of variance in scale scores. The instrument is located in this reference:

Worrell, F. C., & Schaefer, B. A. (2004). Reliability and validity of Learning Behaviors Scale (LBS) scores with academically talented students: A comparative perspective. *Gifted Child Quarterly, 48,* 287–308.

*Life Skills Development Scale-Adolescent Form (LSDS-B; Darden, Ginter, & Gazda, 1996). This 65-item self-report scale provides a reflective measurement of an adolescent's perceived life skills. It is suggested that the scale be used with ages 13–18. The subscales include interpersonal communication, problem solving, physical fitness, and identity development. Each may be used to monitor progress during interventions. The total scale shows an internal consistency (a) of .94, with each subscale ranging from a = .72 to .87. More information about the scale and its appropriate use may be found in this reference:

Darden, C. A., Ginter, E. J., & Gazda, G. M. (1996). Life Skills Development Scale–Adolescent Form: The theoretical and therapeutic relevance of life-skills. *Journal of Mental Health Counseling, 18,* 142–163.

*Metacognitive Awareness Inventory (Kearney, 2010). The instrument uses an 18-item survey using a Likert format to identify metacognition in academic settings. Most research using the scale has been in the discipline of math, but the stems for each item could be used in any discipline. The instrument is located in this dissertation:

Kearney, L. J. (2010). *Differences in self-concept, racial identity, self-efficacy, resilience, and achievement among African-American gifted and non-gifted students: Implications for retention and persistence of African Americans in gifted programs* (Doctoral dissertation). Available from ProQuest Dissertations and Theses database. (UMI 3404513)

The instrument is also used in this reference:

Sperling, R. A., Howard, B. C., Miller, L. A., & Murphy, C. (2002). Measures of children's knowledge and regulation of cognition. *Contemporary Educational Psychology, 27,* 57–79.

Activities and Accomplishments Inventory (AAI; Milgram & Hong, 2001). This self-report instrument for high school students assesses activities and accomplishments in areas like science, computers, mathematics, literature, social activities, drama, music, art, dance, and sports. The instrument has reported validity demonstrated by longitudinal studies showing predictive validity of the AAI with vocation in adulthood. The instrument is located in this reference:

Hong, E., & Aqui, Y. (2004). Cognitive and motivational characteristics of adolescents gifted in mathematics: Comparisons among students with different types of giftedness. *Gifted Child Quarterly, 48,* 191–201.

Preferred Method of Instruction (Krogh, 2010). Part 1 of this Javits Student Survey assesses students' preferred method of instruction in grades 2–5 and asks the students to provide reasons for the choice. Part 2 assesses inductive versus deductive learning preferences by presenting information and asking the students to choose the order of learning. Part 1 and Part 2 assess preferences across all disciplines. The instrument is located in Appendix A of this reference:

Krogh, J. (2010). *The effects of the models of teaching on student learning.* (Doctoral dissertation). Available from ProQuest Dissertations and Theses database. (UMI No. 3418088)

Multicultural Assessments

*Cross-Cultural Counseling Inventory-R (LaFromboise, Coleman, & Hernandez, 1991). This instrument assesses cross-cultural competence with young adults using three subscales: beliefs/attitudes, knowledge, and skills. It contains 20 items with an internal consistency reliability (a) reported at .95. Validity studies confirm a three-factor structure with all items loading on the hypothesized factor. The instrument is located in this reference:

LaFromboise, T. D., Coleman, H. L., & Hernandez, A. (1991). Development and factor analysis of the Cross-Cultural Counseling Inventory-Revised. *Professional Psychology: Research and Practice, 22,* 380–388.

*Multidimensional Inventory of Black Identity (MIBI; Kearney, 2010). The MIBI is a research instrument used to measure racial identity along three dimensions: centrality, ideology, and regard. The instrument does not render a composite score. It has been used for research in gifted and talented and may be found in this dissertation:

Kearney, L. J. (2010). *Differences in self-concept, racial identity, self-efficacy, resilience, and achievement among African-American gifted and non-gifted students: Implications for retention and persistence of African Americans in gifted programs* (Doctoral dissertation). Available from ProQuest Dissertations and Theses database. (UMI 3404513)

It is also used in the following references:

Sellers, R. M., Rowley, S. A., Chavous, T. M., Shelton, J. N., & Smith, M. A. (1997). Multidimensional Inventory of Black Identity: A preliminary investigation of reliability and construct validity. *Journal of Personality and Social Psychology, 73,* 805–815.

Sellers, R. M., Smith, M. A., Shelton, J. N., Rowley, S. J., & Chavous, T. M. (1998). Multidimensional model of racial identity: A reconceptualization of African-American racial identity. *Personality and Social Psychology Review, 2,* 18–36.

*The Multigroup Ethnic Identity Measure (Phinney, 1992). This self-report instrument provides a measure of ethnic identity. Four general aspects of ethnic identity are assessed: positive ethnic attitudes and sense of belonging, ethnic identity of achievement, ethnic behaviors or practices, and other group orientation. It is appropriate for use with all ethnic groups and may be used with adolescents. Internal consistency reliability for a high school sample was a = .81. Additional information may be found in these references:

Phinney, J. S. (1992). The Multigroup Ethnic Identity Measure: A new scale for use with diverse groups. *Journal of Adolescent Research, 7,* 156–176.

Worrell, F. C. (2007). Ethnic identity, academic achievement, and global self-concept in four groups of academically talented adolescents. *Gifted Child Quarterly, 51,* 23–58.

Products/Performance Assessments

*My Way . . . An Expression Style Inventory (Kettle, Renzulli, & Rizza, 1998). This 50-item Likert-scale inventory was designed to assess how interested students are in developing different types of products. Factor analysis produced 10 factors or components. Reliability for the scales ranged from .72 to .95. The instrument may be found in this reference:

Kettle, K. E., Renzulli, J. S., & Rizza, M. G. (1998). Products of mind: Exploring student preferences for product development using My Way . . . An Expression Style Instrument. *Gifted Child Quarterly, 42,* 48–61.

*Student Product Assessment Form (SPAF; Renzulli & Reis, 1997). This rating scale is composed of 15 items designed to assess both individual aspects and overall excellence of products. Each item is rated using three related parts: the key concept, item description, and examples. Instructions for rating products are included on the form. The form may be used in a variety of disciplines and with all grade levels. Levels of agreement among raters on individual items of the scale ranged from 86.4% to 100%. The authors reported a reliability coefficient between raters who assessed the same set of products on two occasions with a period of time between ratings. A copy of the instrument may be retrieved from http://www.gifted.uconn.edu/sem/pdf/spaf.pdf.

Six-Trait Assessment for Beginning Writers (Northwest Educational Regional Laboratory). This assessment identifies strengths in primary students' writing and allows a qualitative indicator to be assigned to the work according to the traits illustrated. It could be used with a student as a self-assessment or as a progress-monitoring tool. The assessment is written specifically for beginning composition writers. The assessment may be retrieved from http://apps.educationnorthwest.org/toolkit98/six.html#begin.

Resource: Texas Performance Standards Project. This website includes performance-based assessment tools for students in grade 4 through high school. Tasks are also included and are scaffolded according to the developmental level of the student. The assessments may be used in the disciplines of language arts, mathematics, social studies, and science. The tools may be used as summative and formative assessment of learning. Information on the tasks and assessment tools may be retrieved from http://www.texaspsp.org.

Resource: Webquest Design and Evaluation Rubrics. These websites contain information on evaluation of WebQuest performance. The teacher link on the second website has sample WebQuests with standards and student work examples (in some cases). The materials are appropriate for all grade levels if modifications are made for reading ability. An evaluation rubric is included and it may be used as a self-assessment for students who create WebQuests. All materials may be retrieved from these sites:

http://projects.edtech.sandi.net/staffdev/tpss99/mywebquest/index.htm
http://projects.edtech.sandi.net/staffdev/buildingblocks/p-index.htm

Social/Emotional Assessments

*Goals and Work Habits Survey (Schuler, 1994). This 35-item scale assesses perfectionism by using a Likert-type scale. The assessment uses six subscales: concern over mistakes, personal standards, parental expectations, parental criticism, doubts of actions, and organization. The internal consistency reliability of the total scale during piloting was a = .87. The assessment may be found in Appendix A of this reference:

Schuler, P. A. (1999). *Voices of perfectionism: Perfectionistic gifted adolescents in a rural middle school.* Storrs: University of Connecticut, The National Research Center on the Gifted and Talented.

It may be retrieved from http://www.gifted.uconn.edu/nrcgt/reports/rm 99140/rm99140.pdf.

*Harter's Self-Perception Profile for Adolescents (Harter, 1988). This 45-item questionnaire measures eight domains of self-concept and a general domain of self-worth. The self-concept domains measured are social competence, physical appearance, behavioral conduct, scholastic competence, romantic appeal, close friendship, job competence, and athletic competence. The reliability ranges from a = .62 to .94, and the factor structure appears to support the domains. Further information about the instrument is reported in this reference:

Harter, S., Whitesnell, N. R., & Junkin, L. J. (1998). Similarities and differences in domain-specific and global self-evaluation of learning disabled, behaviorally disabled, and normally achieving adolescents. *American Educational Research Journal, 35,* 653–680.

*Peer Competition Rating Scale; Teacher Competition Rating Scale; Self-Competition Rating Scale (Schneider et al., 2006; Schneider, Woodburn, del Pilar Soteras del Toro, & Udvari, 2005). All of these instruments measure perceptions of competitive goal orientations with middle and high school students. The Peer Competition Rating Scale has 16 items that address task-oriented and other-referenced competition in the scholastic and athletic domains. The Teacher Competition Rating Scale has eight items that address the students' competition goal orientation in the scholastic domain. The 19-item Self-Rating Competition Scale measures the participant's own perception of his or her competition orientation. The self and teacher reports correlate and yield the same factors when examined through factor analysis. Internal consistency ranges from a = .55 to .82 across all scales. More information is reported in these references:

Schneider, B. H., Soteras de Toro, M. P., Woodburn, S., Fulop, M., Cervino, C., Bernstein, S., & Sandor, M. (2006). Cross-cultural differences in competition among children and adolescents. In X. Chen, D. C. French, & B. H. Schneider (Eds.), *Peer relationships in cultural context* (pp. 310–338). New York, NY: Cambridge University Press.

Schapiro, M., Schneider, B. H., Shore, B. M., Margison, J. A., & Udvari, S. J. (2009). Competitive goal orientations, quality, and stability in gifted and other adolescents' friendships: A test of Sullivan's theory about the harm caused by rivalry. *Gifted Child Quarterly, 53,* 71–88.

*Psychological Well-Being Scale (Ryff, 1989). This 84-item instrument measures six domains of psychological well-being in adolescents. The subscales include autonomy, environmental mastery, personal growth, positive relations with others, purpose in life, and self-acceptance. Internal consistency ranges from a = .86 to .93 with correlations on test-retest of r = .81 to .88 on an unspecified time interval. A confirmatory factor analysis supported the six-factor structure. More information may be found in these references:

Jin, S., & Moon, S. M. (2006). A study of well-being and school satisfaction among academically talented students attending a science high school in Korea. *Gifted Child Quarterly, 50,* 169–184.

Ryff, C. D. (1989). Beyond Ponce de Leon and life satisfaction: New directions in quest successful aging. *International Journal of Behavioral Development, 12,* 35–55.

*Student Social Attribution Scale (Bell & McCallum, 1995). This instrument assesses the causal attributions (ability, effort, chance, and task difficulty) for success and failure by using social situations of students in grades 4–6. The student rates each situation on a Likert scale to determine causal attributions. The correlations for test-retest on a 2-week interval were r = .74 to .84, and internal consistency on initial studies was a = .76 to .93. More information may be found in this reference:

Bain, S. K., & Bell, S. M. (2004). Social self-concept, social attributions, and peer relationships in fourth, fifth, and sixth graders who are gifted compared to high achievers. *Gifted Child Quarterly, 48,* 167–178.

Communication Skills and Competencies. This rubric may be used to rate written and verbal communication skills in high school students. It is a self-report assessment and focuses on strengths and weaknesses, which makes it appropriate for progress monitoring communication skills. The rubric can be retrieved from http://www.uwgb.edu/clampitp/Communication%20skills.htm.

Empowering Gifted Behavior Scale (Jenkins-Friedman, Bransky, & Murphy, 1986). This rating scale is used to identify patterns of enabling and disabling perfectionistic behaviors in gifted students at all grade levels. The teacher rates 11 items that identify the degree to which students might demonstrate perfectionism. The assessment may be found in Appendix B of this reference:

Schuler, P. A. (1999). *Voices of perfectionism: Perfectionistic gifted adolescents in a rural middle school.* Storrs: University of Connecticut, The National Research Center on the Gifted and Talented.

It may be retrieved from http://www.gifted.uconn.edu/nrcgt/reports/rm 99140/rm99140.pdf.

Teacher Social Rating (Coie & Dodge, 1988). This teacher-rating instrument assesses social function in relation to peers. Interrater reliability on initial studies was 100% across four different raters. More information may be found in this reference:

Bain, S. K., & Bell, S. M. (2004). Social self-concept, social attributions, and peer relationships in fourth, fifth, and sixth graders who are gifted compared to high achievers. *Gifted Child Quarterly, 48,* 167–178.

Resource: Leadership Instruments. More information about leadership instruments is reported in these references:

Shaunessy, E., & Karnes, F. A. (2004). Instruments for measuring leadership in children and youth. *Gifted Child Today, 27*(1), 42–47.
Oakland, T., Falkenberg, B. A., & Oakland, C. (1996). Assessment of leadership in children, youth and adults. *Gifted Child Quarterly, 40,* 138–146.

Resources for Program Planning and Evaluation

*****Classroom Instructional Practices Scale (Johnsen, 1992).** This checklist is designed to measure how teachers organize their classrooms in adapting for learner differences in content, rate, preference, and environment. The description of each area is hierarchical, beginning with the least adaptive classroom practice for individual differences and progressing to the most adaptive classroom practice. Interrater reliability was reported at .92. The instrument may be found in this reference:

Johnsen, S. K., Haensly, P. A., Ryser, G. R., & Ford, R. F. (2002). Changing general education classroom practices to adapt for gifted students. *Gifted Child Quarterly, 46,* 45–63.

*****Classroom Observation Scales, Revised (VanTassel-Baska et al., 2003).** This checklist is designed to evaluate teacher behaviors as related to gifted education. A student observation form and manual are also available on the website. The document contains information on appropriate use and interpretations and may be retrieved from http://cfge.wm.edu/COSR%20Form.pdf.

The instrument may be found in this reference:

VanTassel-Baska, J., Feng, A. X., Brown, E., Bracken, B., Stambaugh, T., French, H., . . . Bai, W. (2008). A study of differentiated instructional change over 3 years. *Gifted Child Quarterly, 52*, 297–312.

VanTassel-Baska, J., Feng, A. X., MacFarlane, B., Heng, M. A., Tee, C. T., Wong, M. L., . . . Kohng, B. C. (2008). A cross-cultural study of teachers' instructional practices in Singapore and the United States. *Journal for the Education of the Gifted, 31*, 338–363.

*Teacher Observation Scales for Assessing Programs (Peters & Gates, 2010). The purpose of the Purdue University Gifted Education Teacher Observation Form (TOF) is to provide useful "feedback to teachers as to the prevalence of gifted education pedagogical effective practices in their classrooms" (p. 179). The Teacher Observation Form contains 12 items that address these areas: content coverage; clarity of instruction; motivational techniques; pedagogy/instructional techniques; opportunity for self-determination of activities by student; student involvement in a variety of experiences; interaction between teacher and student, student and peers; opportunity for student follow-up on activities and topics on their own; emphasis on higher level thinking skills; emphasis on creativity; lesson plans designed to meet program, course, and daily objectives; and appropriate use of classroom technology. Observers use the TOF during 30-minute blocks in which they sit quietly in the classroom, mark their observations on the form, and make notes concerning what they observe. The overall alpha reliability estimate was .95. The instrument may be found in the following reference:

Peters, S. J., & Gates, J. C. (2010). The teacher observation form: Revisions and updates. *Gifted Child Quarterly, 54*, 179–188.

*Teacher Rating of Student Performance (Johnsen & Ryser, 1997). This assessment measures the degree to which students meet overall program objectives. The instrument consists of 26 items to be rated by the teacher using a 4-point Likert-type scale. Internal consistency reliability for the instrument is .9678. The instrument may be found in the following reference:

Johnsen, S. K., & Ryser, G. R. (1997). The validity of portfolios in predicting performance in a gifted program. *Journal for the Education of the Gifted, 20,* 253–257.

Educator and Student Evaluation Surveys (VanTassel-Baska, 2006). These surveys examine student and educator perceptions of the gifted education program. Educator areas include identification, program/curriculum, communication, staff development, and administration. The surveys are found in the following reference:

VanTassel-Baska, J. (2006). A content analysis of evaluation findings across 20 gifted programs: A clarion call for enhanced gifted program development. *Gifted Child Quarterly, 50,* 199–215.

Fast-Paced Class Evaluation Survey (Lee & Olszewski-Kubilius, 2006). This one-page survey uses a 5-point Likert scale. Examples of the questions included whether teachers pretest to see what students know before teaching a unit, group students into clusters for instruction based on previous knowledge of subject, allow students to proceed at their own individual pace, and so on. The survey may be found in the following reference:

Seon-Young, L., & Olszewski-Kubilius, P. (2006). A study of instructional methods used in fast-paced classes. *Gifted Child Quarterly, 50,* 216–237.

Parent Questionnaire Regarding Child's Gifted Class Performance (PQCP) (NRC/GT at UGA, 1993). The PQCP is comprised of 22 items on a 5-point Likert-scale and was developed to determine parents' perceptions of their child's performance in the gifted program. Areas include the parents' relationship with the school, the parents' perception of their child's adjustment to the gifted program, and the parents' perception of the benefits of the gifted program. The PQCP may be useful in program evaluation. The SRSP may be found in Appendix E of this reference:

Hunsaker, S. L., Frasier, M. M., Frank, E., Finley, V., & Klekotka, P. (1995). *Performance of economically disadvantaged students placed in gifted programs through the Research-Based Assessment Plan.* Storrs: University of Connecticut, The National Research Center on the Gifted and Talented.

The reference may be retrieved from http://www.gifted.uconn.edu/nrcgt/ reports/rm95208/rm95208.pdf.

Scale for Rating Student Participation in the Local Gifted Education Program (SRSP; Renzulli & Westberg, 1991). The SRSP is used to obtain a gifted education teacher's rating of a student's performance in the gifted program. The SRSP is a 10-item rating instrument with a five point Likert-scale. The instrument is internally consistent with an alpha reliability coefficient reported to be .95. The SRSP may be useful in program evaluation and studies that might examine the relationship between identification with classroom performance. The SRSP may be found in Appendix D of this reference:

Hunsaker, S. L., Frasier, M. M., Frank, E., Finley, V., & Klekotka, P. (1995). *Performance of economically disadvantaged students placed in gifted programs through the Research-Based Assessment Plan.* Storrs: University of Connecticut, The National Research Center on the Gifted and Talented.

The reference may be retrieved from http://www.gifted.uconn.edu/nrcgt/reports/rm95208/rm95208.pdf.

Talents Unlimited Lesson Plan and Teacher Self-Rating Scale (Newman, Gregg, & Dantzler). This scale is used to evaluate the implementation of the Talents Unlimited model. Educators rate themselves on each of the talents. A copy of this scale may be found in the following reference:

Newman, J. L., Gregg, M., & Dantzler, J. (2009). Summer enrichment workshop (SEW): A quality component of The University of Alabama's gifted education preservice training program. *Roeper Review, 31,* 170–184.

Resource: Gifted Education Unit Reference Series: Creativity, Leadership, Visual and Performing Arts (Colorado Department of Education). This Colorado Department of Education booklet contains copies of a Creativity Product Assessment (p. 17), CREATIVITY Rating Scale (pp. 18–19), Leadership Talent Scale (pp. 28–29), Leadership Development Triad Model (pp. 34–35), and other assessment resources in creativity, leadership, and visual and performing arts. They may be used with students of any age, but are most appropriate for late elementary to high school students. References and rating scales may be retrieved from http://www.cde.state.co.us/gt/download/pdf/Creativity.pdf.

Resource: The Connie Belin & Jacqueline N. Blank International Center for Gifted Education and Talent Development. This website contains published texts and resources for acceleration and grade skipping. *Guidelines for Developing an Academic Acceleration Policy* and *A Nation Deceived* are available for download. A web-based math acceleration guide is also available (for a fee). The materials are appropriate for all grade levels. Information may be retrieved from http://www.education.uiowa.edu/belinblank/Research.

Resource: Frasier Talent Assessment Profile (F-TAP; Frasier, 1992). The F-TAP is used to organize multiple assessments used during the identification process. Quantitative data are recorded on a graph producing a profile of each student's strengths and weaknesses. The F-TAP may be found in Appendix C of this reference:

Hunsaker, S. L., Frasier, M. M., Frank, E., Finley, V., & Klekotka, P. (1995). *Performance of economically disadvantaged students placed in gifted programs through the Research-Based Assessment Plan.* Storrs: University of Connecticut, The National Research Center on the Gifted and Talented.

The reference may be retrieved from http://www.gifted.uconn.edu/nrcgt/reports/rm95208/rm95208.pdf.

Resource: State Advisory Council for Gifted and Talented Education and the Kentucky Department of Education Behavioral GT Coordinator Handbook. This handbook describes how to create behavioral assessments, curriculum-based measures, and performance assessments and contains a variety of assessment instruments in Section 5 and in the Appendix. Retrieve a copy of the appendix at http://www.wku.edu/kage/GiftedHandbook.

Authors' Note

Assessments with an asterisk (*) have technical information.

About the Editor

Susan K. Johnsen is a professor in the Department of Educational Psychology at Baylor University in Waco, TX, where she directs the Ph.D. program and programs related to gifted and talented education. She is editor of *Gifted Child Today* and *Identifying Gifted Students: A Practical Guide*, coauthor of the *Independent Study Program*, *Using the National Gifted Education Standards for University Teacher Preparation Programs*, *Using the National Gifted Education Standards for PreK–12 Professional Development*, and author of more than 200 articles, monographs, technical reports, and other books related to gifted education. She has written three tests used in identifying gifted students: Test of Mathematical Abilities for Gifted Students (TOMAGS), Test of Nonverbal Intelligence (TONI-4) and Screening Assessment for Gifted Elementary and Middles School Students (SAGES-2). She is past president of The Association for the Gifted (TAG), Council for Exceptional Children and past president of the Texas Association for the Gifted and Talented (TAGT).

About the Authors

Cheryll M. Adams is the Director of the Center for Gifted Studies and Talent Development at Ball State University and teaches graduate courses for the license in gifted education. She has authored and coauthored numerous publications in professional journals, as well as several books and book chapters. She serves on the editorial review boards of *Roeper Review*, *Gifted Child Quarterly*, and *Journal for the Education of the Gifted*. She has served on the Board of Directors of the National Association for Gifted Children, has been president of the Indiana Association for the Gifted, and currently serves as president of The Association for the Gifted, Council for Exceptional Children.

Jane Clarenbach is the Director of Public Education at the National Association for Gifted Children (NAGC). She coordinates NAGC's advocacy and legislative initiatives and promotes gifted education and NAGC through her work with the media and state and national organizations. Clarenbach is an attorney with more than 25 years of advocacy experience in Washington, DC.

Alicia Cotabish is one of two Principal Investigators of STEM Starters, a federally funded Jacob K. Javits project, and the Associate Director of the Mahony Center for Gifted Education at the University of Arkansas at Little Rock. Dr. Cotabish was formerly the program administrator and teacher of an award-winning gifted program in Arkansas.

Reva Friedman-Nimz is an associate professor in the Department of Curriculum and Teaching at the University of Kansas, where she has been responsible for degree and graduate certificate programs in gifted/talented/creative child education for more than 30 years. A former high school teacher and teacher of gifted students (elementary and secondary), she continues to educate general education and gifted education teachers about the learning and personal needs of gifted and talented students, to counsel bright youngsters and their families, and to collaborate with K–12 teachers. Her writings focus on the psychological factors that impact the development of gifted young people and on using models that develop students' talents and strengths. She has served on the boards of the National Association for Gifted Children (NAGC) and The Association for the Gifted (TAG), Council for Exceptional Children. Currently, she serves on NAGC's Professional Standards Committee. On the state level, she is a board member of the Kansas Association for the Gifted, Talented, and Creative.

Donna Y. Ford is a professor of special education at Vanderbilt University, where she prepares teachers in gifted education, multicultural education, and working with students and families who live in poverty. Dr. Ford consults nationally on topics and issues such as underrepresentation and recruiting and retaining Black students in gifted and AP classes, closing the achievement gap, and designing rigorous multicultural lesson plans. She is the editor of several books, including *Multicultural Gifted Education* and *Reversing Underachievement Among Gifted Black Students*, and numerous articles and book chapters. She has been a board member of the National Association for Gifted Children and serves in various leadership positions for other organizations. Dr. Ford has received several awards for her work.

Tarek Grantham is an associate professor in the Department of Educational Psychology and Instructional Technology at the University of Georgia (UGA). He teaches courses in the Gifted and Creative Education Program and has served as program coordinator for its on-campus and online graduate programs. His research addresses recruitment and retention of diverse youth (particularly African Americans) in gifted and advanced programs. In his area of research, Dr. Grantham emphasizes mentoring, parent advocacy, multicultural education, and "upstander" attitudes to enhance motivation, leadership, and talent development among diverse youth. Dr. Grantham has consulted with schools, community groups, and parents on issues of underrepresentation and underachievement among culturally diverse students in gifted education. Dr. Grantham is the coeditor of *Gifted and Advanced Black Students in Schools: An Anthology of Critical Works*.

Thomas P. Hébert is a professor in the Department of Educational Psychology at the University of Georgia, where he teaches graduate courses in gifted education and qualitative research methods. His research interests include social and emotional development of gifted students, culturally diverse gifted students, underachievement, and problems faced by gifted young men. He is the author of *Understanding the Social and Emotional Lives of Gifted Students*.

Sandra N. Kaplan is a professor of clinical education, Rossier School of Education, University of Southern California. She is past president of the National Association for Gifted Children (NAGC) and the California Association for the Gifted (CAG). She has been a teacher and administrator of gifted programs in an urban school district in California. She has authored articles and books on the nature and scope of differentiated curriculum for gifted students, including *Using the Parallel Curriculum Model in Urban Settings, Grades K–8* and the *Curriculum Development Kit for Gifted and Advanced Learners*. She has been nationally recognized for her contributions to gifted education, receiving the Award for Excellence from The Association for the Gifted (TAG), Council for Exceptional Children and the Gifted Distinguished Award of Service from NAGC.

Bill Keilty teaches for Hamline University in the gifted certificate program. He is a long-standing member of the Minnesota Department of Education's Gifted Advisory Board. He serves on the executive board as the legislative liaison for the Minnesota Educators of the Gifted and Talented. Bill designed, implemented, and directs the Lighthouse Program for the highly gifted, a unique program that takes the lid off and nurtures kids ages 5–17 to their true potential. Dr. Keilty is married and the father of four gifted boys, who introduced him to this field.

Sally Krisel is the Director of Innovative and Advanced Programs for Hall County Schools in Gainesville, GA, and a part-time faculty member at the University of Georgia. She leads innovative programming initiatives that employ practices traditionally associated with gifted education in order to help teachers recognize and develop the creative and cognitive abilities of all students, including those who are gifted and talented.

E. Wayne Lord is an associate professor and department chair in Educational Leadership, Counseling, and Special Education at Augusta State University in Augusta, GA. He received the 2006 NAGC President's Award for his support and positive influence on gifted education policy. Dr. Lord's previous educational experiences include teaching at the middle and high school levels, working at the district level in staff development, and coordinating gifted programs at the South Carolina State Department of Education.

Chrystyna V. Mursky serves as the State Director for Gifted Education at the Wisconsin Department of Public Instruction. She holds bachelor's degrees in zoology and elementary education, a master's degree in curriculum and instruction, and a Ph.D. in educational policy and leadership. She was a member of the workgroup that wrote the NAGC Pre-K–12 Gifted Programming Standards and a contributing author to *RtI for Gifted Students*.

Julia Link Roberts is the Mahurin Professor of Gifted Studies at Western Kentucky University. She is the Executive Director of The Center for Gifted Studies and the Carol Martin Gatton Academy of Mathematics and Science in Kentucky. Dr. Roberts is a member of the Executive Committee of the World Council for Gifted and Talented Children and a board member of The Association for the Gifted, Council for Exceptional Children and the Kentucky Association for Gifted Education. Dr. Roberts received the first David W. Belin NAGC Award for Advocacy. She is coauthor of *Strategies for Differentiating Instruction: Best Practices for the Classroom* (2009 Legacy Award for the outstanding book for educators in gifted education by the Texas Association for the Gifted and Talented), *Assessing Differentiated Student Products: A Protocol for Development and Evaluation*, and *Teacher's Survival Guide: Gifted Education*. Dr. Roberts directs programming for children and young people who are gifted and talented as well as professional development for educators and parents.

Tracey N. Sulak is a doctoral candidate in the Department of Educational Psychology at Baylor University. She earned an M.Ed. in curriculum and instruction with an emphasis in gifted and talented. Her research interests are learning disabilities, assessment, and educational environments, and she has multiple publications and presentations in each of these areas. Her educational experiences include teaching in public and private educational settings as well as serving as an instructor in the special education program at Baylor University.

Joyce VanTassel-Baska is the Smith Professor Emerita at The College of William and Mary in Virginia, where she developed a graduate program and a research and development center in gifted education. Formerly, she initiated and directed the Center for Talent Development at Northwestern University. She has also served as the state director of gifted programs for Illinois, as a regional director of a gifted service center in the Chicago area, as coordinator of gifted programs for the Toledo, OH, public school system, and as a teacher of gifted high school students in English and Latin. Dr. VanTassel-Baska has published widely, including 27 books and more than 500 refereed journal articles, book chapters, and scholarly reports. Her major research interests are on the talent development process and effective curricular interventions with the gifted.